DRUNKEN COMPORTMENT
A Social Explanation

FOUNDATIONS OF ANTHROPOLOGY

Advisory Editors

Melvin Ember, *Human Relations Area Files, New Haven, Connecticut*
Joyce Marcus, *University of Michigan, Ann Arbor, Michigan*
Gary M. Feinman, *The Field Museum, Chicago, Illinois*

DRUNKEN COMPORTMENT
A Social Explanation
Craig MacAndrew and Robert B. Edgerton

MAORI WARFARE
Andrew P. Vayda

THE SCIENCE OF CULTURE
A Study of Man and Civilization
Leslie A. White

DRUNKEN COMPORTMENT
A Social Explanation

CRAIG MacANDREW
University of California, Irvine
Irvine, California

and

ROBERT B. EDGERTON
University of California, Los Angeles
Los Angeles, California

With a New Foreword by
Dwight B. Heath
Brown University
Providence, Rhode Island

PERCHERON PRESS
A Division of Eliot Werner Publications, Inc.
Clinton Corners, New York

Library of Congress Control Number 2002113046

This Percheron Press paperback edition of *Drunken Comportment: A Social Explanation* is an unabridged republication of the edition published by Aldine in 1969 supplemented with a new foreword by Dwight B. Heath.

ISBN 0-9719587-6-9

Copyright © 2003 Percheron Press
A Division of Eliot Werner Publications, Inc.
PO Box 268, Clinton Corners, New York 12514
http://www.eliotwerner.com

Printed in the United States of America

Foreword to the Percheron Press Edition:

MacAndrew and Edgerton's Singular Contribution

Ethanol (also called ethyl alcohol, ETOH, or C_2H_5OH) is a simple chemical compound that is commonly produced by the natural process of fermentation with no human intervention. At the
same time, it is an important artifact as the only type of alcohol
(among many) that is commonly ingested by human beings. As
such it has come to have many and varied connotations in different cultural contexts.

Peoples around the world have variously viewed beverages
containing ethanol as staples, a gracious complement to other
foods, or a poison. Some treat this peculiar substance as a medicine, others as a tonic or an analgesic, while still others shun it
as a dangerous and addictive drug. It is commonly thought to
stimulate the appetite and aid digestion. The same individual
may use it sometimes as an energizer and at other times as a
soporific, a stimulant or relaxant, a euphoriant or depressant. It
is widely acclaimed as a natural adjunct to sociability, although
many also turn to it to aid them in retreat or withdrawal. Even
the law is confused and confusing, treating it as exculpatory or
mitigating in some situations and as aggravating or compound-
ing the blame in others.

Whether alcohol is viewed as a benign gift from some super-natural being to humankind or as a curse and a blight, it is clear that attitudes, meanings, and values must be considered in addition to chemistry, biology, and their interactions with physiology if we are to understand how it affects behavior. It is as a contribution to that ambitious enterprise that this modest book is important. I would not have recommended its republication if I did not consider it to be a major work. It is one of only a few books that can truly be said to have had a major impact on our understanding of alcohol use and its outcomes. Part of its importance is specifically anthropological, generally social and cultural, but it is also relevant to our understanding of science as a way of knowing.

****

Both the organization and writing style are elegantly simple and simply elegant, resulting in a book that is both a joy to read and a stimulus to think about drink, drinking, and drunken comportment in ways that few people do without a little help. In an era when we are constantly confronted with scientific evidence about the benefits of moderate drinking—evidence that is compelling because of its derivation from so many studies, conducted on such large and diverse populations in all parts of the world and reported by reputable scholars and scientists who have no apparent interest in the direction of the results—it is a good time to reconsider policies and programs that are too often based on what appears to be common sense but that just happen to be wrong and outdated.

By combining historical, ethnographic, and cross-cultural data at a time when few scholars or professionals paid much attention to them, MacAndrew and Edgerton demonstrated that the dominant image of alcohol as primarily a pharmacological agent that selectively suppressed certain parts of the brain was grossly inadequate to account for the enormous range of variation that had been recorded with respect to drinking and related human behavior. According to the simplistic models of the time, a dose of alcohol was a direct toxic assault on the central nervous system. It was thought to depress "the higher centers of the brain," inhibiting "power of judgment" or overriding inhibitions.

These, in turn, supposedly caused "loss of control" or "disinhibition" in the drinker so that he or she did things that he or she otherwise would not do. This "common-sense" model dominated even the few textbooks and scientifically authoritative volumes that were available on the subject in the middle of the twentieth century.

One problem with this view is that there are several societies where alcohol does not have the power to disinhibit. Another problem is that in other societies changes occur that bear little relation to the level of alcohol in the blood, with exaggerated pseudointoxication or quiet withdrawal and even stupor (with no misbehavior) a normal and expected outcome of a single drink. Then, too, it is commonplace that one kind of drink is said to result in disinhibition, or that one kind of place where people drink is conducive while others are not. In those few societies where we do have data that allow us to look at drinking over the trajectory of history, we sometimes find periods that are free of such disinhibition and others that are marred by its apparent frequency.

This book challenged the prevailing wisdom of the time, an especially sensitive stance inasmuch as biology, chemistry, physiology, and other "hard sciences" were dominating the emerging multidisciplinary field that has subsequently come to be known as alcohol studies. MacAndrew and Edgerton were writing at a time prior to the preoccupation with genetics in connection with alcohol, but one in which other kinds of simple answers were being sought for many of the same complex questions. Pharmacological or biochemical forces then held sway, and this little book did much to steer some away from accepting those simplistic determinisms. Certainly it argues strongly against the notion of alcohol as an automatic disinhibitor, a unique or peculiar pharmacological agent that somehow dissolves the superego.

This book represents one of the few instances in which a sociocultural perspective has been used to directly challenge the conventional view of a phenomenon (specifically, drunken comportment). At the same time, these authors offered a rival theory to explain why such behavior so often deviates from that which is normally acceptable. What they called a "social explanation" brought into focus a whole new corpus of information that many who were interested in alcohol had not encountered before. They dealt with different kinds of data from anthropology, sociology, history, and other disciplines that tended often to be regarded as "soft" (in view of their predominantly qualitative treatment of information, with more emphasis on attitudes, values, norms, and context)—all of those elements that are nowadays understood by the term "environment" or "setting." There are still some who consider such variables to be uncomfortably elusive when compared to the rigorous quantification that is superficially interpreted as the hallmark of the scientific method, but there are few who would dismiss the importance that such variables may have—especially in relation to an alien culture.

There are several points that emerge from MacAndrew and Edgerton's broad-ranging description and analysis of drinking and its sequelae. Fundamentally (and importantly) they remind us that drinking often results in no negative outcomes whatsoever—a fact that tends to be overlooked in a field that has long appeared to be almost obsessed with pathology. In addition, they demonstrate that even where drinking is regularly followed by some form of misconduct, such "changes for the worse" generally occur only within certain socially defined limits in the sense that they are neither random, nor excessive, nor directed at inappropriate individuals. Rather than being the outcomes of a total suppression of morality, they can better be described as occurring within an altered morality, providing a kind of "time-out" from some of the stricter precepts and a sort of excuse based on temporarily diminished responsibility. (Something similar often occurs episodically in connection with community festivals such as Carnaval or Mardi Gras or at bachelor parties, soccer games, or on other special occasions.)

There does not appear to have been a major agonizing reappraisal of the important implications among medical and legal practitioners at the time this book appeared, at least not in many public venues, but it is clear that a more widespread recognition and acceptance of the importance of social and cultural factors soon became evident on the part of many influential spokespersons—in ways that opened many minds, some granting agencies, and even a few bureaucrats. A variety of "biopsychosocial" approaches to alcohol were articulated; a movement to decriminalize public drunkenness gained momentum; and ethnic, cultural, and subcultural variations in drinking patterns and their outcomes were recognized as relevant to public health and social welfare.

****

In the decades since this book was originally published, there have unquestionably been many and important changes in both anthropology and alcohol studies. The nature of those changes, however, does little to diminish the evident validity and relevance of what these authors said or how they arrived at their conclusions. In fact, one of the most important of those changes is the increasing emphasis that is given to social and cultural aspects of alcohol use and its outcomes, which are often lumped together as sociocultural or environmental. Another is the recent recognition of the importance that drinking patterns have as variables intervening between sheer volume of alcohol consumption (which has long been a focus of attention) and the wide range of so-called alcohol-related problems, which were long said to occur in direct proportion to consumption.

Although social scientists have been paying close attention to drinking patterns—in simplest terms, who drinks what, where, when, how, with whom, while doing what, and how they feel about it—epidemiologists and public health workers have tended to dismiss such details as interesting but anecdotal. They have focused instead on sheer quantity of alcohol consumption per day, week, or year.

Until very recently the World Health Organization was vocal in its opposition to the wide variety of alcohol-related problems, and various publications from that organization insisted that such problems occurred in a universal and constant relationship to alcohol consumption (although the nature of that relationship was not always clearly spelled out). Among such alcohol-related problems were included an ample range of phenomena, some of which are physiological, others psychological, social, economic, or other. They are as varied as liver cirrhosis, absenteeism at work, spouse or child abuse, difficulties at school, addiction or dependence, and traffic accidents. All such problems were said to occur in a direct proportion to consumption of alcohol, whether in an individual or in similar proportion to the average per capita consumption in a group, community, society, or nation. However sensible such a view may appear to be, it is not supported by empirical evidence—even in those few nations where the most outspoken theorists have lived and worked for many years.

In recent years it has become increasingly evident that how much people drink tends (with very few exceptions) to be less important than how people drink. Two drinks each day for a week are very different in their outcomes from fourteen drinks on a Saturday night. People at home or in a cocktail lounge generally behave very differently from people in a bar or pub, even after having had the same number of drinks. Children who are introduced to drinking in a ritual context are unlikely to view it as something that would make them appear more sexy or mature, whereas those who are warned by their elders not to drink tend to view it as a tempting forbidden fruit that is likely to mysteriously transform them for the better. Not surprisingly those for whom alcohol is a normal part of daily life, enjoyed with meals at home among the family, generally learn to use it without problems and to feel sorry for those who do not know how. By contrast, those who choose to drink in defiance of their elders tend to do so with the aim of risk taking and deviance, often hidden from more experienced drinkers, with no guidelines and with social support only from others who are similarly inclined; problems are commonplace in such an ambivalent context. Unless imbedded in sacred meanings and values, prohibitions have rarely succeeded—throughout history and around the world.

To a great extent it is what people have learned about what is forbidden, allowable, acceptable, encouraged, or rewarded that shapes their choices and actions, whether drunk or sober. This delightful little book explains with crystal clarity how and why that formerly mysterious process works. To have done so briefly and with no resort to jargon was a masterly job of analysis and exposition on the part of MacAndrew and Edgerton, aptly commemorated with this reprinting.

Dwight B. Heath

Preface

IT IS A FUNDAMENTAL dictum of the scientific enterprise that the propositions that constitute its corpus of knowledge at any given moment are ever subject to reexamination and possible replacement. Nor is this a matter of mere empty rhetoric, for when the weight of conflicting evidence reaches a certain point, previously accepted propositions are in fact replaced by propositions that are more compatible with the existing state of knowledge.

But this is something of an idealization of how things actually proceed. The scientific enterprise, after all, is an essentially social enterprise, and its practitioners are quite other than just so many pristine embodiments of pure rationality. Rather, intellectual commitments, friendships, moral and esthetic predilections, and often whole lifetimes of professional activities (to name but a few of the "irrelevant," *i.e.*, practical, considerations that might intrude) are frequently vested in the scientific status quo. Thus, it sometimes happens that even when "the weight of the evidence" tilts the scales dramatically in favor of the new, the replacement process does not proceed automatically or even dispassionately. Indeed, the history of every scientific discipline contains examples in which the extent of the discrepancy between warranted fact and conventionally accepted theory has had to become downright scandalous before the point of maximal forbearance was exceeded and the old at last gave way to the new.

So much for things in general. The present effort is addressed to a reconsideration of the conventional understanding of one aspect of man's relationship to alcohol—the proposition that alcohol, by virtue of its toxic assault upon the central nervous system, causes the drinker to lose control of himself and to do things he would not otherwise do. It will be our contention that the disjunction between this, the conventionally accepted formulation of alcohol's effects upon man's comportment, and presently available fact concerning what people actually do when they are drunk is even now so scandalous as to exceed the limits of reasonable toleration.

Contents

And it must be added too, that superstition and error and fantasy of all kinds do become incorporated in ordinary language and even sometimes stand up to the survival test (only, when they do, why should we not detect it?).

J. L. Austin

DRUNKEN COMPORTMENT

1 *The Conventional Wisdom*

WHETHER WE DRINK HEAVILY, moderately, or are totally abstinent, we all possess a host of common-sense understandings concerning the effects of alcohol on man. The bits and pieces
of "evidence" upon which these shared understandings are based
come to us from a wide variety of sources—parents, peers, schools,
books, magazines, radio and television programs, movies, and, of
course, our own everyday experiences. Nor is there anything systematic about either the ordering or the timing with which this or
that piece of "evidence" is presented to us. Indeed, in their composite, these presentations give every appearance of being not so
much an ill-conceived as an unconceived potpourri, in which
"random access" is the sole governing principle. Yet, however
diverse our "source materials" and however fortuitous our actual
contacts with them, they have produced a high degree of unanimity
among us concerning what we take to be at least certain of the
effects of alcohol on man.

Everybody knows, for example, that "drinking and driving don't
mix." And if our own personal experiences have not been such as
to convince us that this is so, we need only consult our local newspapers, for a day seldom passes without mention of a serious ac-

cident in which the intoxication of one or another of the drivers
is reported to have been causally implicated. Sometimes the accident is judged sufficiently newsworthy to warrant extended national coverage, as, for instance, when the drunken driver is an
engineer and the vehicle is a train. Thus, under a Washington
dateline, a recent UPI story read in part:

> A government agency charged Monday that beer drinking had "sub-
> stantially impaired" the condition of the engineer of a train that
> derailed at the Montana-Idaho border June 10, killing a child and
> injuring 272 others. . . . The Interstate Commerce Commission
> finding estimated that five minutes before the train derailed the
> engineer was legally under the influence of intoxicating liquor ac-
> cording to Montana state law.

And in the face of a continuing stream of research findings that
specify in ever greater detail the adverse effects of alcohol on one
or another sensorimotor component of driving performance—findings that appear in popularized form under such captions as "Five
Beers Called Enough to Impair Car Driver" and "Can You
Drink and Drive? Psychological Tests Say You Can't"—no one
seriously questions the good sense of the dictum, "If you drink,
don't drive; and if you drive, don't drink."

But our understanding of the effects of alcohol on behavior is
not confined to the recognition that alcohol adversely affects sundry of our sensorimotor capabilities. We also know that drinking
can affect the manner in which we comport ourselves with others.
Thus, for instance, when Ogden Nash puckishly observed that
"Candy is dandy, but liquor is quicker," he, too, was commenting
upon something that everybody knows—namely, that while a
woman's resistance to a man's amorous advances may undergo
gradual erosion by gifts and kindnesses of one sort or another, this
same effect can often be brought to pass far more rapidly with the
aid, say, of a few martinis. And while the validity of this bit of
tactical advice to the amorously inclined is regularly confirmed
—or so we think—by accounts of drunken comportment even
from some of the more remote corners of the world, we feel little
need to go so far afield in our search for confirmation. The "proof,"
after all, is everywhere around us, as witness the following account
of the doings of a young teaching assistant and a female student
taken from a recent report (Group for the Advancement of Psy-

chiatry, 1966) dealing with present-day sexual practices on the American college campus:

> At a small party in the instructor's apartment, Betty, a junior, became intoxicated and the teacher had intercourse with her after the party. He thought little more about it, and was surprised and very distressed to be summoned by the dean two days later. There he learned that the girl had gone to the dean, stating that she had been attacked and forced into relations when her inebriated state made it impossible for her to protest effectively. The teacher stated that he had in no way used force, and that he believed that the girl had been an active participant (p. 95).

Most of us, however, count such an unhappy aftermath to "a good night's fun" as the exception rather than the rule, for in ever-increasing numbers we are coming to agree that if drinking and driving don't go together, drinking and partying most emphatically do. Furthermore, we presume that we know *why* they do. We all know, for instance, that the relative carefreeness of the cocktail party is often due in no small measure to the effects of the cocktails themselves. We know, that is, that in most "party" situations drinking is typically accompanied by a general spirit of relaxed good feeling. We know, too, that as the hours pass, we are likely to see more laughing and joking—sometimes off-color— and that, a little further down the road, behavior is likely to become increasingly "unguarded." In fact, if it is a really *good* party some of the participants can usually be counted upon to become "drunk enough" to do things that are truly "out-of-character."

We are aware, too, that such periods of insouciance cannot with certainty be counted on to remain so forever. For when alcohol flows, everybody knows that the result is not always an uninterrupted interlude of good fellowship. We all know, for instance, that when people drink, the odds are appreciably increased that some unpleasant incident—a not-so-innocent flirtation, an argument, a fight, or whatever—will ensue. Indeed, of such incidents as these we are all too well aware. But we have learned both to accept and to expect the bitter with the sweet, and we do not usually find ourselves inordinately surprised or dismayed when, say, a "drunken" quarrel takes place before our very eyes. Although regrettable, such episodes have nothing of the mysterious about them, for "After all, they were drunk, weren't they?"

Nor do we feel in any way at a loss to comprehend the phenomenon of wholesale drunken brawling. Instances of this, too, are routinely reported in the pages of our daily newspapers, and we regularly come upon stories such as the following, which took place —of all places— in the relatively prosperous and usually sedate city of Santa Barbara, California. Under the caption, "Six Arrested as Fight Erupts at Youth Dance," the story reports that:

> Six youths were arrested, car windows were smashed and several persons suffered minor injuries at midnight Friday when students from two rival high schools here rioted at a crowded dance at the city Recreational Center . . . [The] assistant youth supervisor was struck in the face as she attempted to turn on bright lights on the dance floor after fighting started. . . . A dozen policemen responded to a call for help from recreation officials at the auditorium filled with more than 1,100 students.

It was further reported that, after quelling the riot, the lieutenant in charge of the police detail suggested by way of explanation for the disturbance that "A few of the boys evidently had been drinking." To our mind, the significant thing about this remark is that neither the officer who uttered it, the reporter who wrote up the story, nor the wire service that carried it felt any need to spell out its "obvious" explanatory relevance to the disturbance in question.

But of what does this "obviousness" consist? What exactly *do* we know—or *think* we know—about the phenomenon of drunkenness from the vantage point of the middle decades of our twentieth-century Western experience?

Historically and to this day our common-sense understanding of the effects of alcohol on man has rested upon a seemingly self-evident proposition. This proposition holds that alcohol is a substance of such potency —such "psychopharmacological" potency, we would now say—that its action within the body both impairs the performance of sundry of our sensorimotor skills and alters the character of our social comportment. Nor is this formulation in any sense unique to our common-sense understanding, for its hold upon the scientific imagination is just as deeply ingrained. Thus, this proposition may fairly be said to constitute the very cornerstone of what *everybody* knows about the matter.

But how is it that alcohol is capable of producing these changes?

In regards its deleterious effects upon our sensorimotor capabilities—those doings that we talk about under such headings as locomotor ability, motor coordination, visual acuity, reaction time, and the like—there is widespread agreement, bolstered by significant supporting evidence, that the performance decrements we observe are due to alcohol's toxic assault upon the operation of one or another functionally relevant internal bodily mechanism. And while the empirical specification of the exact nature of alcohol's toxic action and of such things as the relationship of the resulting alcohol-produced performance decrements to differing blood-alcohol levels, etc., is available for the most part only in rough outline, everyone agrees (and correctly, we believe) that, at least in principle, it is only a matter of time until the complete story is in. In this connection, then, the conventional understanding of alcohol's workings has served us very well indeed.

As for the effects of alcohol upon changes in our comportment, much the same would appear to be the case. Certainly those who address this topic typically write *as if* these two orders of change are essentially of a piece and that the conventional understanding of alcohol's workings possesses an equally self-evident relevance to both. Thus, in a recently published manual on the pharmacology and toxicology of alcohol prepared by the Committee on Medicolegal Problems of the American Medical Association (Harger, 1959), we are informed that alcohol produces changes in comportment by impairing the higher brain functions and that one of the results of such an alcohol-induced impairment is "loss of inhibitions." The statement continues that:

> The inhibitions are our moral brakes. The chief distinction between man and the lower animals is that the former exercises many more inhibitions. Without them he could hardly live a civilized life. . . . Concentrations of alcohol in the brain and blood far below those necessary to produce detectable muscular incoordination will cause a blunting of the sense of caution and normal restraints (p. 13).

Leon Greenberg (1953), a long-time chairman of Yale's Department of Applied Physiology and one of the founders of the Yale Center of Alcohol Studies, says much the same:

> A blood concentration of about .05 per cent of alcohol, which in a person of average size results from drinking two or three ounces of

whiskey, depresses the uppermost level of the brain—the center of inhibitions, restraint and judgment. At this stage the drinker feels that he is sitting on top of the world; he is "a free human being"; many of his normal inhibitions vanish; he takes personal and social liberties as the impulse prompts; he is long-winded and can lick anybody in the country. Such a man has undergone an obvious blunting of self-criticism. . . . Contrary to old and popular belief, alcohol does not stimulate the nervous system. The illusion of stimulation results from the removal of inhibitions and restraints (p. 88).

W. H. Neil (1962), writing in a recent medical journal, provides a quasi-specification of the neurological process that is conventionally presumed to underlie this "loss of inhibitions":

It is a well-known fact that the effect of alcohol is primarily upon the nervous tissue in the body and that these effects are always depressing. However, not all nervous tissue is equally susceptible to the effects of alcohol. The more primitive types of nervous tissue, namely, portions of the brain common to both man and the lower animals, have a higher degree of resistance to the effects of alcohol than do the more specialized forms of nervous tissue which are present for the most part in man, but also to some degree in the higher animals. From early in childhood, man develops specialized brain cells which restrain or inhibit actions that might be of an antisocial character. For instance, if another driver turns suddenly into your lane of traffic, you may have an immediate impulse to ram him. However, the nerve cells governing social restraints prevent you from doing so because certain unhappy consequences would result. Thus you are kept from indulging in antisocial behavior. However, if the restraint nerve cells are paralyzed by alcohol, this impulse to ram the other car probably will be carried out. Some have said that such an unsocial act results from a stimulation of impulses, but it actually is not a stimulation of these impulses but a paralysis of the restraints (pp. 2–3).

Chafetz and Demone (1962), in their recent treatise on "alcoholism and society," provide the following statement of the conventional understanding of how alcohol comes to alter our comportment:

The apparent "stimulation" from alcohol is the result of the lower brain centers being released from higher brain controls. This reduces inhibitions, and behavior which is untoward when the individual is sober becomes acceptable. For example . . . an always proper, ladylike woman may become obscene and promiscuous when intoxicated (p. 9).

The medical profession's fidelity to the conventional wisdom has been even more recently set forth by Marvin Block (1965), who is perhaps the American Medical Association's leading spokesman on alcoholism:

> Since alcohol depresses the powers of judgment, drinking may re-lease inhibitions . . . As far as sexual behavior is concerned, it is well-known that alcohol reduces the inhibitions of individuals and removes the controls. The individual becomes careless and will often do things under the influence of alcohol that he would not do if his judgment were not impaired. Therefore, impairment of the judgment by alcohol may cause sexual behavior that would not occur were he not exposed to the loss of control that alcohol brings about (pp. 219–20).

That this formulation is in no way peculiar to American medicine is indicated in a recent British treatise on alcoholism written by Kessel and Walton (1965):

> After a few drinks . . . the first thing to be depressed is the power of restraint. The inhibition of our actions or our wishes which we all of us adopt in order to get on with our fellows is the product of the highest mental processes and it is these that are impaired first. When the curb that we normally place on our instinctual urges goes, unguarded behavior comes to the fore and these released im-pulses are forcefully expressed. . . . sometimes the drinking facil-itates a group mood of dejection or of anger, and people have had their passions so inflamed by alcohol that they carried out cruel, senseless, irrevocable actions from which, if the highest mental processes were functioning intact, each individual would recoil with disgust (pp. 26–27).

Nor, finally, is there anything peculiarly contemporary about this formulation of alcohol's workings. While Aristotle's observa-tion that wine drinkers have a tendency to sleep on their stomachs and beer drinkers on their backs has long since been relegated to the status of oblivion, Plato's contention that drunken-ness brings out much that is otherwise dormant within us has been unreflectively accepted right along. In early Rome, for instance, there was a strict prohibition on women's drinking "lest thereby they fall into some disgrace," as Valerius Maximus discreetly put it. And, in the first century A.D., according to the classical scholar Arthur McKinlay (1945), Pope Clement I warned "of the deadly association of wine and women; he criticizes women for reveling in luxurious riot, gulping down wine so as to make a show of themselves, and hiccuping ostentatiously like men; he advises boys and girls to keep away from wine as an arouser of the passions" (pp. 14–15). Scarcely distinguishable, this, from the warning emblazoned on an Anti-Saloon League poster of 1913, which read in part:

> *Alcohol inflames the passions*, thus making the temptation to sexsin unusually strong. *Alcohol decreases the power of control*, thus making the resisting of temptation especially difficult. . . . *Avoid all alcoholic drink absolutely*. The control of sex impulses will then be easy, and disease, dishonor, disgrace and degradation will be avoided.

Or consider the scarcely veiled warning contained in the following excerpt from an educational tract of a British religious society (Society of Friends, 1935) issued in 1934:

> Judgment, modesty, reason, shame, prudence are all impaired by a little alcohol. In other words, alcohol narcotizes first those powers of self-criticism and inhibition by which we normally judge and control our conduct; and when this control is relaxed, a man's physical impulses, imperious enough at the best of times, may sweep him into acts unworthy of his better nature. . . . A boy's or girl's downward slide begins, more often than not, at a moment of excitement or carelessness, when alcohol has lulled the powers of self-control (p. 11).

While most of the above quotations have been largely sexual in focus, it was never held that alcohol's effects on comportment were limited to this sphere. Witness, for example, "the eight kindes of drunkennesse" observed in sixteenth-century England by Thomas Nash (1592), a contemporary of Shakespeare and a friend of Marlowe:

> Nor haue we one or two kinde of drunkards onely, but eight kindes.

The first is Ape drunke, and he leapes, and sings, and hollowes, and daunceth for the heauens: the second is Lion drunke, and he flings the pots about the house, calls his Hostesse whore, breakes the glasse windowes with his dagger, and is apt to quarrell with any man that speakes to him: the third is Swine drunke, heauy, lumpish, and sleepie, and cries for a little more drinke, and a fewe more cloathes: the fourth is Sheepe drunke, wise in his owne conceipt, when he cannot bring foorth a right word: the fifth is Mawdlen drunke when a fellowe will weepe for kindnes in the midst of his Ale, and kisse you, saying; By God, Captaine, I loue thee; goe thy waies, thou dost not thinke so often of me as I do of thee, I would (if it pleased GOD) I could not loue thee so well as I doo; and then he puts his finger in his eie, and cries: the sixt is Martin drunke, when a man is drunke, and drinkes himselfe sober ere he stirre: the seuenth is Goate drunke, when, in his drunkenness, he hath no minde but on Lechery: the eighth is Foxe drunke, when he is craftie drunke, as many of the Dutch men bee, that will neuer bargaine but when they are drunke. All these *species*, and more, I haue seene practised in one Company at one sitting, when I haue beene permitted to remaine sober amongst them, onely to note their seuerall humors (p. 467).

Similarly, the early American physician Benjamin Rush (1811) in discussing some of the diverse "symptoms" of drunkenness which he had observed, wrote specifically of:

Certain extravagant acts which indicate a temporary fit of madness. These are singing, hallooing, roaring, imitating the noises of brute animals, jumping, tearing off clothes, dancing naked, breaking glasses and china, and dashing other articles of household furniture upon the ground or floor (p. 2).

And to these, Rush added in an ascending order of gravity, "Idleness, Gaming, Peevishness, Quarrelling, Fighting, Horse-Racing, Lying and Swearing, Stealing and Swindling, Perjury, Burglary, and Murder" (p. ii).

While it has long been recognized that alcohol often gives rise to various sorts of disruptive changes, probably at no time has more been made of this than during the period of our own domestic debates over prohibition. And in no section of this nation was prohibitionist sentiment more frenetic than in the South. At least one major reason for the Southerners' abiding concern with "the evils of alcohol" was the threat to domestic tranquility that they widely presumed to be resident in the drunken Negro. Speaking on the floor of the House of Representatives in 1914 in support of his resolution for a prohibition amendment, Congressman Hobson of Alabama (quoted in Sinclair, 1962) provided the following "theoretical" grounds for this presumption:

> Liquor will actually make a brute of a Negro, causing him to commit unnatural crimes. The effect is the same on the white man, though the white man, being further evolved, it takes a longer time to reduce him to the same level (p. 29).

Most prohibitionists, however, refused to accept the notion that this assumedly alcohol-induced primitivization recognized any color line. Booker T. Washington (quoted in Sinclair, 1962), for instance, in a generous display of egalitarianism opined that "Two-thirds of the mobs, lynchings, and burnings at the stake are the result of bad whisky drunk by bad black men and bad white men" (p. 30).

Returning now to the present, we suggest that in their general import there is no *fundamental* difference between the theory implicit in the warnings, say, of Pope Clement I or the Anti-Saloon League and the recent statement of C. Nelson Davis (1962), Psychiatrist-in-Chief of the Malvern Institute for Psychiatric and Alcoholic Studies:

> In alcoholism, the equation is simply expressed: Man plus alcohol equals psychopathic behavior. Man minus alcohol equals a normally disciplined person. When alcohol is added, you change the behavior pattern. . . . There is a myth that man plus alcohol equals the true person. Nothing could be further from the truth. To be your real self you must have control of all your faculties. Alcohol removes the power of control over behavior (p. 1).

But why go on? The essential force of the conventional understanding has been both clear and constant through the ages. When we are drunk we sometimes do things that we would "never" do when we are sober. And whether we choose to explain this fact in terms of some neurological or quasi-neurological version of an alcohol-induced "cortical disinhibition" or, as the psychoanalysts do, in terms of an alcohol-induced paralysis, dissolution, or castration (take your pick) of the superego, we are simply selecting different words to express an essentially similar conception of how this assumedly self-evident loss of restraint comes about. The general thrust of the position is unvarying: *Just as changes in the efficiency with which we exercise our sensorimotor capabilities are consequent upon the action of alcohol on our innards, so too are changes in the manner in which we comport ourselves with our fellows.*

But has the sway of alcohol over our comportment in fact been demonstrated, as it has (at least to a sufficient degree to convince us that we are on the right track) in the case of various of our sensorimotor performances? Candidness requires that we answer this question in the negative, for consider what such a demonstration would necessarily entail. Since what is being asserted is the existence of a causal relationship between events in *two* coordinate domains—the domain of one's innards, and the domain of one's social comportment in the world of everyday life—the very *possibility* of demonstrating that the events in the former domain are causal of the events in the latter requires the prior accomplishment of a rigorous description of the events in each. And not even the most cavalier spokesman for the causal role of alcohol on comportment has ever claimed that *this* has been done. Indeed, insofar as the sphere of comportment is concerned, we have scarcely even begun our descriptive task.[1] But barring the attainment of such descriptions, it stands as a matter of elementary logic that even if, say, the brain physiologists were fully to accomplish their task of explicating the effects of alcohol on the human brain in the most minute and final detail, we would remain no better informed

1. Hans-Lukas Teuber (1959) made much the same point in his evaluation of the present state of knowledge concerning the relation between cerebral lesions and alterations in behavior: "The greatest difficulty in the use of abnormal physiology stems from incomplete or incorrect description of behavioral changes. We tend to substitute casual observation or clinical beliefs for the necessary analyses of altered performance" (p. 158). But the adequate description of comportment does not simply await the appearance of persons of sufficient energy and dedication to go out and "do it." For a brief consideration of the essentially philosophical difficulties that are inherent in such an enterprise, see, for example, Peter Winch (1958). A more general treatment of the issue is contained in Ludwig Wittgenstein (1953). The radically *serious* concern with this problem—the problem of the description of human conduct—is the core concern of what Garfinkel (1967) and his colleagues have termed "ethnomethodology."

concerning the relationship *between* this now fully explicated state of affairs, and the purportedly resultant changes in man's comportment than we are today.

Lacking such a demonstration, the most that one can legitimately assert concerning the assumedly self-evident causal role of alcohol on man's comportment is that it constitutes a *possible,* but to this date unsubstantiated, explanation of why people's comportment so frequently changes after they have made their bodies alcoholed. The formal status of such a claim is only, and at best, that of an *hypothesis.*

In the next three chapters we shall present evidence to the point that, although this hypothesis is a possible explanation of why people comport themselves differently when they are drunk, it is a most dubious explanation.

2 "Some People Can Really Hold Their Liquor"

IN CHAPTER 1 we tried to show that the conventional understanding of alcohol's workings has it that once alcohol is inside us, its toxic action produces changes in two fundamentally different kinds of behavior. First, its pernicious action on our innards is held to result in a marked impairment in our ability to perform at least certain of our sensorimotor skills. And with this aspect of the conventional understanding we have no quarrel. In the face of the available evidence, it is impossible to imagine how one could seriously doubt that the presence of alcohol in the body does, in fact, produce various sensorimotor performance decrements. Nor can one dispute the fact that alcohol in sufficiently high concentrations produces grave and even fatal bodily malfunctioning. In this profound sense, then, there can be no question that alcohol *is* the potent change-producer that everyone claims it to be.

The conventional understanding also insists, however, that alcohol depresses the activity of "the higher centers of the brain," thereby producing a state of affairs in which neither man's reason nor his conscience is any longer capable of performing its customary directive and inhibitory functions. It is with this aspect of the conventional understanding that we now propose to take issue.

We have already noted that, despite its near unanimous acceptance, the formal status of this supposition that alcohol is a "moral" as well as a sensorimotor incapacitator is only and at best that of an hypothesis. Just what, after all, is the empirical warrant for the contention that alcohol reduces man to the status of a mere creature of his now unrestrained impulses? Well, the argument goes, one has but to open his eyes and look around, for the evidence is everywhere. Haven't we all seen people do things when they were drunk that they would not *think* of doing (would not think *seriously* of doing) when they were sober? To this we would reply that of course we have. But we would hasten to add that this is not *all* we have seen; and as John Dewey never tired of reminding us, we must accept consequences impartially.

In point of fact, while changes in comportment of the sort that we customarily construe as disinhibited are certainly a sometime corollary of drunkenness, they are anything but an *inevitable* corollary. While the sheer occurrence of changes between one's "sober" and one's "drunken" comportment is beyond question, it is an equally incontestable fact that these changes are of a most incredible diversity. Relative to our comportment when sober, we may, for instance, become boisterous or solemn, depressed or euphoric, repugnantly gregarious or totally withdrawn, vicious or saintly, ready at last to say our say or stoically noncommittal, energetic or lackadaisical, amorous or hostile . . . but the list could be continued for pages. The point is that, with alcohol inside us, our comportment may change in any of a wondrously profuse variety of ways. Indeed, it is precisely this variability that constitutes the problem. For how can the conventional understanding of alcohol *qua* disinhibitor possibly accommodate the fact that even within our own culture people who have made their bodies alcoholled differ so drastically both within and among themselves in their subsequent doings? Thus, while we are all aware, for instance, of the connection between drunkenness and such things as promiscuity and crime, we also know that everyone who gets drunk does not, *ipso facto*, become promiscuous and/or criminal. Furthermore, even in regard to those who do, we know that they do not comport themselves in such a fashion on *every* occasion that they lift a few. How is it, we would ask (and the question is not an idle one), that the same man, in the same bar, drinking approximately the same amount of alcohol, may, on three nights running, be, say, surly and belligerent on the first evening, the spirit of amiability on the second, and morose and withdrawn on the third? Are our impulses—the very wellsprings of conduct, by most accounts—really so frivolous? And what, finally, of the person about whom we say, "He can really hold his liquor?" In the absence of anything observably untoward in such a one's drunken comportment are we seriously to presume that he is devoid of inhibitions?

But there is little to be gained by laboring this point any further, if only because everyone—including even the most vociferous spokesman for the conventional wisdom—is already perfectly familiar with these sorts of puzzles as they pertain to drunken comportment in our own society. Familiarity, in this case, however, would seem to have given rise to nothing; for despite their patent relevance to the evaluation of the conventional understanding, the puzzles have been and continue to be ignored.

How, then, to proceed? Perhaps by turning from the seen-but-unnoticed puzzles with which the variability of drunken comportment confronts us in our everyday lives and looking instead to "the same" phenomena as they naturally occur in cultures which are foreign to our own, we shall stand a better chance of creating that necessary "shock of recognition" which apparently must precede a willingness to take these everyday puzzles seriously. This, at any rate, is our hope. For whatever may be the final judgment as to the merit of the alternative formulation that we shall advance in later chapters, of this much we are firmly convinced: the conventional explanation cannot possibly account for what is actually going on.

One or another form of alcoholic beverage has long been consumed in the vast majority of the world's societies. Although the descriptive literature on these hundreds of societies usually fails to provide specific accounts of how people actually conduct themselves when drunk—and where mention is made, it typically takes the form of but a passing remark—the ethnographic literature does contain sufficient documentation to support the following generalization: When people are drunk, not only are various of their sensorimotor capabilities impaired (there are no exceptions in this regard), their comportment often changes as well. And to this we would add as a secondary generalization that when changes in comportment *are* reported, more often than not they take the form of "changes-for-the-*worse*."

The Abipone Indians are a good example of a people whose comportment undergoes such a metamorphosis once they have alcohol inside them. When first described in the early 1800's, the Abipone were warlike, tent-dwelling horsemen who traversed the great plains of the Paraguayan Chaco. Martin Dobrizhoffer (1822) describes their natural state as follows:

> The Abipones, in their whole deportment, preserve a decorum scarce credible to Europeans. Their countenance and gait display a modest cheerfulness, and manly gravity tempered with gentleness and kindness. Nothing licentious, indecent, or uncourteous, is discoverable in their actions. In their daily meetings, all is quiet and orderly. Confused vociferations, quarrels, or sharp words, have no place there. They love jokes in conversation, but are adverse to indecency and ill-nature. If any dispute arises, each declares his opinion with a calm countenance and unruffled speech: they never break out into clamours, threats and reproaches, as is usual to certain people of Europe. These praises are justly due to the Abipones as long as they remain sober: but when intoxicated, they shake off the bridle of reason, become distracted, and quite unlike themselves (Vol. 3, p. 136).

"Quite unlike themselves" indeed, as Dobrizhoffer's sharply contrasting account of Abipone comportment during a drinking party vividly illustrates:

> Disputes are frequent among them concerning preeminence in valour, which produce confused clamours, fighting, wounds and slaughter. . . . It often happens that a contention between two implicates and incites them all, so that snatching up arms, and taking the part, some of one, some of the other, they furiously rush to attack and slay one another. This is no uncommon occurrence in drinking parties and is sometimes carried on for many hours with much vociferation of the combatants, and no less effusion of blood (Vol. 2, pp. 436–37).

Clearly, this transformation in Abipone comportment from a taciturn civility to outright savagery is admirably in accord with what one would expect if alcohol were in fact the disinhibitor that the conventional wisdom takes it to be.[1] Nor are similar examples hard to come by; societies in which such Jekyll-to-Hyde transformations occur are to be found in virtually all parts of the world.

But, and here is the rub, it is not *always* so. Consider, for example, the anthropologist C. Nimuendajú's (1948) account of the Yuruna Indians, a warlike, head-hunting tribe living in the Xingu region of South America's tropical forest. While the Yuruna drink substantial quantities of *malicha* (which they make from fermented manioc root), not only do they fail to become "disinhibited," they withdraw entirely into themselves and behave much as though no one else existed (p. 238). Nor can it be said that the Yuruna constitute "the exception which proves the rule" (whatever that may mean). The Yuruna are but one of many societies in which persons consume appreciable, and in some cases prodigious, quantities of alcohol without displaying anything like the wholesale changes-for-the-worse that characterize Abipone drunkenness. In fact, in many of these societies there is scant evidence of *anything* that might reasonably be termed "disinhibited." Over the course of this chapter, we shall want to examine several such societies which have recently been studied in some detail.

What we actually find when we examine the phenomenon of drunkenness as it occurs throughout the world is a series of infinite gradations in the degree of "disinhibition" that is manifested in drunken comportment. Because of this, it might be well to begin by taking a closer look at a society in which the inhabitants' comportment falls somewhere *between* that of the Abipone and that of the Yuruna. For an example of such a society we move to the Peruvian Andes, to the Indians of Vicos as described by the anthropologist William Mangin (1957). The *hacienda* of Vicos is a largely self-contained community inhabited by approximately 1,800 Indians who, being in large measure both geographically and culturally isolated from the ongoing "life of the nation," have retained much of their traditional way of life. What of drinking and drunkenness in this *hacienda*? Ceremonial drinking has existed in Peru since pre-Conquest times, and to this day drinking remains an integral feature of both formal and informal community life in

1. But even with the Abipone, these changes are selective in character. See Chapter 4, pp. 76–77.

Vicos. Here is Mangin's depiction of the present-day drinking practices of these Indians:

> In Vicos, small children are given corn beer and everyone over 16 years drinks (*aguardiente*). Drinking by most adults, particularly adult males. is usually followed by drunkeness, and in many instances a man or woman may be drunk for several days in succession. The incidence and frquency of drinking and the amounts consumed seem to be very high. Drinking is a social activity, however, and drinking customs are integrated with the most basic and powerful institutions in the community. Drinking and drunkeness do not seem to lead to any breakdown in interpersonal relations, nor do they seem to interfere with the performance of social roles by individuals (p. 58).

Mangin's overall evaluation is that for the Vicosino the role of alcohol is "prevailingly integrative" in nature. While he does suggest that the frequency of violence seems to increase when people are drunk, his statement is a cautious one, for he goes on to add that "drunk or sober, there is actually very little violence in Vicos. Few fights were noted during the field investigation. And of those noted, the same two men seemed to be involved most of the time" (p. 63). Regarding other manifestations of what we usually consider to be "drunken impulsivity," he writes:

> Sexual activity of a premarital variety appears to increase during fiestas, but may not be a function of drinking. Several male informants told the author that they purposely stayed sober at times during fiestas so that they could "escape" with a girl. Extramarital sexual activity, which is a disruptive force in Vicos culture, seems to occur mostly when individuals are quite sober. . . . Most of the crimes committed by Vicosinos during the field study were carried out while sober. In only two cases (one of which occurred before the [21 month] field study and one during it) could it be documented that drunkeness was associated with criminality (p. 63).

Thus, while something or other of an apparently "disinhibited" sort may occasionally occur when the inhabitants of Vicos are drunk, the paucity of specifically drunken transgressions contained in the above roster places Vicosino drunken comportment in sharp contrast to that of the Abipone.

We turn now to an examination of five societies in which not even *this* degree of drunken "disinhibition" is to be found. For our first example, we select the anthropologist Dwight Heath's (1958) account of drinking among the Camba of Eastern Bolivia. The Camba, who number approximately 80,000, are a mestizo people, the descendants of colonial Spaniards and indigenous Indians. Having rejected traditional tribal ways of life, a few Camba live as independent land-owning agriculturalists or as squatters, but most work as tenants on one or another of the vast *haciendas* into which the area is divided. From the owners or managers of these *haciendas* they receive food, housing, clothing, and a small wage in exchange for their labor. Because of the primitiveness of the infrastructure of the Bolivian economy and the natural barriers that limit even nonmechanized transport, those Camba whom Heath studied have been effectively isolated from extensive contact with other population centers. As a result, their way of life has undergone only slight modification since the Spanish colonial period.

As for their drinking, the Camba drink a distillate of sugar cane, which, with good reason, they call *alcohol*. Chemical analysis has shown this beverage to be 89 percent ethyl alcohol—approximately twice as potent as a good scotch or bourbon. And the Camba drink this beverage *undiluted*! Furthermore, with the exception of a few who have joined one or another fundamentalist Protestant sect, all Camba drink and "most of them become intoxicated at least twice each month" (p. 498). Because Heath's (1958) description of Camba drinking practices is unusually rich in detail, it warrants extended quotation:

> The behavioral patterns associated with drinking are so formalized as to constitute a secular ritual. Members of the group are seated in chairs in an approximate circle in a yard or, occasionally, in a hut. A bottle of *alcohol* and a single water glass rest on a tiny table which forms part of the circle. The "sponsor" of the party pours a glassful (about 300 cc.) at the table, turns and walks to stand in front of whomever he wishes, nods and raises the glass slightly. The person addressed smiles and nods while still seated; the "sponsor" toasts with "Salud" (health), or "A su salud" (to your health), drinks half of the glassful in a single quick draught, and hands it to the person he has toasted, who then repeats the toast and finishes the glass in one gulp. While the "sponsor" returns to his seat, the recipient of the toast goes to the table

to refill the glass and to repeat the ritual. There are no apparent
rules concerning whom one may toast, and in this sense toasts
proceed in no discernible sequence. A newcomer is likely to
receive a barrage of toasts when he first joins a drinking group, and
sometimes an attractive girl may be frequently addressed, but there
tends to be a fairly equal distribution of toasts over a period of
several hours. To decline a toast is unthinkable to the Camba, although as the party wears on and the inflammation of mouth and
throat makes drinking increasingly painful, participants resort to a
variety of ruses in order to avoid having to swallow an entire
glassful of *alcohol* each time. These ruses are quite transparent (such
as turning one's head aside and spitting out a fair portion) and are
met with cajoling remonstrances to "Drink it all!" Such behavior
is not an affront to the toaster, however, and the other members
of the group are teasing more than admonishing the deviant. After
the first three or four hours virtually everyone "cheats" this way
and almost as much *alcohol* is wasted as is consumed. Also, as the
fiesta wears on, the rate of toasting decreases markedly: during the
first hour a single toast is completed in less than two minutes; during
the third hour it slows to five minutes or more. A regular cycle of
activity can be discerned, with a party being revived about every
six hours. When a bottle is emptied, one of the children standing
quietly nearby takes it away and brings a replacement from the hut.
When the supply is exhausted, members of the group pool their
funds to buy more; they send a child to bring it from the nearest
seller.

The ritual sequence described above is the only way in which
the Camba drink, except at wakes where a different but equally
formalized pattern of behavior is followed (pp. 499–500).

Heath (1958) also provides an hour-by-hour account of the first
of the repetitive cycles into which these extended drinking bouts
are divided:

The Camba usually begin drinking shortly after breakfast. . . . as
a party wears on, the effects of intoxication become apparent. After
two or three hours of fairly voluble and warm social intercourse,
people tend to become thick-lipped and intervals of silence lengthen.
By the fourth hour there is little conversation; many people stare
dumbly at the ground except when toasted, and a few who may
have fallen asleep or "passed out" are left undisturbed. Once a
band or guitarist starts playing, the music is interminable and others
take over as individual players pass out. The sixth hour sees a

renewed exhilaration as sleepers waken and give the party a "second wind." This cycle is repeated every five, six, or seven hours, day and night, until the *alcohol* gives out or the call to work is sounded (pp. 500–501).

Clearly, there can be no question that the Camba get very drunk indeed; gross sensorimotor incapacitation could hardly be more evident. But what of their comportment, and what, specifically, of drunken "disinhibition"?

Among the Camba drinking does not lead to expressions of aggression in verbal or physical form. . . . Neither is there a heightening of sexual activity: obscene joking and sexual overtures are rarely associated with drinking. Even when drunk, the Camba are not given to maudlin sentimentality, clowning, boasting or "baring of souls" (p. 501).

Actually the only change Heath noted between the Cambas' sober and drunken comportment was an increase in "volubility" and "self-confidence." And even this he observed not in the acute stages of intoxication, but only in the early stages of drinking and upon recovery of consciousness. In sum, the Camba drink often and to a point of intoxication that is extreme by anyone's standards, yet the expression of impulsivity is quite unaffected thereby. So much, then, for the "disinhibiting" effects of alcohol upon the Camba.

For a second example of a society in which disinhibition fails to occur during drunkenness, we turn to Gerardo and Alicia Reichel-Dolmatoff's (1961) account of life in the small mestizo village of Aritama, located in northern Colombia. Situated in the tropical foothills of the Sierra Nevada de Santa Marta, Aritama lies in a region that is both geographically and culturally intermediate between that of the more advanced Creoles of the urban and rural lowlands and the autochthonous Indian tribes of the higher mountains. While the Creole lowlanders consider Aritama a backward Indian village, the majority of its inhabitants manifest a tri-ethnic mixture of Indian, Caucasian, and Negro traits. Although their culture is not so untouched as that of the Indians, neither is it so developed as the Creoles, being now at a stage through which the latter have already passed. As contacts with the lowland towns have increased, the inhabitants of Aritama have become acutely aware that many of their customs and ways are "unprogressive"; and change is everywhere in evidence.

As for the character of life in present-day Aritama, we would begin by noting that the people are inordinately self-conscious. Whether with neighbor or with stranger, "They are always afraid of giving themselves away somehow, of being ridiculed because of the things they say or do, or of being taken advantage of by persons in authority" (1961, p. xvii). Not only do they avoid close personal relationships, they have firm cultural support for so doing. Thus, the Reichel-Dolmatoffs (1961) inform us that merely "to ask personal questions and to show interest in other people's lives is, according to local standards, one of the worst breaches of proper conduct" (p. xvii). While they live their lives behind a mask of formal politeness, hostility is endemic to Aritama—as witness, for instance, the fact that immortality is deemed desirable "only insofar as it offers the opportunity for the spirit to take revenge that he was unable to take during his lifetime" (p. 281). So controlled are the adult males that it was only during cock fights—which, interestingly enough, are the sole sport in which any interest is shown—that they were observed to throw off their deep-seated reserve and, in their excitement, become truly spontaneous.

As for the nature of the relations between the sexes, Aritama women look to their unions (whether they be marriage, free union, or concubinage) almost exclusively in terms of economic security, while men see above all a chance to demonstrate their virility by having as many children as possible. Not only are such relationships devoid of mutual trust, the Reichel-Dolmatoffs (1961) state flatly that in all homes, whether or not they are sanctioned by Catholic marriage, "the dominant impression is one of open hostility" (p. 186). Nor is any attempt made to hide this state of affairs. Quite the contrary, while fighting typically takes the form of verbal abuse and violent gestures, physical assaults also occur. Where relative tranquility does prevail between the partners, it is a subject of ridicule; neighbors or friends "try in every way to disturb the apparent harmony by gossip, false accusations, and open insinuations of sorcery" (1961, p. 190). Indeed, hostility between the sexes is so much a part of things that the Aritamans find it quite impossible to accept the fact that in other places couples live together in peace and happiness.

The children of such unions are not desired in and of themselves, but only for their "asset-value." Even in earliest infancy, the child is seldom, if ever, fondled. When he is handled, he is handled roughly—"like a dead weight." Mothers consider suckling to be both tiresome and physically debilitating. When weaning occurs, it is abrupt, being accomplished by rubbing lemon juice or chili peppers on the nipples. The whole affair is taken as a joke and no one pays any serious attention to the infants' consequent rage. The fathers are, if anything, even less supporting; at best they are indifferent to their newborn and at worst they openly verbalize a profound loathing. Throughout childhood a father will rarely even touch his child save to administer punishment. Nor is the death of one's baby likely to evoke deeply felt sorrow. The Reichel-Dolmatoffs (1961) report four recent cases in which small babies died "simply because their mothers were unwilling to make the effort to feed them properly . . ." (p. 89). They report that public opinion took scarcely any notice of these deaths.

Child rearing in Aritama is predicated upon the notion that both "good" and "evil" character traits are inherited; and because of this, a child's "bad" behavior can never be blamed upon his parents' *doings*. Each parent, often in the presence of the other parent, points out to the child the undesirable traits of the other as examples of how one ought *not* to behave. In consequence, once the child understands the nature of these sundry accusations, his respect for his parents is all but obliterated. Thus, while obedience and respect are taught from infancy on, hostility between the generations is the rule: "Both boys and girls throw stones at adults, strike them when angry, or insult them with obscene words. Adults with physical handicaps or old people are mocked and insulted; animals are often beaten mercilessly . . ." (1961, p. 103). Nor is there affection between siblings: "The older ones take away the youngers' food or playthings, beat and push them whenever they can, and try to make them cry" (p. 102).

In adolescence, however, all of this suddenly changes:

His former mobility of facial expression and gesture is transformed. His face becomes a rigid mask of "seriousness" which betrays no emotion. The spontaneity of play gives way to silent deliberation. All conversation is dominated by extreme caution so that no word may betray inner feelings. Routine questions as to health, family, or work are answered with monotonous formulas, and any other inquiry is answered with a stereotyped "I don't know, maybe" (*no*

sé, quizás). . . . A tremendous mechanism is set into motion completely hiding the individual behind a wall of control and formality.
To smile, to laugh, to talk, to ask questions, to joke about people
and things, these are now improper. All the former manifestations
of aggressiveness are gone; no anger, no fit of sudden rage, no obscene language are now indulged in. In their place are aloofness and
apparent indifference. But there is also a certain troubled alertness,
seen in the quick furtive glance, in the nervous twitching of the
hands, in the halting walk. An exaggerated self-consciousness makes
the youth behave as if he were continuously watched, criticized or,
worse still, ridiculed. This inner tension which characterizes the
adolescent continues into adulthood, no balance ever being achieved,
it seems (1961, pp. 112–13).

The stage thus set, we now ask what happens to this "rigid mask
of seriousness" when the Aritamans get drunk? Although illegal,
some thirty to forty primitive distilleries are operating in the general
area of Aritama, and the rum they produce enjoys a reputation
for quality that extends far beyond the immediate area. In Aritama, if anywhere, we would seem to have every reason to expect
that this rum would be consumed in great quantity by the inhabitants and that it would play merry hell with the veneer of formal
politeness and controlled "seriousness" with which they confront
the world. This is not, however, what we find. Instead, the Reichel-
Dolmatoffs (1961) report that although boisterous drunkenness is
very prevalent in the Creole lowlands, in Aritama "Even during
the fiesta season, at marriages, baptisms, or wakes, one hardly
ever sees an intoxicated person, and *those who can be seen are
unobtrusive and silent"* (pp. 196–97; emphasis ours).

Although by prevailing Latin American peasant standards the
people of Aritama are neither heavy nor regular drinkers, drinking to the point of drunkenness does occur. But the resulting comportment is scarcely what one would expect from the members of so
inhibited a society:

> The various stages of intoxication are quite characteristic. After the
> first euphoria accompanied by small talk and a few jokes there
> may be some singing, and someone may go and bring a drum and
> play it for a while, but soon all conversation stops and gloominess
> sets in. There is never open physical aggressiveness of serious
> proportions, nor is there merry socializing, romantic serenading,
> obscene talk, or political discussion of any kind. One man will sing,

perhaps, another play the drum or rattle, while the others sit and listen, drinking in silence and only rarely making physical contacts or attempts at conversation (1961, p. 197).

Neither is the drinking bout the occasion for the youth of Aritama to "sow their wild oats":

Boys of fifteen or sixteen years will occasionally spend a night singing, drinking, and playing music in the company of older men who invite them on such sprees. However, the youth rarely seems to enjoy drinking and takes part in such nightly adventures mainly to demonstrate his new manliness. But as soon as the new status is achieved, *i.e.*, when the boy has left his home, such sprees become rare and are marked by increased seriousness. A man might drink and drum all night long without once losing his composure, without becoming aggressive, sentimental, verbose, or amorous (1961, p. 113).

Even among the gravediggers, a group whose occupational task constitutes one of Aritama's few institutionalized occasions for drinking, the resulting drunkenness is not counted as a reward, but an occupational hazard. That it is totally devoid of enjoyment is obvious from the following account:

They work and drink in silence with tense, harassed faces, digging, carrying stones, drinking again and again until they fall to the ground. Some lie in a stupor in the grass covering the graves of strangers or close relatives; others stumble between the mounds offering their bottles to each other. But there is no joking or story-telling. Only once in a while a man will say, "So we are digging a grave! Doing a good job at it, too. Working hard, drinking hard. Now we are drunk and the job is done" (1961, p. 383).

It is apparent, then, that in Aritama, regardless of the occasion and regardless of the degree of intoxication that is achieved, the "rigid mask of seriousness" remains firmly in place. In Aritama, as with the Camba, it is evident that alcohol lacks the power to "disinhibit."

For our third example we turn to Micronesia, specifically to the small atoll of Ifaluk, which is located about midway between Yap and Truk in the heart of the Caroline Islands. This half square mile of coral rock and sand, with a total population of approximately

250, has recently been studied by the anthropologists Burrows and
Spiro (1953) and by a team of natural scientists led by Marston
Bates (Bates and Abbott, 1958).

Aside from an occasional trading ship, Ifaluk's contact with the
West was virtually nonexistent through the nineteenth century. Under the nominal control of first Spain and then, briefly, Germany,
the Caroline Islands were taken over by Japan in 1914; following
World War I they were mandated to Japan by the League of Nations. The Japanese retained control until World War II, in the
aftermath of which the Carolines became an American trust territory. Through it all, however, everyday life on this small atoll has
been little affected. Perhaps by good fortune, Ifaluk was gifted
with neither the population, the strategic position, nor the raw
materials to warrant more than passing stabs at "civilizing" by any
of this array of controlling powers.

The people of Ifaluk hold that their population was once much
larger than it is now, and there is a good deal of evidence to suggest
that this is so. For example, while there are 60 married couples in
the present population, there are only 81 inhabitants under 20
years of age (Burrows and Spiro, 1953, p. 5). Since the married
population is not reproducing itself, it is small wonder that in their
regard for the infant there is a total reversal of the Aritama pattern.
Here infants are highly prized and given the most profuse attention and indulgence. Thus, Spiro (Burrows and Spiro, 1953)
writes:

> The infant is idealized and indulged to a degree that is unthinkable
> according to Western standards. . . . no infant is left alone, day
> or night, asleep or awake, until it can walk. To isolate a baby would
> be to commit a major atrocity, for if a baby is left alone, "by and
> by dies, no more people" (p. 257).

And again:

> Babies are constantly being handled, kissed, hugged and played with.
> The people have an inordinate desire to fondle babies, and babies
> are always the center of attention and of attraction in every home
> and in every gathering. . . . A baby knows only smiling and laugh-
> ing faces, soft arms and soft words. No baby is ever handled
> roughly, no baby is scowled at or spoken to with bitterness (p. 245).

Verily, on Ifaluk the infant is king! But by the age of four or five, innocence is lost and so, too, is this affectual paradise. Overt signs of affection are abruptly withdrawn, and the young child is left largely to his own devices. Spiro (Burrows and Spiro, 1953) sums up the starkness of this contrast between age levels as follows: "The minutest frustration of the infant is attended to immediately, whereas much greater frustrations of the child are not only ignored, but often provoke amusement" (p. 275). It does not take great powers of insight to anticipate the consequences of so abrupt a transition: temper tantrums, rivalry for the attention of adults, generalized negativism, fighting, etc.

But on so small an atoll, aggression cannot be allowed to go unchecked. The people of Ifaluk wisely regard cooperation to be the primary social value, and aggression "the most heinous of offenses" (Burrows and Spiro, 1953, p. 276). Thus, from the time that children can speak, their training is directed with an awesome single-mindedness, and with no little harshness, to stamping out all manifestations of discord. And, "Despite the high incidence of aggression in children, this goal of the socialization process is attained with unqualified success, for there are no overt expressions of hostility in the interpersonal relations of Ifaluk adults" (p. 278).

That the resulting harmony is not all that it might be, however, can be seen in their treatment of dogs, for to be a dog on Ifaluk is truly to "lead a dog's life." Spiro (Burrows and Spiro, 1953) notes that "The children, as well as the adults, mistreat the dogs. . . . Children often kick the dogs, pull their tails, and maltreat them in other ways" (p. 278). In a word, Ifaluk, like Aritama, would seem to present a paradigm case of a society in which aggressiveness, inhibited under normal conditions, ought to be manifested with a vengeance under conditions of drunkenness.

Once again, however, this is not what we find. Life on Ifaluk depends on the abundant presence of the coconut palm; its fruit is both the people's basic dietary staple and the source of their alcoholic beverage. The juice, left unstrained, ferments in four days, producing an intoxicant that has been described (Bates and Abbott, 1958) as having "about the strength of good beer" (p. 77). That the ingestion of this intoxicant is often accompanied by dramatic changes-for-the-worse is evidenced by accounts from many parts of Micronesia. Speaking of the consequences of its use on the island of Butaritari in the Gilberts, Robert Lewis Stevenson (published 1912), not without reason, termed it "a devilish intoxicant, the counsellor of crime" (p. 238). That Stevenson's remark was more than an example of mere poetic license is indicated in many other early accounts of life in this area. Consider, for instance, F. W. Christian's (1899) sarcastic account of the aftermath of toddy-drinking festivals in the Gilberts:

> These merry meetings invariably terminated in a fierce free-fight, where men and women joined in the melee with ironwood clubs and wooden swords, thickly studded with sharks' teeth, with which they inflicted ghastly lacerations (p. 165).

And on the islands even closer to Ifaluk, there are many accounts that document a history of violence and discord in the wake of toddy-drinking.[2] Indeed, it was because the chiefs of Ifaluk had observed the deleterious consequences of toddy-drinking on some of the neighboring (and more Westernized) atolls that "they had decided that for the peace and security of the island it would be best if even fermentation were not allowed" (Bates and Abbott, 1958, p. 77). However, "their prohibition works about as well as that tried for some years by the United States. That is to say, those who enjoy drinking fermented toddy . . . make it quietly and drink it without interference" (Burrows and Spiro, 1953, p. 44).

And what happens to their comportment when they do so? According to Burrows and Spiro (1953), essentially nothing: "Some of the men drink glass after glass in the course of an evening. A slightly bleary look about the eyes, and a tendency to be jovial or sentimentally friendly, were the only effects we noticed" (p. 44). Elsewhere, Burrows (1952) wrote that "indulgence in coconut toddy seemed to have a mellowing effect. *We never saw or heard of a 'fighting drunk'*" (emphasis ours, p. 24). In confirmation of these observations we have Bates and Abbott's (1958) account of two farewell parties held in their honor, one given by the young men of Ifaluk and the other by the island's chiefs. Of the first party they report that the toddy "spread a warm feeling of good fellowship through everyone. . . . reality lost all its hard corners, and every man became a brother and the world a paradise"

2. For an extensive statement of the current situation on these islands, see P. R. and P. M. Toomin (1963, pp. 88–94 and *passim*).

(pp. 121–22). Of the latter party they report only that "we were all very gay, because we liked each other so much; and very sad because we would have to part so soon" (p. 122). As with the Camba and the people of Aritama, again the question arises: How is it that on Ifaluk, where one would expect that alcohol would have a field day in releasing pent-up hostility, it has mysteriously lost all force?

For a fourth example of a society in which alcohol proves itself to be strangely incapable of producing disinhibition, we turn to the rural Japanese fishing community of Takashima, as observed in 1950–1951 by the anthropologist Edward Norbeck (1954). A community of 33 households and 188 inhabitants, Takashima is located on a small island in the Inland Sea. It lies about a quarter of a mile off the Japanese coast, and is almost directly opposite the mainland town of Shionasu, where the children go to school and where the adults market, attend meetings of the area's fishing cooperative, etc. Aside from such contacts as these with Shionasu, most of Takashima's inhabitants have little to do with any outside communities, their attention being directed in large measure simply toward making ends meet. Although almost all Takashima males are fishermen, most households do have small plots of land that the women keep under intensive cultivation. Land suitable for agricultural production is very limited on Takashima, however, and since none is ever put up for sale, it is come by only through inheritance. Still, with the exception of purchased rice, the diet of the typical household is largely confined to what members of the household have themselves raised or secured. Through the sale of their excess fish, however, they are very much a part of the money economy, and the amount of money a household possesses is the chief factor in determining its social prestige within the community.

The basic social unit of Takashima society is the household which usually embraces at least three generations and often four. Child rearing, economic affairs, entertainment, and traditional religious observances all revolve around the household. How do the members get along? Norbeck (1954) states that although there is a strong feeling of attachment between most couples, quarreling, although shameful, is considered a normal part of domestic life: "The usual course of such quarrels [being] that the wife eventually gives in, but often not until she has had her say" (p. 51). In so circumscribed a community as Takashima, little occurs that does not almost immediately become common knowledge. Not only is the state of one's domestic relations an open book, but "the habits, reactions, capabilities, and failings of each person are well-known to all other persons" (Norbeck, 1954, p. 115).

Since Takashima's inhabitants are thrown into almost inescapable contact with each other, it is not surprising that the ideal man should be one with whom all relations are smooth. Although he should not be affable to the point of self-effacement, neither should he be "pushing."

> He must never seem to contradict others or openly express opinions at variance with others. He adjusts his actions in accordance with the status of those with whom he has intercourse; elders must be respected and all shades of age and sex distinctions and their attendant behavior patterns are taken into account. . . . Actions or transactions without precedent leave the average person at a loss and are avoided as much as possible (Norbeck, 1954, p. 115).

Still, frictions do arise, and in situations that might become discordant, the usual and preferred course of action is that of avoidance. If avoidance is impossible (which is not infrequently the case), self-control is relied upon to sustain the tranquility of the community. And to good effect, for "beyond the initial situation when tempers and voices may rise briefly, overt expression of dislike or anger toward other persons is not made beyond the confines of one's own household" (p. 117).

So much, then, for the expression—or more correctly, the suppression—of aggression in Takashima. We would now note that in the area of sexuality things are kept similarly "under wraps."

> Rules of sex morality for women are strict, and an illegitimate child is a calamity which brings disgrace to the household and near ruin to the luckless girl. The average young man demands a virginal bride, and in the rare case when a groom fails to regard this as a matter of major importance, his parents will nevertheless demand it. Even the most wayward girl is well aware of the premium placed on chastity and knows that even one slip, if it becomes known, will almost surely prevent her from making a good marriage (Norbeck, 1954, p. 161).

As with aggression, so too with things sexual—the expectation determines the reality. Norbeck writes that "the Takashima girl is now almost invariably a virgin at the time of her marriage" (1954, p. 162). Furthermore, there has not been a single case of illegitimate birth within the *buraku* of Takashima for twenty years, and there has been only one case of even suspected adultery in approximately the same period. Nor does this puritanical orientation relate only to sexual activity; outright obscenity is considered *yaban* ("uncivilized"), the custom of the distant past. Indeed, even the nonprurient discussion of things sexual is considered a *hazukashii tokoro* ("an occasion for embarrassment"), and the subject is usually avoided. Even the custom of "dating," a custom of which the inhabitants of Takashima are well aware, is considered "too bold and daring" (p. 173). So, too, is Western-style dancing, which, although attempted by some, is also considered "a little new and bold for the *buraku*" (p. 85).

So much, then, for the constrictions placed upon everyday affairs in Takashima. It, too, would seem to be an ideal example of a community in which alcohol's purported ability to disinhibit would produce waves of truly tidal proportions. Let us now look at what actually happens. Norbeck (1954) describes a conventional drinking occasion as follows:

> Feasts, and particularly wedding feasts, are the most pleasurable social occasions of life, for even during difficult times strong effort is made to have food and liquor available in liberal quantities at these times. . . . When stomachs are comfortably full of banquet food and the liquor has begun to evince itself, the gathering becomes highly informal. . . . A common form of conviviality is to call upon everyone to render a song. There is hesitation at first until someone bolder than average . . . has sung a song. From that point there is no difficulty, and even the most unaccomplished singers take their turns. Applause follows every turn, and as the party spirit waxes, someone rises and dances to his own singing or to that of others. The party has now reached its height, and several dancers may perform at once. Men, usually careful to avoid bodily contact with other persons, throw their arms affectionately about one another in an excess of friendliness (pp. 87–88).

Such celebrations commence before nightfall and continue until midnight or later. That the participants do, in fact, become quite

drunk is evidenced by Norbeck's (1954) observation that those
drunken guests who must return to the mainland are "carefully
shepherded by their wives and the more clear-headed men for fear
of falling from the small boats and drowning during the crossing
to Shionasu" (p. 88).

Or consider Norbeck's description of the "slambang drunk"
(1954, p. 156) that occurs during the Autumn Festival:

> "[It] is the one occasion of the year when young unmarried men
> (from about sixteen years of age upward) may, without censure,
> become thoroughly drunk. . . .
> Many of the youths are already drunk by the time the *sendairoku*
> (portable shrine) is assembled, although, traditionally, serious drink-
> ing does not occur until later. It is customary to carry the shrine,
> weaving and staggering, back and forth along the main path center-
> ing about the community hall for an interval of perhaps an hour
> while children and adults watch. . . . [Following this] the young
> men, many of them weaving from drink and all sweating profusely,
> convene at someone's house where they continue drinking until
> [all] the *sake* is consumed (p. 155).

Although more of the participants remain sober today than formerly, the Autumn Festival and its aftermath is still an occasion for
boisterous drunkenness. The participants do not, however, become
quarrelsome, for the day of the Festival is formally defined as a
day in which personal animosities are forgotten.

Not all drinking in Takashima is confined to such formal or
quasi-formal occasions, however. Norbeck (1954) writes, for instance, that in the aftermath of a session of gambling—and
gambling, while somewhat cyclical, is endemic among Takashima
males—"winners are expected to be extravagant with their easily
gained money and are chided by their opponents into spending if
they are not liberal in the purchase of *shochu* and *sake*" (p. 85).
Given the fact that "money is the prime topic of conversation for
most men [and that] their thoughts appear to revolve constantly
around the cost of material objects, and the amount of money
possessed by other (and richer) individuals" (p. 206), one would
expect the resulting drunkenness to be particularly acrimonious.
This is not the case, however, for Norbeck gives the following as
his summary depiction of the effects of alcohol upon the Takashima
drinker:

Reactions to alcohol are usually rapid. For many persons the first obvious reaction is a flushing of the face; often only a few of the tiny cups of *sake* or *shochu* will produce a vivid glow. This quick and intense flushing is considered both embarrassing and ugly, but it is also amusing and the subject of friendly jokes. Continued drinking soon results in a good-natured drunkenness, camaraderie, laughter, jokes, songs and dances, which are considered the inevitable result if not the objective of continued drinking (p. 72).

In summary, Takashima—with its insistence upon interpersonal harmony and its rigorously inforced puritanical approach to all things sexual—would seem to be still another society that should be ideally susceptible to alcohol's toxic effects. But not only does alcohol fail to produce tidal waves of aggression and sexuality, it does not even produce ripples. Thus, Takashima joins the list of societies in which alcohol has somehow lost its sting.

We turn now to a fifth and final example of a society in which drunken "disinhibition" *ought* to occur, but does not. This time we examine the town of Juxtlahuaca, in the state of Oaxaca, Mexico, as described by the anthropologists Kimball and Romaine Romney (1963). Juxtlahuaca has a population of approximately 3,600 people, 3,000 of whom are of mixed Spanish and Indian descent, speak Spanish, live in the central town, and differ little in their way of life from the inhabitants of the hundreds of other towns that make up village Mexico. Our interest in Juxtlahuaca, however, lies not in these townsmen, but in the remaining inhabitants—some 600 Mixtec Indians who live as agriculturalists in the *barrio* of Santo Domingo, a "neighborhood" set off from the rest of the town by a deep ravine. These Indians (all members of the *barrio* are Mixtec Indians) speak Mixteco first and Spanish second, if at all, for their heritage derives not from village Mexico, but from their indigenous Indian culture, which has existed in the area for at least the past 2,000 years.

Juxtlahuaca, then, is a town divided. While most of its inhabitants—the Spanish-speaking townsmen—live and work much as do villagers all over Mexico, the Mixtecan minority maintain a distinct language and culture within the confines of their relatively isolated *barrio*. Separate they are, but equal they are not, for the townspeople look down upon the Indians, and they avoid interaction with them wherever possible. The Romneys (1963) report that when interaction does occur, "derogation of Indians by townspeople and deference to townspeople by Indians seem to be the accepted pattern of behavior" (p. 563). Nor are the Mixtecans any better off economically: industry is nonexistent, animal husbandry is of little economic importance, land is scarce, and price levels—both of the goods the Indians must purchase and of the agricultural products they must sell—are set by the townspeople. In short, "it is difficult to make ends meet in the *barrio*, and it is virtually impossible to become rich" (p. 585).

In light of all this, it is small wonder that the Indians' main identifications center on the *barrio* itself and that "none identify much with the larger town of Juxtlahuaca, let alone with the state" (Romney and Romney, 1963, p. 561). Since their experience provides them scant cause to expect much from the outside world, their primary efforts are directed to the maintenance of the reputable character of their membership in the *barrio* proper. What sort of conduct does this entail? The Romneys summarize the character of Mixtec interaction as follows:

> In his relations with other men in the barrio the Indian pattern is adjustive and permissive, while within the town the Spanish pattern is one of ordering and dominating. The statuses of leadership in the barrio . . . are thought of as obligations rather than something to be striven for competitively. . . . [Indeed] envy and competitiveness are regarded as a minor crime. An Indian in a position of prominence never gives orders to his fellows. He may point out the pattern to be followed in a ritual or suggest practical modes of action, but this is in the manner of dispensing knowledge, not of dominating others either by force of personality or by authority of position. . . . Group decisions are made by consensus rather than by majority rule or dictatorial fiat. . . . [In a word] adjustment without friction is the goal, and, if this proves to be impossible, withdrawal rather than domination is the answer (1963, p. 565).

Thus, the Mixtecans place a high value on tranquility; and in the face of abundant reason to expect the contrary, their everyday life is, in fact, remarkably serene. In addition to the threat of ostracism from the ongoing life of the *barrio*, two additional factors to account for the tranquility of normal life are suggested by the Romneys. First, throughout childhood the parents place great emphasis upon training in the control of aggression. For example, (and the examples are numerous), most mothers reported that the sole reason for which they would physically punish their children would be to prevent them from fighting back. Secondly, the Mixtecans share a deeply held pattern of beliefs concerning the causal role of jealousy, anger, and aggression in the production of illness, which acts as a strong deterrent even to remaining in situations that *might* give rise to such emotions. The result of this three-pronged attack appears to be highly successful, for while Indian informants were able to recall specific acts of aggression that had occurred within their lifetimes, all were agreed that such instances were extremely rare. Furthermore, during their full year of residence among the Mixtecans, the Romneys neither witnessed nor heard of a single instance of sober aggression.

Clearly, then, the Mixtecan is a person who is rarely if ever overtly aggressive when he is sober. But what happens when alcohol assaults the higher centers of the Mixtecan brain? Once again we would seem to have legitimate grounds for expecting all hell to break loose. In fact, however, although these Indians drink truly prodigious amounts of alcohol—frequently to the point of passing out—*nothing of the kind occurs*. While the drunken comportment of the Spanish-speaking townspeople follows a pattern quite in keeping with what the disinhibition theory would predict (among them, drunken violence is commonplace), and while the Indian inhabitants of the *barrio* are aware of such drunken changes-for-the-worse in the townspeople, the Romneys (1963, p. 611) report that the Indians specifically deny that alcohol is capable of producing aggression in themselves. And indeed, although the Romneys witnessed numerous instances in which the Mixtecans drank themselves into states of gross intoxication, even at the fiestas during which "the men generally drank a great deal [they] were never observed to become loud or aggressive" (p. 611).

The Romneys (1963) did observe one instance of Mixtecan aggression during their year long study. When they asked the cause of this outburst they were informed that although Pedro was drunk at the time, "[he] had gone to the city to work in the past and there had picked up the habit of smoking marijuana. . . . [Prior to the outburst] he had been smoking marijuana; and, in their opinion, it was only a combination of the marijuana and drinking that could give rise to and account for such aggressive behavior" (p. 609). The Romneys (p. 686) also report a second variant case—that of an adult Mixtecan male whose drinking patterns and drunken aggressivity resembled that of the townspeople. But this person was variant in *most* crucial respects. His wife was Mexican (not Mixtecan), he was the only adult male in the *barrio* whose primary means of support was other than agricultural (he worked in the central part of town as a secretary in the mayor's office, being one of but three *barrio* adults who was considered literate), and, because his identification was with the townspeople, he participated in none of the ceremonies of the *barrio*. In a word, whether drunk or sober, he was very un-Mixtecan both in outlook and in action. So much, then, for drunkenness in Juxtlahuaca.

We have now presented five societies—the Camba, Aritama, Ifaluk, Takashima, and a Mixtec Indian *barrio*—in which the "disinhibiting" effects of alcohol are nowhere to be seen. Even during periods of extreme intoxication, the inhibitions that are normally in effect *remain* in effect. Drunken persons in these societies (and in others like them which we could have selected in their stead) may stagger, speak thickly, and become stuporous, without any corresponding display of changes-for-the-worse. Alcohol *can* be consumed—and, in many societies it *is* consumed—in immense quantities without producing any appreciable changes in behavior save for a progressive impairment in the exercise of certain of one's sensorimotor capabilities. Indeed, the only significant change in comportment reported for any of these societies is an increased volubility or sociability. But it is difficult to attribute even this to the direct action of alcohol, for such changes often begin quite early in the drinking process—they often begin, that is, *before* any appreciable degree of actual bodily intoxication could possibly have taken place.

That such societies should exist argues tellingly against the conventionally accepted notion that alcohol is a substance whose toxic action so impairs man's normally operative controls that he becomes a mere creature of impulse, inexorably doing things that he would not do under normal conditions. In a word, if alcohol were a "superego solvent" for one group of people due to its toxic action, then this same disinhibiting effect *ought to* be evident in *all* people. In point of fact, however, *it is not*. This is the first puzzle with which we confront the conventional wisdom.

3 *"Now-You-See-It-Now-You-Don't"*

The Sway of Time and Circumstance
Over Drunken Comportment

IN A BARREN PORTION of the Lower Sonoran Desert—
part of what is now southern Arizona and northern Sonora, Mexico
—live a group of Indians who call themselves *tohono au' autam,* the
"Desert People." We know them as the Papago, the inhabitants
of an area so inhospitable to homesteading or ranching, so devoid of
economic resources, and so vulnerable throughout history to attack
by Apache raiding parties that their contacts with the agents and
agencies of civilization have until recent years been remarkably
few. Furthermore, since their lands contained little, if anything,
that anyone else might want, those contacts that did occur were
almost uniquely free of conflict. For instance, when the American
cavalry made its appearance, as it eventually did in every area of
the Southwest, it did not come to subdue the Papago, but the Papago's traditional enemy, the Apaches; and in this effort the Papago became the cavalry's eager allies.

Historically, the Papago have been agriculturalists. But to be

agriculturalists in a desert area which boasts an annual rainfall of
but about five inches is to be dependent on the capriciousness of the
rains to a degree we can scarcely imagine. The Papago did not
confront their dependence on the coming of the rains in a spirit of
blind passivity, however. Once each year they engaged in a practice
that they believed to be instrumental in *making* the rains occur;
and much that is most interesting about their traditional way of life
relates to this annual undertaking. The rationale for this effort is
contained in one of their more important myths. It seems that one
day Elder Brother, their deity, noticed the dryness of their soil and
decided to remedy the situation. He placed beads of his perspiration
in the ground and circled the spot in ceremonial fashion for four
days, at the end of which time a saguaro cactus had sprouted, grown
to its full stature, and borne fruit. Elder Brother took this fruit,
mixed its juice with water, and said, "Let me see if we can not
make rain with this to refresh the thirsty soil." With this (the myth
continues), the mixture became wine, and rain began to fall. Thus,
it is held, did the Papago learn to make wine from the fruit of the
saguaro; and thus, too, did they come to learn that by drinking this
wine in annual religious ceremony they achieved the power to "pull
down the clouds," thereby insuring their survival for yet another
year.

So it became customary that when the figlike saguaro fruit was
ripe (conveniently, it ripened just at the end of the dry season), the
Papago went forth from their villages and gathered up this fruit
in great quantities, allocating some to the common store and some
to their private preserves. After sufficient fruit had been collected,
the wine was made—the ceremonial wine in one large batch and
the rest in numerous smaller family batches.

Since the Papago were but a loose confederation of remote villages scattered throughout the vastness of their barren desert abode,
the formal properties of their drinking ceremony varied from one
village to another. The anthropologist Ruth Underhill (1938)
provides the following description of one version of the ceremony:
When the wine was ready for consumption, the Indians gathered
around in a large circle outside the sacred rain house. From the
rain house four cupbearers emerged, each carrying a basket containing the wine. These baskets they brought to four medicine men,
each of whom was sitting in the circle at one of the four points of
the compass. The medicine men then proceeded ritually to cleanse

the wine by rubbing their hands around the baskets. Next, a speech of admonition was delivered to all the participants, stressing the Papago virtues of peacefulness and harmony. Following this, the baskets were passed counterclockwise around the circle, a cupbearer dipping out a portion for each participant and saying as he offered the beverage, "Drink friend. Grow beautifully drunk." The recipient drank and then sang of the glories of dizziness, of the clouds, and of the rain a-coming. And so the ceremony continued, with each man duty-bound to drink to the point of saturation, "even as the rain-soaked earth is saturated." The baskets were refilled again and again from the communal supply; and when this supply was finally exhausted, the formal ceremony was at an end. At this point the participants repaired to their houses where they proceeded to consume their private preserves throughout the night.

That the Papago did in fact get drunk—often "falling-down drunk"—on such occasions has been attested to by all observers. Edward Davis (1920), for instance, in describing a version of the wine ceremony practiced in the village of Quitovaquita in the summer of 1920, writes that "some of the young men, still able to walk, went around to every Indian house and touched every man on the shoulder with a stick of saguaro wood—a summons to go to the tizwin house and get drunk. This [summons] could not be disregarded. . . . Often the men would vomit, then proceed to drink again, and this might happen several times during the night. All drank, both men and boys, until there was not a sober one in the village" (pp. 174–75). Underhill (1938) records a similar observation. Writing of her experiences at Papago wine ceremonies during the early 1930's, she reports, "The young dandies reddened the soles of their feet so that when they fell over, drunk, the beautiful color would show" (p. 31).

What of the Papagos' comportment during these traditional festivities? Carl Lumholtz (1912), describing his experience at such a ceremony about 1909–1910, reported that although he had been told that in earlier times quarrels of long standing were settled at the ceremony, this was no longer the case and that "it was a good tempered crowd" (p. 125) of drunkards that he observed. Davis (1920) confirms the pacific character of the participants, stating flatly that during the wine ceremony that he observed "there was neither quarreling nor fighting" (p. 176). And Underhill (1938), summarizing her observations of several such ceremonies states:

"I, who have seen it [the wine ceremony] often, have never seen
the intoxication lead to anything more violent than song" (p. 22).[1]
Indeed, as Underhill stresses, it is entirely consistent with the
ostensible function of drinking in traditional Papago culture that
"the words which mean 'drunken' and 'dizzy' are, in the Papago
language, sacred and poetic words, for the trance of drunkenness
is akin to the trance of vision" (p. 40). So much, then, for *traditional* Papago drunkenness. It is evident from the independent
reports of Lumholtz, Davis, and Underhill that under traditional
circumstances the Papago, like the members of the societies discussed in the previous chapter, could "really hold their liquor."

But there is booze and there is booze. As one elderly Papago
put it in discussing the cactus wine, "Ours is good liquor. It does
not make you fight and think unhappy thoughts. It only makes you
sing" (Underhill, 1936, p. 47). Not so, however, the white man's
brew. This same informant, reflecting upon the introduction of the
latter among the Papago, reminisced as follows:

> There were white men here and there on our land . . . as there
> never had been. So our men began to learn to drink that whiskey.
> It was not a thing you must drink only once a year like our cactus
> cider. You could drink it any time, with no singing and no speeches,
> and it did not bring rain. Men grew crazy when they drank that
> whiskey (p. 51).

For many years these "two kinds of drinking" existed side by side,
with the American government attempting quite unsuccessfully to
enforce a ban on both. But in their ceremonial observances, the
Papago were passively recalcitrant; when the pressure on one community to suspend observance of the wine ceremony became intense, the inhabitants simply attended the ceremony in another
village. "Do the whites not understand that we have no water
except what comes from the sky? We have no canned food, so we
need the corn to feed our children. We have no automobiles so we
need the hay for our horses. Why then do they say we should not

1. Underhill (1939) does note that although the Papago had a good deal
of sexual freedom even in normal circumstances, there were times when the
rules were entirely abrogated. Thus, during the wine ceremony "men and
women were absolved from marriage bonds and the light and 'playful'
woman was glorified" (p. 197). But such absolution also occurred during
both the scalp dance and the girls' puberty dance—and alcohol played no
part whatsoever in either of these latter ceremonies.

drink the cactus liquor?" (Underhill, 1938, p. 21). Efforts to pro-
hibit the wine ceremony were as unsuccessful as they were inept,
and, to make a long story short, all governmental attempts in this
direction were finally abandoned in 1933.

But in that same year the Civilian Conservation Corps came
into being, and for the first time many Papago youth were drawn
into the wage-labor nexus—a development that the tribal elders
opposed on the grounds that with money in their pockets the young
would come to lose their commitment to the old ways, "to disregard
parental authority, begin drinking and get into trouble" (Joseph,
Spicer, and Chesky, 1949, p. 26). And so it came to be. Joseph
and her co-authors, reporting the situation on the Papago reservation in the mid-1940's, noted, among other things, that "much of the
old religion has disappeared. In most parts of the Reservation people
say that the old men who know the ancient ceremonies are dying
off and that no one else has learned how to conduct them . . ."
(p. 73). At the same time, however, secular drunkenness had
increased tremendously. Some indication of the resulting changes in
the Papago's hitherto peaceable drunken comportment is contained
in the following summary of wives' reactions to secular drinking:

> The women do not mind the drinking itself; what troubles them is
> that it is done in the wrong spirit. Drinking should bring happiness
> and singing, as it does in the wine ceremony, not cruelty and fight-
> ing. Women say that they sometimes talk to their husbands but
> that "they don't pay any attention." Others simply leave home until
> their husbands sober up (Joseph et al., 1949, pp. 76–77).

While in earlier times everyone, and perhaps most particularly
the children, had looked forward to the wine ceremony in joyful
anticipation—"Everybody sang. We felt as if a beautiful thing was
coming. Because the rain was coming and the dancing and the
songs" (Underhill, 1936, p. 10)—by the mid-1940's this was no
longer true:

> During the fiesta the small child learns of a new danger. He finds
> that men, perhaps his father and uncles, at times, behave strangely.
> His female relatives snatch him out of the way and whisper,
> "Drunk!" in the same tone they use to warn him of ghosts. He
> learns to run away when drunks lurch near him and to ignore them
> completely when they accost him; sometimes he witnesses brawls or

other violence. By the time he is five, he has probably developed a strong fear of drunkenness, but he views it as something to be expected at a fiesta (Joseph *et al.*, 1949, p. 129).

In the 1950's, the sale of liquor to the Indians was at last legalized. The entirely predictable result was that alcohol consumption increased greatly among the Papago and that "many men and women, too, [are] now regular 'sots and wine-o's' " (Poe, 1964, p. 148). With the Papago, then, we appear to have caught—in mid-passage, as it were—an historical change both in the meaning of drunkenness and in the comportment that accompanies it. Now the Papago, like so many other tribes before them, are fast becoming (if they have not already become) "just another bunch of drunken Indians" for whom drunken changes-for-the-worse are all too prevalent. Of this we shall have a good bit more to say in Chapter 6.

We turn now to the Society Islands for a second example of a culture in which drunken comportment has undergone marked changes over historical time. When Captain Samuel Wallis, commanding *H.M.S. Dolphin*, sighted Tahiti (the principal island in the Society group) in June of 1767, he became the first European to discover this fabled island of love and beauty.[2] All Europe was soon to read of this tropical paradise, where every vision was beautiful, and where the women were said to be as lovely as they were eager to extend every possible favor to visiting Europeans. When Count Louis de Bougainville independently chanced upon Tahiti less than a year later, his account "confirmed" that the Noble Savage did in fact exist; and the Western imagination has never been quite the same. For Rousseau, and for all succeeding Romantics, the words of Bougainville have never ceased to echo: "I thought I was walking in the Garden of Eden."

As more and more European vessels arrived at Tahiti, however, the fabric of Tahitian life began to alter. And while Tahiti suffered less from the intrusive rewards of "civilization" than did many other Pacific islands, the coming of the Europeans was a good deal less than an unmitigated blessing. Among the many "gifts" of these first European interlopers were such dubiously beneficient introductions as muskets, fleas, venereal disease, and alcohol. It is the Tahitian response to this latter offering that we want to consider. Specifically, we shall attempt to document that their comportment

2. Although Tahiti is but one island in the Society Island group, "Tahiti" is sometimes used, and we shall sometimes use it, as a generic term for the whole of the Society Islands.

while "under the influence" has been anything but uniform over the years.

Before Captain Wallis' visit, Tahiti, like the other islands of Polynesia, had no alcohol. Rather, the Tahitians, as other Polynesians, drank kava, a beverage they made from the root of the plant *piper methysticum*. While kava was generally monopolized by the chiefs and priests, it was in general demand and was drunk by any man who could obtain it. The effects of kava were said to be quite uniform—drinkers became pleasantly relaxed and fuddled, and when they fell asleep, as they usually did after imbibing heavily, they had pleasant dreams. No one—neither the Tahitians nor the first Europeans who, seeing kava being drunk, decided to try it for themselves—ever thought of it as more than a mild tranquilizer. Certainly it was never construed as a "disinhibitor." [3] In contrast, from the moment of its first introduction, alcohol *was* so construed.

The crews of European sailing vessels of the late eighteenth century were anything but models of temperance. Such ships carried large quantities of alcoholic beverages, but no matter how much they carried, it seems that it had all been consumed by the time they returned to port. The *Dolphin*, for example, carried rum, brandy, beer, and wine; at that time the official liquor ration aboard ships of the Royal Navy was one gallon of beer per man per day. When the *Dolphin* reached Tahiti, her liquor stores were still ample, and throughout her stay, both men and officers received their regular liquor rations without interruption. It is clear from the accounts of Wallis' stay on Tahiti that the natives had frequent opportunity to observe the effects of alcohol upon more than one British sailor.

Furthermore, as was often the case when these early explorers met the native inhabitants of strange lands, the British officers offered alcoholic beverages to some of the more important of the natives. One of Wallis' officers, George Robertson, records such an event involving a dinner to which the chief priest of Tahiti, one Tupaia, was invited. On a table laden with an immense feast, there was an array of spirits including claret, Madeira, port, rum, brandy grog, and London porter, from which all partook. However, while the British drank their customary large amounts, Tupaia only tasted the wine and the grog, decided that he liked neither, and settled for water (Rowe, 1955, p. 171).

---

3. Nor is it so construed today. See Edwin Lemert (1967).

That this was not a unique reaction is evidenced by the fact that when subsequent ships visited Tahiti, the Tahitians continued to display a definite distaste for alcohol. Bougainville makes no mention of alcohol in his chronicle, but the third explorer to reach Tahiti, Captain James Cook, had with him Sir Joseph Banks, and Banks (published 1963) recorded a most significant development. Cook's expedition arrived in Tahiti in 1769, two years after Wallis' discovery, and once again Tupaia, in this instance accompanied by other priests and chiefs, was invited on board. This time the occasion was the birthday of King George III, and as a warrant of their loyalty and affection to the King, the Tahitians were induced to drink to the King's health. In a short time all the celebrants, Tahitians and Englishmen alike, became "roaring" drunk. Although Banks does not describe their resulting comportment, he does make it clear that the Tahitians who were present disliked the experience and wanted no repetition of it. Indeed, summarizing the Tahitians' overall reactions to alcohol during the course of his stay on the Island, Banks wrote:

> Some there were who drank pretty freely of our liquors and in a few instances became very drunk but seemed far from pleased with their intoxication, the individuals afterwards shunning a repetition of it instead of greedily desiring it as most Indians are said to do (Vol. 1, p. 346).

Three years later, in 1772, the first Spanish explorers, sailing under Captain Don Domingo de Boenechea, arrived on Tahiti, and they too offered liquor to the natives, Again, the Tahitians drank sparingly or refused it altogether. Fray Joseph Amich, a priest accompanying Boenechea, wrote of the Tahitians that while they were very fond of their native kava, "the wine on board the frigate did not appeal to them" (published 1914, p. 85).

Although we do not have an unbroken chronicle of the ensuing years, early Spanish accounts suggest that this distaste for alcohol continued for at least the next few years (Hakluyt Society, 1914). It did not, however, continue for very much longer than that, for when Vancouver put into Tahiti in 1791, he reported that the then reigning paramount chief, Pomare, and his followers "had become addicted to strong European Spirits" (Langdon, 1959, p. 74). Thus, Vancouver reported that on one occasion Pomare came aboard his ship, the *Discovery*, consumed a bottle of brandy and "became so violent that four strong men were required to hold him down . . ." (Godwin, 1930, pp. 50–51).

And when John Turnbull, an English adventurer-chronicler, arrived in Tahiti in 1802, he found that Vancouver's remarks were, if anything, an understatement. Turnbull (1813) wrote that Pomare would mooch liquor from every European ship that reached Tahiti, and that he was so "addicted to the use of such liquors [that] he would go to any length to procure them" (p. 134). Turnbull also described the effects of this liquor upon Pomare and those about him as "dreadful," with the men becoming angry and violent, and the women silly and childish (pp. 146–47). He noted, too, that women who were normally treated with kindness were often struck by their drunken husbands, and that members of the Tahitian royal family typically became "outrageous and brutal when intoxicated" (p. 147):

> The effects of their inebriety were really horrible. Otoo the young king was so furious in his fits of intoxication, that I am persuaded he would make no scruple of killing his subjects out of mere ferocity (p. 149).

Certainly, by Turnbull's time there can be no question that the Tahitians had had ample occasion to see what alcohol did to the crews of European trading ships and whalers, which were visiting Tahiti in ever greater numbers. James Morrison, former boat-swain's mate on the *Bounty*, tells of one such European "model" of drunken decorum. Returning to Tahiti with one group of the muti-neers from the *Bounty*—the other group of mutineers had gone on to Pitcairn Island, where their drunken debauches helped lead to their virtual extinction (Shapiro, 1964)—Morrison found that there was one European already residing on the island. This man, an English sailor named Brown, had been forced off a previous ship as a hopeless incorrigible. Morrison kept a careful chronicle (published 1935) of his stay on Tahiti, and in it he recorded that after his first meeting with Brown, a local chief produced a letter signed by his former captain, T. H. Cox, wherein Brown was referred to as "an Ingenious handy Man when sober but when Drunk a dangerous fellow" (Morrison, 1935, p. 79). Morrison also records that his band of mutineers set up more than one still on the island, as Brown himself had most probably done even earlier. And Turnbull (1813) wrote that the Tahitians had somehow obtained several grape plants which had grown to maturity by the time of his arrival. He further recounted that one day the Tahitians' desire for alcohol grew so imperative that a number of men pulled the still green grapes from the vines and ate them in anticipation of instant intoxication, and that when the grapes failed to produce this desired effect, the enraged Tahitians tore all the grapes from the vines.

Although the first missionaries reached Tahiti in 1797, their efforts did not become concerted for another twenty years, and missionary control did not really begin to be achieved until the late 1830's. It was during the period prior to this stabilization of power that Tahitian drunkenness seems to have displayed its most violent aspect. Thus, when William Ellis (1853), one of the more scholarly of the missionaries, arrived in Tahiti in 1817, he summarized the documents left by his immediate predecessors as follows:

> Intemperance at this time prevailed to an awful and unprecedented degree. . . . [The natives] exhibited, in a proportionate degree, all the demoralizing and debasing influences of drunkenness. . . . Whole districts frequently united, to erect what might be termed a public still. . . . When the materials were prepared, the men and boys of the district assembled in a kind of temporary house, erected over the still. . . . In this employment they were sometimes engaged for several days together, drinking the spirit as it issued from the still, sinking into a state of indescribable wretchedness, and often practising the most ferocious barbarities. . . . Under the unrestrained influence of their intoxicating draught, in their appearance and actions they resembled demons more than human beings. Sometimes in a deserted still-house might be seen fragments of the rude boiler, and the other appendages of the still, scattered in confusion on the ground; and among them the dead and mangled bodies of those who had been murdered with axes or billets of wood in the quarrels that had terminated their debauch (Vol. 2, pp. 130–32).

In 1830 the Belgian trader Moerenhout, writing about conditions in the port town of Papeete, referred to the deplorable effects of liquor upon the Tahitians, who, he said, "are only too easily given to drunkenness; thus one soon saw, everywhere, only drunks, at any time, on all sides, day and night, women and men" (1837, Vol. 1, p. 312). And a missionary from the London Missionary Society recorded of his visit to the Islands in 1832 that he was "perfectly astounded at beholding the scenes of drunkenness which prevailed . . ." (Williams, 1837, p. 405).

Frederick Bennett (1840), the captain of a whaler that put into Tahiti in 1834, was able to say no better of the Tahitians than that "nothing short of the most complete inebriety will satisfy them" (Vol. 1, p. 125). And to this he added that it was a common sight to see "debauched islanders parading the settlement in a state of riotous intoxication . . . yelling like demons, until, incapable of further advance, they expended their last gleam of reason in seeking the nearest shed for a swinish repose" (Vol. 1, pp. 125–26). And Mrs. Thomas Mortimer (1838), who wrote "of the labours of the first missionaries in the South Sea Islands," commented sadly on the fact that the many sailors who visited the Islands at this time had great success in trading liquor for native goods and that, in consequence, "Drunkards might often be seen lying senseless on the beach, or quarreling and fighting with each other till blood was shed" (p. 401).

In the ensuing years, violence continued to be referred to by European visitors. For example, when Captain Sir Edward Belcher (1843) attempted to leave the island in 1841 after a stay of almost a year, he was implored by the local queen to remain in order that she might be protected against the king, who "in a fit of intoxication" had recently attempted to "kill her with a stone" (Vol. 2, p. 10).

Such accounts as these make it abundantly clear that within a relatively short period of time the Tahitians' initial distaste for both alcohol and the resulting state of drunkenness became transformed to a more familiar portrait—that of still another native people with an insatiable craving for liquor. And, as in so many other "primitive" societies, when they succeeded in satisfying this craving, the resulting drunkenness was accompanied by marked changes-for-the-worse.

But *not* so today. Barnaby Conrad (1962, p. 148), for instance, has recently reported of contemporary drinking practices that, while most Tahitians get drunk on week-ends, their comportment is remarkably amiable in character. The present state of affairs has also been examined in some detail by the sociologist, Edwin Lemert, and by the psychiatrist, Robert Levy, both of whom agree with Conrad that the Tahitians' present-day drunken comportment is essentially nonviolent. Lemert (1964) notes that not only is drunken aggression uncommon, but when it does occur it is a pretty bland affair, "being mostly verbal, or random pushing and slapping.

Stones or weapons are never used" (pp. 367–68). Levy, who recently spent three years in ethnographic research in the Society Islands, most of it in an isolated community on the island of Huahine, provides a more detailed account of contemporary Tahitian drunkenness that confirms Lemert's observations in all significant respects. The inhabitants of Huahine drink beer, red Algerian wine, and illegally home-brewed orange beer in considerable amounts, sometimes over a period of several days. Of their resulting drunken comportment, Levy (1966) writes that "public aggressive behavior is very rare, even in crowds of people who have been drinking for two or three days" (p. 314). And again, "If there was little violence under ordinary conditions, there also seemed to be little under conditions of personal breakdown, including drunkenness. Drinking was common, particularly during the two yearly festivals. [But] with the exception of a few incidents, the people were as unhostile drunk as sober" (Levy, in press). Indeed, it would appear that the present state of affairs could scarcely be in sharper contrast to that earlier time when Tahitian drunkenness was accompanied by all manner of violence, for, as one of Levy's informants put it, it is now the case that, "If you have been feeling angry, you drink and the anger goes away. You just want to enjoy yourself, you don't pay any attention any more . . ." (In press).

We have now followed the Tahitian reaction to alcohol through three successive periods. In the first, Tahitians rejected alcohol, either refusing it altogether or, if they drank it once, choosing to avoid it on subsequent occasions. In the second period, Tahitians drank heavily and avidly and, when they were drunk, they were notably violent, with bloodshed a not uncommon outcome. In the present period, the Tahitians continue to drink, often heavily, but now their drunken comportment is pacific in character.

What could possibly have transpired? While at each of these three stages we *have* been talking about alcohol, its effects upon Tahitian comportment have changed—and changed dramatically —from one stage to the next. And when we place the Tahitian example alongside that of the Papago, our puzzle is twice compounded. For while with the Tahitians the historical progression has been from overt violence and aggressivity to civility, with the Papago it has been precisely the opposite. In a word, it would seem that alcohol's ability to "disinhibit" is sometimes as capricious as the course of history itself.

And there is no end to this sort of bafflement. For still another example in which time and circumstance have combined to determine the character of drunken comportment, we want now to examine the drunken doings of those many thousands of cattle-herding Bantu tribesmen who inhabit that great swath of land that is the high veld of southern and southeastern Africa. These tribesmen drink a native grain beer that not only is the *sine qua non* of most of their secular festivities, but plays an essential role in most of their religious rituals as well. For these Africans, beer has long served a multitude of purposes—to enliven a social gathering, to solemnize a birth or a death, to propitiate supernatural beings, etc. And as the occasion of their drinking differed, so, too, did the nature of their drunken comportment. Thus, there was awed silence on many religious occasions, easy-going conviviality during casual everyday drinking, boisterous hilarity and increased sexual freedom during some of their secular ceremonies. But within the context of traditional practices—and this is the point—their doings conformed to their understanding of what the occasion called for.

·An illustration of the "appropriate-to-the-occasion" character of their drunken comportment is available in the anthropologist Hugh Ashton's (1952) account of one of these tribes, the Basuto. The Basuto are avid beer-drinkers for whom the most important social occasion is the feast; and while feasts are held in connection with many ceremonies, both secular and religious, they are also given (as they put it) "just for the sake of a party." Drinking is a principal attraction of every feast, and the success with which any given feast is viewed is determined largely by the quantity and strength of the beer that is provided (p. 93). Typically, everyone drinks from a communal drinking pot that is passed from person to person. The men drink rapidly, the women more slowly; and at most feasts substantial amounts of beer are consumed.

But there is certainly nothing unique in any of this. It is when Ashton describes the participants' comportment at these various feasts that his account becomes intriguing. For although he is talking about the *same* people, drinking the *same* native beer, he emphasizes the fact that what these people do when they have this beer inside them is highly variable, and that this variation is in strict accordance with the demands of the occasion:

People's behaviour at feasts and other social gatherings is generally quiet and dignified. They talk a lot, usually topical trivialities, with a gusto which varies greatly with the occasion. On formal occasions they are restrained and sedate, but their behaviour varies considerably with the nature of the occasion. Thus the opening celebrations of boys' and girls' initiation allow wide licence to men and women, as the case may be, and the former particularly are liable to become quite unrestrained; weddings and witch doctor seances . . . are jolly; funeral feasts are quiet, sometimes almost lugubrious. Feasts that are primarily family affairs, such as weddings, the return of the bride, or various small rites . . . are more or less informal, depending on the importance of the occasion and the status of the host, and the guests may laugh, joke and enjoy themselves in a friendly and free (but not licentious) manner" (p. 94).

On all of these occasions, Basuto comportment is free of rancor. However, there are certain beer drinks (such as those held at the conclusion of communal work parties) during which the participants are likely to become both noisy and quarrelsome. But Ashton informs us that even on these latter occasions the quarrels almost never reach the point of actual physical violence.

For a second account of traditional tribal beer-drinking in this area, we quote from the description given by anthropologist E. J. and J. D. Krige (1943) of Lovedu drinking on their native reserve:

A typical beer-drinking scene meets the eye. The centre of the picture is a large pot of beer placed in a rounded depression made for it in the courtyard. Beside it stands a flat winnowing basket containing long-handled calabash cups from which the beer is drunk. . . . The guests have ranged themselves on either side of the beer pot, women on one side, men on the other. . . . There is no hurry. Each one drinks at his leisure and conversation flows freely. . . . It is a pleasant social gathering and all the latest gossip is discussed. Small children toddle about in between the drinkers and may even be given a little of the beer" (p. 26).

The Kriges add that while such beer-drinking results in "a state of exhilaration," Lovedu beer parties remain quite orderly from start to finish, with all participants maintaining a proper sense of decorum throughout.

' But when this traditional Lovedu drinking pattern is altered— when, for instance, the Lovedu move only a few miles from their reserve to work on European farms where "beer can never be used in its full cultural context"—the Kriges report that their drunken comportment becomes "pathological" (1943, p. 297). That "excesses" are often displayed in this latter situation is evidenced by the frequently voiced lament of the local white farmers concerning "the demoralizing effect of beer" on the natives (p. 297).

Over the course of time, the towns, cities, and farms of the Europeans have come to attract ever larger numbers of Africans who, as they have abandoned their tribal areas, have also abandoned their traditional drinking practices. We want now to take a more detailed look at these changes by focusing on the sort of drunken comportment one finds among these tribesmen in *urban* South Africa. Specifically, we shall direct our attention to Rooiyard, an African slum neighborhood on the outskirts of Johannesburg, as described by the sociologist Ellen Hellmann (1948). These slum "yards," as they are called in South Africa, are, among other things, the centers of the illegal beer-brewing trade, and they are also the locus of the serious social disturbances that go along with this trade. Rooiyard is but one of a large number of small, densely populated areas of ramshackle dwellings in which Africans who live and work in Johannesburg are quartered. Disease among the inhabitants of Rooiyard is rife, crimes of all sorts are a daily occurrence, beer-drinking is the most common form of recreation, and, although the production of native beer is illegal throughout Johannesburg, virtually every woman in the slum yard both brews and sells it regularly (p. 91). While this illicit brew differs little if at all in its alcoholic content from that produced on the tribal reserves (it being about 4 to 5 per cent in both cases), the situation in which it is consumed is markedly different.

> The restraints observed at a beer drink under tribal conditions—the relationship of host and guests, the demand that dignity be maintained, the opprobrium consequent upon unseemly behaviour, the frequent separation of the sexes— cannot be maintained in surroundings where beer is bought, and where the relationship between host and guest is converted into one between seller and purchaser. Of the traditionally prescribed etiquette and procedure of beer-drinking prevailing in the kraals (native reserves) nought is left in Rooiyard (p. 91).

And accompanying these changed circumstances, Hellmann reports the following changes in comportment:

Intoxication frequently leads to the quarrels and stabbing affrays which are such a common feature in Rooiyard beer-drinks. Barely a week-end, when the sale of beer is most active, passed without some casualty occurring from fights during the course of which many Natives were quick to resort to the use of knives. . . . Practically without exception, competition for women is the cause of fights. Usually the struggle for the favours of a woman is an individual affair between two men. It does occur, however, that tribesmen aid each other and the danger of a lengthy and organised fight is then greatly increased. . . . Apart from actual quarrels, it has happened that men, intoxicated to the point of being unconscious of their surroundings, have run amok in the yard, stabbing blindly (p. 92).

Even in the urban slum of Rooiyard, however, it is not always thus. Hellmann (1948) reports that on certain occasions the natives organize formal dances, concerts, and parties, and at such times, even though beer drinking is a paramount feature of the entertainment, there is no violence. Instead, we hear only of "convivial" drinking, of "singing and dancing," and of "merriment and pleasure" (pp. 17, 45–46, and *passim*). That at these more formal gatherings beer drinking once again follows many of the otherwise absent traditional practices is evident, for example, in Hellmann's description of a girl's puberty ceremony at which the traditional host-guest relationship was reasserted. About this ceremony Hellmann notes that while the hosts had provided an abundance of beer for the occasion, "the revelry continued in an atmosphere of general goodwill and gaiety till the dawn" (p. 72).

Yet such instances of drunken tranquility among the urban natives are rare indeed, for volume after volume addressed to the problem of drunkenness in South Africa chronicles the fact that when the urban Bantu migrants get drunk, violence is the typical outcome. In fact, so troublesome has the drunken comportment of the urban Bantu become that over the years the government has found it necessary to impose a series of increasingly severe laws prohibiting their consumption of liquor. Despite these laws, however, African drinking in the cities of South Africa has been described not simply as a "problem," but as a "national menace." Indeed, this menace has been held to include everything the most fervent prohibitionist might possibly imagine: disease, poverty, prostitution, family dissolution, and rampant violence. Although during the single year of 1950, more than 250,000 cases of liquor offenses by

Africans were prosecuted in the city of Johannesburg alone, it is widely believed that "the menace" was scarcely dented thereby. Thus, the anthropologist Laura Longmore (1959) recommends, as have many familiar with South Africa, that the government must act rapidly if the urban Africans are "to be protected from their inordinate thirst, which is debasing and demoralizing them and impoverishing their families" (p. 228).

In summary, then, we have here an example in which the peoples of a large area, who for centuries were able to drink alcoholic beverages without any "trouble" within their own tradition-bound world, find themselves somehow incapable of handling alcohol once they have departed tradition for the world of the European. While the beverage of the South African Bantu has not changed, the circumstances surrounding its consumption most certainly have. And as these circumstances have changed, so, too, has their drunken comportment.

But what people do when they are drunk is almost everywhere situationally variable, and it is often dramatically so. While the examples from which we could draw to exemplify this point are legion, we trust that it will be sufficient to present a few brief accounts in which the situationally variable nature of drunken comportment will be apparent upon even the most casual inspection. For our first example we turn to James Ritchie's (1963) description of a small Maori community located in the center of North Island, New Zealand. According to Ritchie, Maori drinking in this community falls into one of two general classes— drinking "sessions" or drinking "parties." Drinking *sessions* are exemplified by a group of friends who gather, say, on a Saturday afternoon and slowly but steadily consume liquor over a period of four to five hours. "The men will sit in the sun, talk, sleep, listen to the radio, particularly for the race results, and drink" (p. 80). The prevailing atmosphere of drinking sessions such as the above is anything but euphoric, being rather "drowsy, relaxed, and possibly a little depressive" (p. 80).

Maori drinking *parties*, however, stand in sharp contrast to all this—they are "gay and noisy" and usually last the night through. Nor is this all that differentiates the session from the party. Ritchie (1963) reports that the comportment of the participants in the two situations is equally different. "In the later stages of parties, violence is quite common (out of six parties held in one week-end four finished with a fight). There is also a sexual undertone at parties which is quite absent from sessions" (p. 80). Ritchie suggests, then, that while drinking in sessions gives rise to a "peaceful (though often depressive) insulation," Maori comportment at parties "is often aggressive, usually egocentric and self-enhancing" (p. 88).

We now shift our attention to the anthropologists Thomas and Hatsumi Maretzki's (1963) description of life in the small, rural village of Taira, on the northeast coast of Okinawa. The 700 or so inhabitants of Taira make their living—as have many generations of their ancestors before them—from their nearby fields, the forest, and the sea. Life in Taira is so peaceable that the services of the village's one policeman are seldom needed. As the Maretzkis put it: "Policing the village itself is not a difficult job. The absence of crime and the low incidence of quarrels, disputes, and brawls would seem to make policing unnecessary" (p. 411). They report further that the rare quarrels that do occur are either the product of domestic financial problems or arise when the participants have been drinking (p. 411). Thus, in Taira, as in so many societies, everyday tranquility is subject to drunken disruption. But only sometimes, for as with the Maori, so too with the inhabitants of Taira—there are "two kinds of drinking."

The villagers of Taira, particularly the men, find many occasions for the drinking of sake. It is consumed by both sexes at many of their parties and ceremonies, and by men alone at the end of a day of work and at some all-male gatherings. When men drink together, especially if they are young men, the relaxed good-fellowship that ordinarily exists between them sometimes gives way to quarreling and even to brawling. As the Maretzkis described these all-male occasions, "If enough sake is available, parties can become noisy. Occasionally a fight or quarrel starts later in the evening after everybody has drunk steadily" (1963, p. 389).

Things are quite different, however, when men and women drink together, as they do when they celebrate their many village holidays. The Maretzkis describe such holiday festivities as follows: "By the time men—and a little later women—have been served food and drink in some quantity, there is no more stiffness in the room, for with every cup of sake animation and voice volume increase" (1963, p. 451). As the customary reserve between the sexes diminishes, men and women tell off-color jokes and mimic each other. By way of illustration, the Maretzkis describe the comportment at one such celebration as follows:

> As [they] imbibe more sake, they become gayer, and more talents are unleashed. Amusing presentations of a husband and wife, in which sometimes aggression and sexual interaction are acted out playfully, are received with great hilarity by the audience. If such a suggestive performance is given by an old woman and a young man, it seems to appear even funnier (p. 452).

Despite the apparently "disinhibited" antics of both young and old on such occasions, and despite the prevailing sexual innuendo, these parties are completely free of drunken aggression. Thus, the Maretzkis state that:

> Not a single event that we attended was marred by any serious unpleasantness. No guest was ever seen to become sick, although some men drank themselves into a stupor. Here and there a paper screen may be broken as a result of a tumbling body, or a hard bang against a thin panel may set the house shaking. But the end of such a feast would be nothing more uproarious than a group of singing celebrants seeking further entertainment from house to house (pp. 452–53).

In summary then, when men and women drink together, drunken aggression never occurs, but when men drink by themselves, it does.

For a somewhat different example of the situationally variable nature of drunken comportment, we now turn to the anthropologist William Madsen's (1967) account of the Nahuatl-speaking Indian village of San Francisco Tecospa, one of several Indian villages located in the administrative subdivision of Milpa Alta in the Federal District of Mexico. Although the Mexican government has done much to bring its Indian population into the mainstream of national life, the Indians of Milpa Alta, like those of many other sections of the country, are reluctant to abandon their traditional ways. The Tecospan views himself in the first instance as a member of his community, secondly as an Indian, and only thirdly, if at all, as a Mexican national. While he willingly accepts those technological advances that will better his material position, "he wants no part of the efforts to change his identity, his primary loyalties, or his 'spirit' " (Madsen, 1967). The nature of this Indian identity is the

way of one's ancestors; the primary loyalties are to family and to
community; and the "spirit" is one of peaceful cooperation within a
network of essentially egalitarian respect relationships. And in
Tecospa, respect is accorded to all who adequately satisfy the duties
that go with their respective stations in life. A man is expected to be
a good farmer, and a woman, a good homemaker; and any attempt
to outshine one's fellows or to aggress against them is considered
highly improper.

The Indians of Tecospa, then, are traditionalists, and they are
wedded to the land. This land, besides producing maize, beans,
and squash, produces the maguey plant from which they make
pulque, their native intoxicant. From pre-Conquest times to the
present, *pulque* has been considered a holy beverage—"the milk of
our mother" (the Virgin) as they now put it—and an integral
part of Tecospan life from conception to the hereafter. Madsen
reports that expectant mothers often take an extra serving of
pulque for "the one inside" them; and that the dead are buried
with tortillas and *pulque* to sustain them on their trip to the next
world, where, immediately upon their arrival in heaven, they begin
to raise crops, not the least important of which is the maguey plant.
Since the Tecospans' *pulque* is a product of their land—the land in
which their ancestors lie buried and in which they themselves will
someday repose—they believe it to be discernibly different from and
superior to that produced anywhere else. Furthermore, while they
avoid water "like the plague," they view *pulque* as a healthful
drink. Not only do they hold that its ingestion gives rise to feelings
of contentment and harmony, they believe that it serves to *counter-
act* anger and other emotions which, if allowed to run their course,
would threaten their spiritual and physical well-being and make
them antisocial.

Since solitary drinking is considered a sign of degeneracy (and
is in any case virtually unknown), drinking in Tecospa is almost
always a group activity. While they usually begin their drinking
with ritual toasts and countertoasts, these formalities tend to be
relaxed as the evening progresses, and they frequently drink to the
point of collapse. About their comportment during such gatherings,
Madsen (1967) says the following:

> Within these drinking groups, any display of aggression or hostility
> toward a fellow drinker is regarded as unthinkable. One is drinking

a sacred beverage produced in the village by his host and it is a time
for sharing of common identities rather than [for] an airing of individual differences or disagreements. In such a drinking group made
up exclusively of Tecospans, I have never heard people argue in
anger or display physical violence. Rather, group intoxication inten-
sifies the feeling of community and oneness. . . . The greater the
mutual sharing of *pulque*, the greater is the feeling of unity.

In a word, despite the high degree of intoxication the Tecospans
achieve, when they drink among themselves, the sharing of *pulque*
symbolizes social and spiritual brotherhood, and violence is unheard
of.

But the Tecospans do not confine their drinking to such gatherings as these. And at these other times conflict and violence *do*
occur. During a village fiesta, for instance, Indians from several
neighboring communities may assemble, and on these occasions the
Tecospans often become involved in drunken disputes with the
outsiders. While such disputes are typically smoothed over before
they give rise to violence, fights have occasionally erupted between
groups from different villages. Conflicts are even more frequent
when the Tecospans attend the fairs and fiestas held in the surrounding market towns. On such occasions they are often ridiculed by the
mestizo townspeople, and if they are "drunk enough to answer
back in kind," fighting not infrequently ensues.

The Tecospans, then, present us with an example of a people
who, when they drink *pulque* among themselves, typically have
only feelings of contentment and harmony. But when they drink in
the company of outsiders, whether these outsiders are Indians or
mestizos, the outcome is often quite the opposite.

For a final and dramatic example of the impact of the situation
upon drunken comportment, we turn to the anthropologist Francis
Huxley's (1957) account of a Tupi-speaking Indian tribe who inhabit a remote jungle area between the Gurupi and the Turi
Rivers in northern Brazil. These Indians call themselves *caápor*
or "wood-dwellers," but others know them as the Urubu (literally,
"vultures"), the name apparently deriving from their war cry,
Urubu ne u!"—"Vultures eat you!" And indeed, until very recent times (the Urubu were finally pacified only in the mid-
1920's), they did practice ritual cannibalism upon their enemies.
Nor is their warlike past an entirely closed book, for, although the
Urubu have given up cannibalism, Huxley informs us that even

now "there are a number of enemy Indians who still live in the jungle nearby, and should an Urubu meet one of them arrows are certain to fly" (p. 98).

The Urubu drink a manioc beer, the making of which is surrounded with various taboos, for they believe that "a magical transformation" is taking place. Specifically, they believe that the alcohol thus produced is a spirit, that in drinking it this spirit takes possession of them, and that this spiritual possession (*i.e.*, drunkenness) makes them *kaú*, "crazy." Thus they call their beer *kaú-i*, which literally means "crazy water."

According to Huxley, who spent several months among the Urubu, there are two sure indications of whether two tribesmen are on good terms with one another: the first is whether they want to live in the same village, and the second is whether they fear getting drunk together. Since the Urubu "know" that they lose their self-control when they are drunk, they seldom attend feasts with people with whom they have quarreled. They shy away from such encounters not because they are afraid of fighting; to be a willing and able fighter is to be "hard," and in the Urubu scheme of things "hardness" is the paramount virtue. Rather, their reticence is predicated on the recognition that doing injury to one's own tribesman is scarcely proper, and that since one "loses control" when he is drunk, the outcome might be tragic. Huxley relates one instance in which this bit of practical circumspection went unheeded. It seems that Caro and Toí had a quarrel, a short time after which Caro staged a feast to which Toí, among others, was invited. At the urging of his mother-in-law, and against his own better judgment, Toí attended. Huxley (1957) describes the ensuing events as follows:

> Everyone got drunk, including Caro. Towards morning, when the others were happily singing in their hammocks, he started up suddenly, stamped the ground in a rage and shouted. . . . There was a chief from another village present, who tried to calm him down —"Go back to your hammock, you're drunk; we're happy, we're singing. Go back to your hammock and sleep." But Caro took no notice, he just went on stamping and shouting till he rushed over to where Toí was sitting, pulled the red cap he wore from his head, and struck at him with a machete. One blow got him behind the right ear . . . one on the nape of the neck, one below the left ear, and another over the heart. Luckily for him, Caro only used the

flat of the machete blade so that he wasn't hurt much; luckily, too, all the other Indians immediately threw themselves on top of Caro and held him down, while the women and children ran off into the jungle (p. 112).

That the consequences of Urubu drinking can be of more tragic moment is exemplified in Huxley's (1957) account of the single instance he knows of in which a Urubu killed a fellow tribesman. It seems that at another Urubu feast one of the celebrants got "wildly drunk" and "picked up a machete and whirled it around his head in a sudden outburst of animal spirits; then, drunk as much with a feeling of power as from cauin [manioc beer], he rushed into a hut slashing at houseposts as he went. Unfortunately for him, the second housepost he struck was really a man, whom he killed outright" (p. 110).

So much, then, for the Urubu's loss of control when he is drunk. We would now note that his "crazy water" has sometimes played another and quite different role. To bring out the magnitude of the contrast between these "two kinds of drunkenness," we must first say something about the ferocity of the inter-tribal wars that were endemic between the Urubu and various of their neighboring tribes. In the old days, a Urubu was considered to be a man only after he had killed an enemy and fathered a son. And since the Urubu were almost constantly at war, most of those who were not killed off in battle had little trouble in achieving manhood. Once begun, these tribal wars that so engaged the energies of the Urubu were very difficult to stop. Not only was the ever-assertable claim to blood vengeance a potent force in their continuation, the political organization of the Urubu and the surrounding tribes was such that tribal leaders did not possess the power to enter into binding negotiations on behalf of their fellow tribesmen. Thus, Huxley (1957) writes that "Peace [could] only be reached through a personal agreement between every member of each tribe: they [had] to meet each other face to face and somehow turn their common hostility into friendship" (p. 110). And how was this miracle of reconciliation brought to pass?—"*by getting drunk together,* by dancing together and learning each other's songs . . ." (p. 110, emphasis ours). How is it that in a situation such as this—a situation that would seem to be so propitious to the unleashing of yet another wave of inter-tribal blood-letting—the drinking of *kaú-i* gave rise instead to a spirit of forgiveness and reconciliation? What sort of answer will do, save that the Urubu deemed these assemblages to be neither the time nor the place for such bloody carryings-on? And where does this leave the notion that alcohol is a toxic disinhibitor?

As we have already said, additional examples of the situationally variable character of drunken comportment are available virtually without end. Nor is there any reason to go so far afield to find them. Everybody knows, for instance, that the drunken comportment typically found in an Irish pub bears scant resemblance to the often equally drunken comportment manifested by the participants at an Irish wake. But even this example is farther afield than is necessary, for the same sort of variability is present everywhere around us. Consider, for example, the contrast between the comportment that is typically displayed at a genteel cocktail party and that at a typical fraternity party. Yet we continue to speak—and, presumably, to *think*—of alcohol as a toxic disinhibitor.

In this chapter we have attempted to indicate the sway of time and circumstance over how people comport themselves when they are drunk. That these factors do exert such a sway constitutes the second puzzle with which we confront the conventional wisdom.

4 Disinhibition and the Within-Limits Clause

The Problem of Drunken Changes-for-the-Worse

UP TO NOW WE HAVE BEEN engaged in documenting the fact that there are societies scattered throughout the world in which the ingestion of alcohol is followed by comportment that is variously and significantly at odds with that which the conventional formulation of alcohol *qua* toxic disinhibitor would lead us to expect. Specifically, we have presented a series of firsthand accounts of drunken comportment that stand in support of the following propositions: (1) There are societies whose members' drunken comportment fails to exhibit anything of the sort which might reasonably be described as "disinhibited"; (2) there are societies whose members' drunken comportment has undergone marked transformations over historical time; and (3) there are societies whose members' drunken comportment is radically different from one set of socially ordered situations or circumstances to another.

The question now naturally arises as to how adherents to the conventional formulation have attempted to handle this array of

62

DRUNKEN COMPORTMENT

"contrary instances." The answer, to put it bluntly, is that they have elected simply to look the other way. But while a puzzle ignored is scarcely a puzzle solved, what other course is open to them? It is our contention that such examples as we have presented in Chapters 2 and 3 cannot possibly be brought into alignment with conventional expectations, that they constitute acute puzzles that are incapable of solution by means of the conceptual resources the conventional formulation has at its disposal.

Still and all (at least some of you are doubtless saying to yourselves), the examples that have been presented so far *are* anomalies; that is, they are deviations from, and not instances of, the general run of things. Is it not the case that, insofar as it makes any sense at all to talk about "societies in general" in this sort of context, those in which drunken comportment is characterized by publicly recognizable changes-for-the-worse are by far the most prevalent? And is it not to account for precisely these sorts of changes that the conventional formulation of alcohol *qua* toxic disinhibitor is specifically intended? Further, is it not so that, while the examples just presented may indeed leave adherents to the conventional formulation so to say "speechless," this formulation remains both self-evidently and uniquely cogent in its account of the far more important (because far more troublesome) phenomena that are its very *raison d'être*—drunken changes-for-the-worse? And if all of this is so, would it not be a very bad bargain to replace the conventional formulation of alcohol's workings with some new formulation that might possibly be devised to account for this potpourri of "exceptions"? In a word, since the conventional formulation does "come through when it counts," is this not sufficient to convince anyone of normal prudence that we ought to stick with it?

This, briefly, is how we see the two sides positioned at this point in the argument. We want now to join the issue by taking a closer look at what the conventional wisdom presumes to be its essential strong point—the notion that it and it alone provides an adequate account of drunken changes-for-the-worse. For if we should be able to show that the conventional formulation of alcohol *qua* toxic disinhibitor is neck-deep in trouble in its own backyard . . . then, we submit, we would have a brand-new ball game.

Recall that, insofar as comportment is concerned, the conventional wisdom takes it to be self-evidently the case that alcohol, by virtue of its toxic assault upon "the higher brain centers," renders the drinker temporarily immune to the action of those internalized constraints ("inhibitions") that normally serve to keep his comportment within proper bounds. With his otherwise operative powers of reason, judgment, and the like thus temporarily immobilized, the drinker becomes but the amoral vehicle for the actualization of his now-unleashed instincts.

And this, or at least something that looks very much like this, seems to be what we find when we examine accounts of those societies in which drunken changes-for-the-worse have the appearance of being in the nature of things. The comments to this effect are typically pithy, as for instance, when Ruey *et al.* (1955, p. 122) say that when the Formosan aborigines are drunk, they no longer observe their otherwise honored taboos. But sometimes the accounts are a bit more detailed. Thus, the missionary-scholar Henri Junod (1962), writing of the Thonga's annual month-long *bukanye* drinking feast as he observed it in Mozambique at the turn of the century, states that:

> Drinking continues day and night, night and day! When the supply is finished in one village, they go to the next. . . . During these weeks some individuals are in a continuous state of semi-intoxication. Orgies on all sides . . . many cases of adultery occur. Men and women forget the elementary rules of conduct. They attend to the wants of nature in the same places, which is taboo under ordinary circumstances . . . (Vol 1, pp. 401–02).

Or consider the anthropologist Owen Rutter's (1929) account of drinking and drunkenness among the Dusun of North Borneo. Rutter states that the drinking bouts often last for days,

> "as long, indeed, as the liquor will hold out. . . . [And that] the effects of these bouts are as unpleasant as they must be harmful. Mercifully, they are not a daily occurrence, but when they are held there are no half measures. . . . there is [a] disastrous effect both on the children who join in the orgies and on the adolescents of both sexes who only too often complete the saturnalia by throwing restraint and morality to the winds (p. 78).

And so it goes in society after society. On initial inspection, the case for the conventionally accepted disinhibition formulation of alcohol's workings appears to be overwhelming. But when we look a little closer, we find that things are not at all as self-evident as they at first appear. We want now to point up what we believe to be a ubiquitous—and for adherents to the conventional formulation, a most unsettling—characteristic of these seemingly incontestably alcohol-induced changes-for-the-worse that the world seems to exhibit in such plenitude.

Let us introduce what we have in mind by way of a personal experience. While doing field work with the Kamba tribe of central Kenya in 1962, one of the authors (Edgerton) was warned on several occasions of a certain native who was said to be "very dangerous" and "totally beyond control" when drunk. The native informants who issued these warnings were themselves genuinely fearful of their fellow tribesman's drunken rages, and several of them were said to have been painfully injured by him during one or another of these episodes. The following verbatim account of Edgerton's first contact with this native is contained in the field notes he recorded at the time:

> I heard a commotion, and saw people running past me. One young man stopped and urged me to flee because this dangerous drunk was coming down the path attacking all whom he met. As I was about to take this advice and leave, the drunk burst wildly into the clearing where I was sitting. I stood up, ready to run, but much to my surprise, the man calmed down, and as he walked slowly past me, he greeted me in polite, even deferential terms, before he turned and dashed away. I later learned that in the course of his "drunken rage" that day he had beaten two men, pushed down a small boy, and eviscerated a goat with a large knife.

Here, then, we have an instance in which a "primitive," to all appearances so drunk as to be quite out of control, nevertheless conducted himself in the same deferential manner vis-à-vis the white outsider as did sober members of his tribe.

While accounts such as the above, in which the ethnographer would seem to have been in some real danger, seldom reach the printed page, many field workers have reported similar experiences. And one fact about their narrations stands out in bold relief: although one occasionally reads or hears of verbal and, more rarely, of mild physical abuse, instances in which an ethnographer has suffered real bodily harm at the hands of "uncontrollably drunken" natives are very rare indeed.

A particularly instructive example of such immunity is contained in the anthropologist Ruth Bunzel's (1940) account of her field work with the Chamula Indians of the then inaccessible *municipio* of Chamula in the Central American highlands. First, however, a word about the Chamula: they are of pure Indian stock, speak a dialect of the Mayan language, and are unanimously regarded by their non-Indian neighbors as " 'bad' Indians, violent, treacherous, and incorrigible trouble makers" (p. 385). And it is not entirely without reason that they are so little esteemed: the village of Chamula was the center of a major eighteenth-century religious uprising, and at the time of Bunzel's investigation it was still regarded as a hotbed of separatist unrest. Indeed, in 1928—a mere three years before her arrival—the Indians of a nearby village had slaughtered their entire 27-member mestizo population. In the village closest to Chamula, a mestizo official had shortly before been lynched "by a mass action of the Indian population" (p. 385). In fact, the Mexican authorities deemed the situation to be of such potential explosiveness that no white person was permitted to live within the jurisdiction.

Although Bunzel arrived under government protection, her decision to work with the Chamula ran counter to the advice of all concerned. Failing in their efforts at persuasion, they advised her, as she put it, "to carry arms, to barricade my door at night and never to go with Indians to their houses" (p. 385). To make matters worse, Bunzel also informs us that:

> In Chamula everyone from the youngest child to the oldest woman drinks. . . . At fiestas the whole town is in varying degrees of intoxication for a day or a week. During one fiesta the writer counted eighty individuals lying in a stuporous condition in the yard of the church and the marketplace. . . . There were certain individuals who in several months of daily contact were never seen sober, others who were raving drunk several times a week, and no one at all who was not seen highly intoxicated on a number of occasions (p. 372).

Nor was the drunken comportment of the Chamula characterized by a spirit of sweet reasonableness: after describing one quite pointless drunken brawl which ended in bloodshed, Bunzel observes that "Fights of this sort are the invariable accompaniment of any fiesta. Sometimes they are the activation of old grudges, but more often they have no basis except that two men full of aguardiente want to fight" (p. 376). Nor, finally, were the Chamula ones to pull their punches: over a six-months period, Bunzel was able to count five murders of which she personally had knowledge. And yet in spite of all this, not only did Bunzel survive her sojourn among the notoriously hostile, physically aggressive, and hard-drinking Chamula quite without harmful incident, but after she had finished her field work and returned to the States, she avowed that "no one could have wished for more solicitous and considerate hosts. I had a lock for my house but I never used it, and went everywhere in perfect safety and without anxiety" (p. 375).

How does Bunzel—a woman, defenseless and alone—account for the fact that not one harmful incident befell her during the several months in which she resided among the violent and often drunken Chamula? "Before going," Bunzel (1940) writes, "I called the members of the Agrarian Committee, which was the prestige group of the community, and told them my purpose in coming, saying that since they were a free people I would come to their village only on their invitation, but that if I should come, they as citizens and members of the Agrarian Committee and the National Revolutionary Party would be held accountable for my life and property. The invitation was delivered. I became a community responsibility . . ." (p. 375). Here, then, we have an example in which a voluntarily obtained commitment to restraint proved somehow capable of withstanding alcohol's toxic assault upon those very brain centers from which the commitment issued in the first place. What Bunzel seems to be saying, if we may extrapolate, is that her "insurance" consisted precisely in the fact that there would be no room for doubt as to where responsibility would reside should any harm befall her. We suggest that this explanation of how she came through her travail without a scratch makes a good deal of sense *if*—but only if—we reject the conventional formulation of alcohol's workings.[1]

We shall have a good deal more to say about this topic of selective immunity in Chapter 6, for it is unique neither to anthropolo-

---

1. It is also worth pondering in this connection that although when they were drunk, the male Chamula were not at all reticent to assault other adult Chamula, their wives included, Bunzel (1940) reports that she "knew of no cases of aggression against children by intoxicated persons" (p. 377).

gists in the field nor to this time in history. For now, however, we will note only that the presence of outsiders can in some societies result in a more general pacification. Thus, in Robert and Barbara LeVine's (1963) account of drinking in Nyansongo, a Gusii community in western Kenya, we read that although alcohol is believed to make men so aggressive that when they drink, "quarrels among them are inevitable, beginning with pugnacious boasting and ending in physical combat," respected outsiders such as themselves not only are immune to such violence, but their very presence "has the effect of inducing a degree of restraint which is absent when only close neighbors and kinsmen are there" (p. 80). In confirmation of this, the LeVines report that although they personally observed no drunken aggression during their stay in Nyansongo, when they were not around, "brothers attacked one another while drinking beer, as bruised faces testified the following day" (pp. 80–81).

It is on the basis of such examples as these that we have come to recognize the operation of what might best be termed a *within-limits clause* governing one's drunken excesses. By this term, "within-limits," we refer to the fact that, with rare exceptions, for even the most seemingly disinhibited drunkard there are limits beyond which he does not go. Although there can be no doubt that the limits governing drunken comportment are often far less confining than those obtaining under conditions of sobriety, it is our contention that the continued existence of limits of *any* kind gives the lie to the conventionally accepted notion that when one is drunk, his now "uninhibited impulses" take over, and his resulting comportment is no longer under control.

Let us look at some more examples. The Ifugao, some 80,000 pagan tribesmen who live in small villages located in the remote mountains and valleys of northern Luzon in the Philippines, have been described in a series of books by Roy F. Barton (1930, 1946, 1963). Barton spent almost ten years among the Ifugao shortly after the turn of the century, and then returned to their villages on several subsequent visits, the last of which was in 1937. He writes that although they occasionally instituted headhunting forays against their traditional non-Ifugao enemies, under normal conditions, they "usually manage to get along with each other without a great deal of actual fighting" (1963, p. 1). But the Ifugao were much given to partying, during which times they

consumed prodigious quantities of rice wine. And their comportment
at such occasions was typically anything but peaceable.

> People from villages near and far, dressed in their new g-strings,
> loincloths, and finery of jewels and scabbard belts, gather at about
> midday to dance, gossip and guzzle. . . . A considerable portion,
> especially of the males, goes in mainly for liquoring-up as expedi-
> tiously as possible, and then, when they begin to gossip, are indis-
> creet in their remarks, so that trouble almost inevitably ensues. Old
> feuds are likely to break out afresh. In any case, the throng is a
> babbling, maudlin one that always becomes more or less quarrel-
> some soon after the liquor has begun to pour into empty stomachs
> . . . (1946, pp. 133–34).

As the drinkfests wore on, the disputes that "almost inevitably"
accompanied them typically intensified to the point of wholesale
brawling—brawling that often resulted in the death of one or more
of the participants. As one after another of Barton's Ifugao informants recounted his or her experiences at such drinkfests, we hear
of five dead at this feast, seven at that one, and so on. Thus:

> At a drinkfest in Montabiong, a drunken brawl broke out in which
> five men were killed, one of them a kinsman. My sister Dukmin
> and I carried him away, already dead, for all the men were engaged
> in fighting (1963, p. 153).

And again:

> I went to Buhne next morning with people carrying home the bodies
> of their slain, thence to Ligauwe and on to Kudug, where there was
> another drinkfest in progress. Five men from Banao, two from
> Buhne, three from Ligauwe, and some from other towns were
> killed. A man had his belly slashed open; his intestines came out
> and he tried to put them back in, slashing meanwhile at everything
> around him with his bolo (1963, p. 170).

Indeed, so probable was such carnage that the feast-giver prayed
not only that his drunken guests would refrain from assaulting each
other, but, knowing that this prayer would likely go unheeded, he
also prayed that the metal of their spears and knives would go limp
and/or that their aim would prove faulty:

I do the *tikom* rite for the irons [spears and knives], so that the drinkfest guests will assemble tomorrow and will drink and drink and get half drunk and drunk. But when they threaten each other with irons the irons will be weak like the stems of young plants and will overshoot the backs of the guests (1946, p. 131).[2]

Barton (1946) adds that since everybody knew that murderous violence was a frequent occurrence at the Ifugaos' drinkfests, "In these days, the government always sends police or constabulary soldiers to keep order" (p. 134). It would seem from all of this that the Ifugao present us with yet another example of a society whose members become uncontrollably violent once alcohol has unleashed their "primitive passions."

But all of the facts are not yet in. Barton (1930, pp. 212–13) also writes, for instance, of a drinkfest in which, among all those in attendance, only *one* became violent. And, too, there are the words of an elderly Ifugao woman, who, after recounting her experiences at several drinkfests which resulted in death, continued as follows:

Now I will tell you about some more drinkfests that I attended. One of the first was in Ubwag. Fighting broke out —what started it nobody ever learned. Twenty men were killed from various regions: two of them, and five wounded, being from our own region of Hingyón. My brother Adunglay kept out of it. We women ran into the house and the men who were not involved ran into the forest (1963, p. 169).

But violence was not inevitable. After describing still another drinkfest which was every bit as bloody as this one, she went on: "My next drinkfest was at Holnad. It was a good drinkfest—no trouble" (1963, p. 171).

Thus, despite the supposed inevitability that violence would occur during Ifugao drinkfests, there were at least some celebrations at which there was little "trouble," and there were others at which there was no trouble at all! Note, too, that even where drunken violence did occur, not all the participants became involved. What is more, despite the fact that women were always in attendance at these parties, Barton (1963, pp. 170–71) recounts only one instance in which a woman was reported to have died at

2. For a more extended account of this rite, see Barton, 1963, p. 194.

the hands of a drunken assailant. And although some women became so intoxicated that they passed out, there is no mention in any of Barton's many accounts of Ifugao drinking that drunken women ever assaulted anyone—male or female. Neither is there a single indication in his voluminous reports that the Ifugao priests who presided over the drinkfests ever became violent; and this in spite of the fact that the priests sometimes became so drunk that they were unable to remember the words of their prayers and had to be prompted by their less inebriated assistants (1963, pp. 103–04). Finally, Barton makes no mention that he himself was ever even threatened, much less assaulted, during the several years he lived among them. In sum, it is evident that for the Ifugao, alcohol is something appreciably less than the full-blown disinhibitor that it initially seemed to be.

For another example of the operation of the within-limits clause, we turn to South America, and to the anthropologist Jules Henry's (1941) account of the tragedy that drunken violence has brought to the Kaingáng Indians of Brazil. Prior to their pacification in 1914, these warlike nomads roamed over vast portions of the highlands of southeastern Brazil, proving themselves formidable opponents of the Brazilian settlers whom they robbed and killed with abandon. Although at the time Henry lived among them (for two years in the 1930's) they no longer directed their murderous assaults against the Brazilians, violence remained very much a part of their lives. Immediately after pacification, the Kaingáng lived and roamed as before, in extended families of fifty or more persons, and when two or more of these extended families met, violence was the typical result. Murders were frequent on such occasions, and (as with the Urubu) each murder precipitated a cycle of blood vengeance that spread from one extended family to another until, when Henry encountered the Kaingáng, their internecine blood-lettings had reduced them to a mere remnant of what had once been a substantial population. And what does Henry say of the role of alcohol in this genocidal decimation?

When the Kaingáng are drunk, their malevolent and fearsome impulses rise to the surface . . . the more one knows about the Kaingáng, the more one is struck by the extent to which the very roots of their being have been undermined and torn by impulses to violence. This is all the more amazing when we remember what affectionate people they seem to be—how much they love to multiply a hundred fold all kinds of personal attachments. Nevertheless, when drunkenness uncovers the Kaingáng personality, it does not bubble over in rivulets of tenderness, but pours out in torrents of violence. The only outlet is murder . . . (p. 69).

With this as backdrop, it is understandable that among the Kaingáng the offer of one extended family "to brew beer" for another became as much a threat as a promise. Nevertheless, when two extended families met, it was common practice for such an offer to be made. Although the reasons are not altogether clear, Henry states that the invited family "never refused an invitation" even though they could not help knowing that their very lives were endangered thereby.

But what happened when only members of a single extended family drank together, as they often did? *Essentially nothing!* Although the members of an extended family might also quarrel among themselves, they never let these quarrels go beyond mild blows. Murder on such occasions was literally unheard of. Indeed, Henry states (1941, pp. 62–63) that over a period of some 200 years, only one murder is known to have taken place *within* an extended family, and in this single known instance, the killing was one of cold-blooded premeditation, with all the participants quite sober!

Ruth Benedict, in a forward to Henry's monograph, neatly summarizes the puzzle the Kaingáng present in the following words:

> The picture of the Kaingáng is a picture of social tragedy. Within the little band of co-travelers they were gay and self-indulgent and settled their quarrels without violence. But the little band was not coextensive with their world, and in that outer world they could only kill . . . (pp. xii–xiii).

In summary, then, the Kaingáng exemplify a society in which the ingestion of alcohol in no way blurred their ability to recognize what was for them a fundamental distinction between in-group and out-group. Nor did it produce the slightest impairment in their ability to comply with the norms regulating the sort of conduct they deemed appropriate to each.

An example of a different sort of familial immunity is contained in Lionel Wafer's account (published in 1934) of his stay among the Cuna Indians of what is now Panama. The surgeon to a band of English buccaneers, in 1681 Wafer suffered an accidental injury during one inland trek that forced him to leave the company of his companions and to spend several months of recuperation among the then virtually unknown Cuna. These Indians were exclusionists to a fault, their history being marked by recurring efforts to retain their racial-cultural integrity in the face of a steady stream of foreign intruders. In the accounts of these efforts there is ample evidence that violence was in no way foreign to their nature. Our concern, however, is not with these often bloody insurrections (the latest of which occurred as recently as 1925), but with what Wafer observed of the relations between the sexes.

Concerning the sexual division of labor among the Cuna, Wafer writes:

> The Men first clear the Plantations, and bring them into order, but the Women have all the trouble of them afterwards; the digging, howing, planting, plucking the Maiz, and setting Yams, and every thing of Husbandry, is left to them . . . the Women also have the managing Affairs within Doors, for they are in general the Drudges of the Family . . . [They] are little better than Slaves to their Husbands . . . (1934, pp. 92–93).

The women did their work both readily and cheerfully, however, and "They observe their Husbands with a profound Respect and Duty upon all occasions . . ." (p. 93).

According to Wafer, the Cuna female's voluntary servitude was never more pronounced than during the frequent male drinking feasts, at which time the women "constantly stand by and attend them"—a task of no small moment since the men "are very quarrelsome in their Drink," and since the feasts might last as long as three or four days (p. 98). Indeed, so quarrelsome did the men become that in order to forestall the possibility of extreme physical harm befalling any of the participants during their drunken revels, they were required to hang their weapons on the ridgepole before imbiding, a practice which, incidentally, the Cuna continue to observe to this day (Stout, 1947, p. 95). Violent or no, however, when in the course of these drinking bouts the husband reached "such a Condition that he can bear up no longer," the wife assisted her husband to his hammock, washed him, and stood by to look after him. Yet, despite the women's patently inferior position which would seem to make them ideal targets for their husbands' "unleashed" drunken hostility, despite the frequently violent character of their husbands' drunken comportment, and despite the ampleness of drunken opportunity, Wafer relates that:

> I never knew an *Indian* beat his Wife, or give her any hard Words. Nor even in the Quarrels which they are wont to have in their Cups, do they shew any Roughness toward their Women who attend them (1934, p. 93).

So much, then, for the inviolability of Cuna womanhood. But the role of the *within-limits clause* is not limited to specifying appropriate and inappropriate targets for one's drunken assaults. It can also determine the *manner* in which a drunkard's "disinhibited aggressive impulses" are expressed.

Thus, consider the anthropologist Ralph Beals' (1945) account of drunken fighting among the Mixe Indians of Oaxaca, Mexico. Beals writes that, unlike the Mixtecs whom we encountered in Chapter 2:

> The Mixe indulge in frequent fist fights, especially while drunk. Although I probably saw several hundred, I saw no weapons used, although nearly all men carried machetes and many carried rifles. Most fights start with a drunken quarrel. When the pitch of voices reaches a certain point, everyone expects a fight. The men hold out their weapons to the onlookers, and then begin to fight with their fists, swinging wildly until one falls down . . . [at which point] the victor helps his opponent to his feet and usually they embrace each other . . . (p. 29).

It is more than a little remarkable, we submit, that the very moment before the combatants fall upon one another in drunken anger, they are still capable of exercising the presence of mind to "hold out their weapons to the onlookers"—lest, we presume, in their coming rage they inflict serious injury on their opponents.

Nor do the "rules-of-proper-combat-when-in-an-uncontrollable-drunken-rage" govern only the propriety or impropriety of weapons usage. Even in societies in which the use of weapons is strictly proscribed, there may still be differing notions of what constitutes proper and improper combat, and these proscriptions, too, may fall under the governance of the *within-limits clause*. In this connection, consider the anthropologist Allan Holmberg's (1950) account of drunken fighting among the Sirionó—an Indian tribe consisting of small bands of nomadic hunters who eke out a precarious existence in the tropical forests of eastern Bolivia. Holmberg states that when the Sirionó drink their native honey liquor, they, like the Mixe, often become so aggressive that brawling frequently ensues. But even though the brawlers are usually so drunk that, as Holmberg puts it, "they cannot stand up," their *mode* of fighting remains rigidly circumscribed. Among the Sirionó, neither the use of weapons *nor fists* is deemed proper. Rather, the brawlers must confine themselves to wrestling; and no exception to this unstated "rule" is tolerated. In describing an occasion in which a drunken Sirionó man struck his opponent with his fist, Holmberg reports that "Everyone began to clamor that he was fighting unfairly, 'like a white man' " (p. 62). While there is certainly nothing in the disinhibition theory of alcohol's workings that would lead us to expect such expressions of righteous indignation to have any effect whatsoever upon the combatants, it is evident that these "mere verbal reminders" *did* work, for Holmberg goes on to report that this same Sirionó "stopped immediately" (p. 62). How is it, we would ask, that the clamor of a morally outraged assemblage of one's peers is capable of returning the "disinhibited" Sirionó drunkard to a proper compliance with the moral proprieties?

If this example is not sufficiently problematic, consider that even an intervention so unlikely to control the uncontrollable as the propitiously uttered whisper can sometimes work this wonder—a fact evidenced both in life and in myth. Thus, among the Ifugao discussed earlier, there is the following legend of the warrior-hero Nahgag and the girl Cuyapi:

> Nahgag met Cuyapi at a canao at Bukyawan . . . and fell in love with her at first sight. The people feasted and danced and danced and sang all night, and Cuyapi sang the sweetest. But Nahgag got drunk and became wild and dangerous, and when some of the others sought to subdue and disarm him, he struck at a pine tree and cut it down with one stroke. Cuyapi liked him for this because it reminded her of her father's prowess, and she whispered in his ear, "If you love and respect me, put down your bolo." Nahgag promptly obeyed (Ramos and Apilis, 1940, p. 104).

There are also many societies in which, regardless of the degree of intoxication achieved, physical aggression remains outside the limits, but periods of drunkenness are the sanctioned occasions for verbally letting off steam. The anthropologist Robert McC. Netting's (1964) account of the Kofyar of West Africa documents such a pattern. The Kofyar are one of many isolated farming peoples of the Nigerian Jos Plateau, who are collectively known as "hill pagans." Like so many African tribal peoples, they are much taken with the drinking of beer. Indeed, as Netting puts it, drinking is the very focus of their culture: "The Kofyar make, drink, talk and think about beer" (p. 376). Netting describes a typical drinking party as follows:

> The drinking of beer appears to be generally connected with increased activity, and such group enjoyments as singing and dancing cannot be imagined apart from it. The beer party also acts as a proper occasion for the discharge of interpersonal tensions in vociferous argument. Large and small areas of friction are exposed for public review and comment in an atmosphere that encourages emotional catharsis. Strict limits are, however, maintained by the practice of submitting quarrels to older men for arbitration and prohibiting physical violence. A clear line is drawn by the Kofyar between verbal aggression which may be expressed freely and potentially dangerous acts (p. 381).

A particularly anomalous example of the relationship between drunkenness and violence is contained in Colonel Meinertzhagen's account (published 1957) of his experiences with the Kikuyu of East Africa during the first decade of the present century. A young British officer at the time, Colonel Meinertzhagen was one of a small handful of British officers and not many more native soldiers who were the sole representatives of the Crown in the whole Kikuyu territory. One evening, Meinertzhagen relates, Kenuthia (a Kikuyu chief) gave a large beer party for his warriors, in the course of which they all became quite boisterous. They surrounded the British camp (euphemistically called a fort) and hurled "rude remarks" at the soldiers who were stationed there. Meinertzhagen became alarmed, and not without cause, for suddenly a rain of arrows fell upon the encampment. But just as Meinertzhagen was about to give the order to open fire, he noted that none of his men had been injured, and on examining the arrows he found that their tips had been covered by protective balls. The next day Kenuthia apologized for the prank, explaining that his men had been drunk at the time. Not long thereafter, a second incident occurred. On this occasion, Kenuthia and some confederates, "obviously drunk," approached the fort and threatened that, since there were so few soldiers stationed there, the Kikuyu intended to attack. The British officer laughed at the reeling chief and his tribesmen and proceeded to exhibit his sangfroid by fining them five goats each. The result? Meinertzhagen reports that not only did Kenuthia and his followers refrain from violence, but "they departed meekly and the next day they paid their fines" (p. 32). Lest the reader think that the Kikuyu were simply playful buffoons who were innocent of serious intent, let him consider the unhappy fate of a British settler who only a few days later had the ill fortune to fall into their hands. Taken to a Kikuyu village, this unfortunate soul was pegged to the ground and his mouth was wedged open; whereupon, the entire village, man, woman and child—*all quite sober*—"urinated into his mouth until he drowned" (p. 50). Putting all this together, it is evident that the Kikuyu were a people who, while capable of the most bestial acts (and the gruesome fate of the captured settler was by no means a unique example) under conditions of sobriety, were at the same time capable of maintaining complete control of themselves when they were drunk.

Where drunkenness is accompanied by violence not against an outsider but against a member of one's own society, the object of one's drunken assault is almost always one's status equal or inferior. But even this is not always the case. Thus, among the Paraguayan Abipone (whose drunken metamorphosis was described in Chapter 2), drinking parties were the sanctioned occasions for settling accounts with their chiefs, as Dobrizhoffer (1822) makes abundantly clear:

> Drunken men frequently kill one another; women quarrel, and often imbrue their hands in one another's blood; young men, fond of glory or booty, rob the Spaniards, to whom they had promised peace, of whole droves of horses, and sometimes secretly slay them: and the cacique [chief], though aware of all these things, dares not say a word. If he were but to rebuke them for these transgressions, which are reckoned amongst the merits, virtues, and victories of the savages, with a single harsh word, he would be punished in the next drinking-party with the fists of the intoxicated savages, and publicly loaded with insults, as a friend to the Spaniards, and a greater lover of ease than of his people. How often have Ychamenraikin, chief

cacique of the Riikahes, and Narè, of the Yaaucanigas, experienced this! How often have they returned from a drinking party with swelled eyes, bruised hands, pale cheeks, and faces exhibiting all the colours of the rainbow! (Vol. 2, p. 103).

However, these same Abipone provide no support whatsoever for Ogden Nash's already quoted bit of proverbial advice to contemporary Conquistadores, viz., "Candy is dandy, but liquor is quicker." Dobrizhoffer (1822) reports that drunkenness among the Abipone did not in any way alter the essentially puritanical relations that normally obtained between the sexes. He states that, even at the height of their often frenzied drinking parties, "You can never perceive the smallest deviation from strict [sexual] decorum. The men are decently separated from the women, the boys from the girls" (Vol. 2, p. 66).

For a related example, we turn now to the anthropologist Monica Hunter's (1961) account of the effects of contact with Europeans on the Pondo of South Africa. Like so many African tribesmen, the Pondo drink large quantities of beer upon numerous ceremonial and secular occasions. Although they are peaceable enough when sober, fighting is now an expected accompaniment of their beer-drinking feasts. Indeed, "Pondo do not consider that an *umjadu* [big feast] is really complete without a fight" (p. 370). As with the Abipone, however, the Pondos' sexual comportment fails to undergo a similar metamorphosis; and this in spite of the fact that "much beer is drunk, and excitement is increased by the crowd and the rhythms" (p. 370). Instead of sexual disinhibition, we find that "At ordinary beer drinks verbal flirtations only are permitted" (p. 369). Hunter concludes that "By giving men and women opportunity to meet, talk freely, and indulge in limited sexual play, the institution of the beer drink helps to canalize sex into socially harmless channels. . . . Lovers may make assignations at beer drinks, but it is not considered seemly that they should be demonstrative in public" (p. 369). Thus, in the case of the Pondo, it would appear that while alcohol "unleashes the aggressive instincts," thereby transforming otherwise peaceable men into brawlers, it canalizes the "sexual instincts" into "socially harmless channels."

Where drunkenness *is* accompanied by a relaxation of the normally operative sexual proprieties, it is not unusual to find the same sort of "selectivity as to object" as we did when we examined drunken aggression. In this connection, consider Bennett and Zingg's (1935) account of the Tarahumara—a group of Indians who inhabit the western region of the Sierra Madre Range of northern Mexico. The Tarahumaras' normal reserve is so great that these authors claim it to be "no exaggeration to say that normal social life could not be carried on without the aid of *tesguino*" (p. 15)—a native alcoholic beverage made from mescal or sprouted corn. With *tesguino* inside them, however, "The silent reserve is broken. Everyone talks, laughs, and smokes. . . . Amidst the fumes of alcohol, the Tarahumara becomes 'human' " (p. 328). According to Bennett and Zingg, then, the primary change in conduct following the ingestion of *tesguino* is a breakdown of their timidity-engendered social isolation—a breakdown that, we would now note, is often accompanied by a radical alteration in the normally chaste relations between the sexes. While the Tarahumara women in the normal course of affairs are described as "abnormally timid and puritanical . . . they become quite free when slightly intoxicated" (p. 361). Indeed, Bennett and Zingg describe the fiestas or *tesguinadas*—in which social drinking plays so paramount a role—as occasions of "licensed promiscuity or wife exchange" (p. 361). But only "within-limits," for these authors go on to add the proviso that:

> The promiscuity does not extend to outsiders. If a Mexican stops at a Tarahumara house for the night, the woman will sleep elsewhere. [And] even though rather drunk, they will not mix with strangers at fiestas (p. 230).

In this instance it is not difficult to discover the role that practical self-interest plays in the maintenance of such selectivity: among the Tarahumara whom Bennett and Zingg studied, and at the time they wrote, it was a publicly appreciated fact of life that "women who are known to have had relations with Mexicans are avoided for fear of disease" (p. 230).

For a final example of the operation of the *within-limits clause,* we move halfway around the world to the Lepchas, as described by the anthropologist Geoffrey Gorer (1938) and by John Morris (1938). The Lepchas are a Mongoloid people who live on the southern and eastern slopes of Mount Kinchenjunga in the Sikkim Himalayas. From earliest Western contact to the present, the Lepchas have with remarkable consistency been characterized as extremely hard-working and industrious, mild of manner, generous, truthful, and respectful of the person and the property of others. They are also characterized as remarkably tolerant—a spirit of *ket ma nin* ("it doesn't matter") being carried to a fine point. Finally, they are magnificently preoccupied with things sexual and, by practically anyone's standards, are inordinately promiscuous. As John Morris has put it, "Sex is, indeed, almost the people's sole recreation, and the most common topic of conversation on practically every occasion" (p. 220). Geoffrey Gorer, in his account of the Lepchas, notes much the same: "Whenever a group of men and women were gathered together for any purpose, however solemn or important, every possible remark was given sexual significance" (p. 260). It was Gorer's further observation that among the Lepchas, "sexual activity is practically divorced from emotion . . . and [is considered] as much a necessity as food and drink; and like food and drink it does not matter from whom 'you receive it . . ." (p. 170). Both Morris and Gorer also report that adultery, which is rampant among the Lepchas, produces no enmity between any of the concerned parties. Thus Morris writes, "During our stay in Lingtem there was not the slightest sign of a quarrel over a woman, and the people thought it laughable that such a thing could happen" (p. 234).

In the Lepcha village of Lingtem, one's active sex life begins early—typically at the age of about ten for the girls and twelve for the boys, with the opposite member an adult in almost every case—and lasts well into the years of senior citizenry. "It is realized that after a certain age women cease to conceive, but there is no break in their sexual activities" (Morris, 1938, p. 237). Since the Lepchas are keenly aware that their population is in marked decline because of a high degree of infertility among the females, they desire children above all things. In consequence of this, "The production of a bastard is no drawback on the girl's subsequent marriage; on the contrary, the fact that she has shown herself fertile makes her if anything more desirable" (Gorer, 1938, p. 174).

There is a line, however, and the Lepchas draw it tightly; incest they consider absolutely horrifying, and such relationships are rigidly proscribed. Should such a union be consummated, it is believed that a year of disaster would befall the community, that a devil would cover the guilty couple with sores, and that should a child result he would be either of evil mind or an idiot, and in any case would be short-lived. At the time of Gorer's presence among the Lepchas of Lingtem, there was one incestuous couple (second cousins by our reckoning) living in the region. And this couple was "coventryized" with a vengeance; they were "shunned as irremediably unclean and contagious; they were exiled from their villages and neighbourhood; neither neighbour nor relative would visit them nor help them; when they die nobody would see to the disposal of their body, nor conduct their souls to paradise" (Gorer, 1938, p. 152).

There is, of course, no universal agreement from culture to culture as to the outer limits of what constitutes an incestuous relationship, and the point we want now to make is that when the Lepcha constructed their definition, they painted with a very broad brush, indeed. They count as incestuous any sexual connection with blood relations for nine generations on the father's side and four on the mother's. In addition, sexual relations between the husband and the following relations-by-marriage are considered equally incestuous: his wife's mother, his wife's elder sisters, the wife of his wife's older brother, his own sons' wives, the wives of his younger brothers, and the wives of his brothers' and sisters' sons. And, similarly, for the wife: her husband's father, her husband's elder brothers, the husband of her husband's elder sister, her own daughters' husbands, the husbands of her younger sisters, and the husbands of her brothers' and sisters' daughters. All of these are one's *num-neu-zong,* and by the age of ten the child is expected to be (and is) aware of this array of fine distinctions that defines the category of the sexually proscribed. Now, an interesting consequence of so broad a definition of what counts as incestuous is that while promiscuity is rampant in Lingtem, there are at the same time additional large numbers of otherwise available sex partners who, but for the incest stricture, would be equally available for purposes of creature comfort but who, because of this stricture, are rigidly defined as "off limits." We want now to examine what happens to this normally operative incest taboo when the Lepchas fall "under the influence" of *chi,* their native alcoholic intoxicant.

Once a year, there is a rice, or harvest, festival where there is much dancing and drinking of *chi* throughout the day. Morris writes that "Anyone who takes part in the dancing must spend the whole of that night in the fields; and on this occasion what is sometimes referred to as 'the greatest license' prevails, the ordinary rules of conduct being completely disregarded" (Morris, 1938, p. 183). Well, not quite "completely"—for Gorer (1938, p. 242) states that although "If a man should see his wife sleeping with another he must never refer to it, not even to his friends," and although all hold that the more copulating couples the better ("for then Talyeu-Nimu and Sangvo-Nimu will be pleased at seeing so many people copulating and will send them a good harvest"), there is one operative proviso: "On that night anybody may sleep with anyone else *provided the rules of incest are not broken*" (emphasis ours). And, needless to say, they are not.

Consider now the Lepchas' lesser festivals. About these, Morris notes that "it is a common sight at monastery feasts to see small children of four or five imitating the act of copulation, and not infrequently being egged on by their inebriated elders, who seem to think this an amusing sight" (1938, p. 235). And at another feast, in honor of some visiting lamas, at which there was much drinking, Morris observed the following:

> I saw a boy of about sixteen attempting to feel the breasts of Tafoor's wife, much to the amusement of the onlookers and the woman herself. She freed herself from his attempted embraces, uncovered one of her breasts and squeezed some milk out of it into her hand. She then ran after the boy and tried to rub the milk on his face. At this there was general laughter. . . . There was a great deal of this sort of sex play. . . . [And as always] the conversation was almost exclusively devoted to sex (p. 269).

Once again, Gorer (1938) notes much the same thing:

> As the drinking continues voices get louder and gestures more vehement and there is a great deal of laughter; most of this laughter arises from obscene remarks . . . the one thing which seems to the Lepchas continually and inexhaustibly funny is sex. There is a certain amount of rough sexual biplay; a young man, or occasionally a young woman, will make a gesture of grabbing at another young man's private parts; this is considered extremely funny. . . . young women set on an old man, strip him naked and chase him around the monastery, and so on . . . (pp. 259–60).

But again, there is a *within-limits* proviso. Gorer informs us that although "sexual conversation and jokes are inevitable and continuous" (1938, p. 260), it remains the case that however drunk the celebrants may become, *"even in jest* direct invitations are not made to people who would count as incestuous" (p. 262, emphasis ours). Thus, when drunk no less than when sober, the Lepchas continue to honor their expanded version of the incest taboo, and not only as it serves to define who is and who is not an available sexual partner. They also honor its determination of who can and who cannot become the recipient of even a jestingly advanced invitation to such a relationship. And this, we submit, is a remarkably circumspect sort of "disinhibition."

But we must somewhere call a halt, for the presentation of additional examples of the operation of the *within-limits clause* could go on and on. In some societies, the drinker becomes euphoric, but neither sexually "loose" nor aggressive. In other societies, certain normally operative constraints on the relations between the sexes may fall, but with no accompanying changes in aggressivity. In still other societies, the opposite may be the case—aggression may become both rampant and unbridled, but without any change whatsoever occurring in one's sexual comportment. And practically everywhere there is wholesale evidence of "object-selectivity." In a word, where instances of what we conventionally take to be drunken "disinhibition" occur, the possibilities are many and so, too, are the realities.

In conclusion, then, since *nowhere* is it the case that once one is drunk, anything and everything goes, we submit that it is highly misleading to construe the state of drunkenness as if it were an interval during which all sense of right and wrong has, as it were, gone on a holiday. Rather, we submit that in their composite the observations that have led us to appreciate the *within-limits* character of drunken changes-for-the-worse constitute an absolutely crucial puzzle with which any theory of the effects of alcohol on man must somehow come to terms. And this, the conventional formulation, which holds that such changes are but so many epiphenomenal manifestations of the instincts unleashed, simply cannot do. This failure constitutes the third puzzle with which we confront the conventional wisdom—and this failure, we submit, is its final undoing.

5 Drunkenness as Time Out

An Alternative Solution to the
Problem of Drunken Changes-for-the-Worse

WE HAVE NOW PRESENTED several bodies of evidence that indicate that the conventional understanding of alcohol's role in producing changes in comportment is anything but the self-evident matter we have customarily taken it to be. In this chapter we shall first develop the general form of an alternative formulation of the relationship between alcohol and man's comportment. We shall then attempt to demonstrate the applicability of this formulation to the phenomenon of drunken changes-for-the-worse. But before doing so, it might be well to recapitulate the essentials of our argument as it has been developed to this point.

We began (in Chapter 1) by noting that in every society in which drinking occurs—our own included—various of peoples' doings are often and in sundry ways recognizably different once they have alcohol inside them. We noted, too, that since similar changes have not been observed to transpire following the ingestion of non-alcoholic beverages, it long ago came to be generally presumed that alcohol was the causal agent in their production. We further noted that for both laymen and professional specialists alike, this age-old supposition still constitutes the unquestioningly accepted core of our contemporary wisdom on the matter. It was our contention, however, that an unprejudiced examination of the available evidence concerning what people actually do when they are drunk does not compel the acceptance of this bit of common knowledge. Rather, such an examination indicates that while there is indeed an abundance of solid evidence to confirm alcohol's causal role in the production of changes in at least certain sensorimotor capabilities, there is no corresponding body of hard documented evidence for the notion that alcohol plays a similar causal role in the production of changes in man's comportment. While we all know that people sometimes do things *after* they have been drinking that they do not otherwise do, and that these drunken doings often have the character of being changes-for-the-worse, this is *all* we know. And because this is all we know, we concluded that although the notion of alcohol *qua* toxic disinhibitor provides a possible explanation for the occurrence of these all too commonly observed changes-for-the-worse, this is all that it provides—a *possible* explanation.

We next turned to the cross-cultural evidence and proceeded (in Chapters 2 and 3) to confront this seemingly self-evident (but actually only hypothetical) formulation of alcohol's workings with two sets of concrete puzzles. How, we asked, can we square the notion that alcohol is a toxic disinhibitor with the fact that societies exist whose members' drunken comportment either (a) manifests *nothing* that can reasonably be classified as "disinhibited"; or (b) is markedly different from one socially ordered situation or circumstance to another? For our part, we suggested that there is no way in which either of these two broad classes of contrary instances might reasonably be aligned with the conventional disinhibition paradigm of alcohol's workings.

Still and all, it has been said that perfection belongs only in heaven; and in our growing sophistication concerning the place of theory in a world of fact, we have come to appreciate that even the best of theories are but partial representations of reality. Thus, although adherents to the conventionally accepted disinhibition theory might find such "evidence to the contrary" as we have presented to be "thought-provoking"—perhaps even a bit unsettling—it nevertheless remains that the problem *par excellence* for any theory of the effects of alcohol on man is the problem of drunken changes-for-the-worse. And since the disinhibition theory has been thought to be uniquely capable of providing a satisfactory explanation for such changes, its adherents might well argue that it would be the height of unreasonableness for them to cancel their subscription to it.

With this consideration firmly in mind, we then turned our attention (in Chapter 4) to the question of just how compelling the conventional explanation of drunken changes-for-the-worse really is. Here our presentation took the form of a series of accounts of societies in which drunken comportment, while manifestly different from that which normally occurs, and while giving the initial impression of being clearly "dishihibited," was found on closer inspection to have remained all the while within certain culturally sanctioned, albeit interculturally variable, limits. Even at their point of greatest departure from the sober run of things, the drunken changes-for-the-worse embodied in these examples went only so far and no farther. And this, we suggested, is a far cry indeed from a state of affairs in which "anything goes." Rather, the evidence seems to indicate that one version or another of what we have called the "within-limits clause" is operative in *every* society in which drunken changes-for-the-worse occur. Furthermore, once we ascertain these limits, we find that they are rarely if ever transgressed.

Thus, however great the difference may be between persons' sober and drunken comportment—and there can be no doubt that these differences are often very great, indeed—it is evident that both states are characterized by a healthy respect for certain socially sanctioned limits. In summary, then, when a spokesman for the conventional wisdom speaks of alcohol as (for example) "the solvent of the superego," and *ipso facto,* of the drunkard's comportment as "a species of blind impulsivity," he would do well to recognize the fact that he is dealing with a form of blindness that operates with its eyes wide open and with a species of impulsivity that possesses the peculiar ability to maintain a keen sense of the appropriate.

Given, then, that even the most "disinhibited" of man's drunken doings bear the mark of an essential "domestication," we submit that the conventionally accepted picture of alcohol as an infrahumanizing substance and of the drunkard as a person who, thus toxically denuded of his civilized veneer, becomes but the amoral instrumentality of his now uncontrolled impulses, is empirically indefensible. Indeed, its empirical warrant is no greater than that for the already exploded derivative notion that such changes-for-the-worse are alcohol's inexorable consequence. In a word, it is our contention that the conventional explanation of drunken comportment is no longer supportable on *any* grounds.

But one does not go about tossing away accepted explanations in the sublime hope that some fine morning something better will come along to replace them. This, at any rate, has not been the course that the sciences, hard or soft, have followed to this point in time. Rather, as Thomas Kuhn (1962) has most recently and compellingly argued, the history of scientific development is replete with examples in which bad theory has been preferred to no theory at all; and, as a corollary, that regardless how inadequate an accepted theory may be, it is an essential precondition for its rejection that a manifestly superior alternative be available to replace it.

The summary of our critique now out of the way, it is to the presentation of such an alternative that we now want to address ourselves. But where to begin? If we can no longer look to alcohol's disinhibiting action on our innards for a single all-encompassing explanation of the fact that people's drunken comportment is often recognizably different from their sober comportment, where, then, shall we look? Since we must begin with what we have, and since all that we have are observations and accounts of what people do when they are sober and what they do when they are drunk, it would seem to be the course of both wisdom and necessity to begin by taking a fresh look at the phenomena themselves. We have found, however, that when we do this we are brought up abruptly by the fact that the way people comport themselves when they are drunk is anything but uniform. And this fact has the following implication for the task to which we now address ourselves: that although an acceptable alternative theory must provide a compelling account of the occurrence of drunken changes-for-the-worse—and, we hasten to add, of the *within-limits* character of these changes— this cannot be its sole concern. A truly adequate alternative must also be capable of furnishing at least the framework for the development of a credible explanation for the occurrence of other drunken outcomes as well.

Let us start, then, with one of these broad classes of "exceptional" outcomes and see just what we are up against. What are we to make of the fact that there are whole societies in which drunken changes-for-the-worse are never or almost never seen? Logically, at least, it would seem that three possible solutions present themselves. The first possibility would be to claim that those societies in which the "disinhibiting effects of alcohol" fail to occur are already totally devoid of inhibitions. That is, this solution would have it that the reason we fail to observe instances of drunken disinhibition in some societies is that these societies are already so inhibition-free that there is simply nothing remaining for alcohol to disinhibit. The problem with this solution resides not in its logic (for it is logically impeccable), but in its lack of coordination with the real world. In simple fact, it stands in flat contradiction to everything we know about social life. No society has *ever* been reported in which *all* inhibitions are absent, and certainly no one would seriously contend that the societies we presented in Chapter 2 can be so characterized. We conclude, then, that this solution to the problem is totally inadequate.

A second possible solution would consist in the claim that, at base, it is differences in genetic makeup from one society to another that account for the corresponding differences we find in drunken comportment. But this solution, too, is impossible to sustain. The stark contrast, for instance, between the drunken comportment of the inhabitants of Ifaluk on the one hand, and that of the inhabitants of Ifaluk's neighboring (and more Westernized) atolls on the other gives the lie to this possibility; for while all concerned are patently of the same genetic "stock," their drunken comportment is very different indeed. And if the reader still entertains any lingering doubts as to the inadequacy of such genetic speculation, let him only reflect on the fact that while one's genetic makeup remains constant from one situation to another, one's drunken comportment (at least for the overwhelming majority of the world's drinkers) most certainly does not. Such considerations as these lead us to conclude that this explanation, too, is a grossly inadequate solution to the puzzle it would purport to solve.

If our analysis is correct to this point, we have but one solution remaining. Since, as we have already seen, the ingestion of alcohol is sometimes followed by the most flagrant imaginable changes in comportment, sometimes by only moderate changes, and sometimes by no significant changes whatsoever, it seems evident that *in and of itself, the presence of alcohol in the body does not neces-*

sarily even conduce to disinhibition, much less inevitably produce such an effect. This is not to say, however, that what one does when he is drunk is a merely capricious affair, for once the socially organized character of drunken comportment is recognized, the notion that it is guided by nothing more substantial than the impulse of the moment can no longer be sustained. And since no one would seriously entertain, much less defend, the possibility that persons are born in possession of all manner of fine distinctions as to what properly goes with what—distinctions that are selectively exercised during drunkenness—we must conclude that drunken comportment is an essentially *learned* affair.

We say that this conclusion is a necessary one, for how else are we to account for such diverse phenomena as the variability that we observe in drunken comportment from one society to another, and the essentially and often minutely organized character of this comportment within each society? How else, for instance, but by assuming that the comportment in question is learned, are we to account for what we found regarding the Mixtec Indians of Juxtlahuaca? Although these Indians (whom we discussed in Chapter 2) knew that alcohol "produced" anger and aggression in the mestizo townsmen, they denied (and correctly) that it was capable of producing such an effect in themselves. We submit that in denying the very possibility of such an outcome, and in comporting themselves in consonance with this denial, the Mixtecans were simply evidencing—both in deed and in word—that they were products of a different course of "social programming." The mestizo townsmen, after all, were not aware (as the Mixtecans were) that anger was intimately connected with the production of illness, and that in consequence such feelings were to be avoided at all costs and in all circumstances. Nor did the *machismo*-oriented mestizos share the Mixtecans' traditional and still reigning values of social harmony and interpersonal tranquility. And because they steered by a different star, the mestizos had not to fear (as did the Mixtecans) the possibility of ostracism from the community when they breached these values, as they so often did in their everyday affairs and, in an even more pronounced fashion, in their drunken revels.

Here, then, is the third possible solution to our puzzle: *Over the course of socialization, people learn about drunkenness what their society "knows" about drunkenness; and, accepting and acting upon the understandings thus imparted to them, they become the living confirmation of their society's teachings.*

This is the general statement of the solution we propose as an alternative to the conventional one. As stated, however, it is far too schematic, for we do not mean to suggest that drinkers are mere automata whose drunken doings amount to nothing more than the preordained running-off of a "program" their society has implanted inside them. While what people do when they are drunk is not what the untrammeled whim (or impulse) of the moment might dictate, neither is it determined in some once-and-forever fashion by something called "Society." It is our prejudice that whether addressing man's sober doings or his drunken doings, no theory of conduct that would gloss or ignore the role of discretion—and more generally, of meaning—in human affairs can hope to get very far. It is with an eye to examining the implications of this prejudice that we want now to look once again at the phenomenon of drunken changes-for-the-worse.

It will be recalled that we began our discussion of the problematic character of these changes (in Chapter 4) with brief mention of three peoples—the Formosan aborigines, the Thonga, and the Dusun—for whom the expectation that drunken transgressions would occur was seldom disappointed. We would now note that these three peoples had something else in common as well—in all three instances, when the drunken transgressions in question occurred, *they were without serious consequence for the transgressors*. Thus, Ruey *et al.* (1955), who spoke of the drunkenness of the Formosan aborigines as a period in which their taboos went out the window, also observed that "When one gets drunk he will not be punished even if he commits a crime" (p. 122). Similarly, Junod (1962), who characterized the Thongas' annual month-long *bukanye* drinking feast as an occasion during which, among other things, "Men and women forget the elementary rules of conduct," also noted that during this celebration, " 'Nau a wa tiyi'—'the law is no longer in force' " (Vol. 1, p. 402). And Rutter (1929), too, who stated that during the Dusuns' drinking parties "almost wholesale license prevails" and that even adolescents throw "restraint and morality to the winds," went on to note that in the eyes of the court, offenses committed at these festivities were typically overlooked on the grounds that "at such times normal restraint was traditionally not to be expected" (p. 163). These accounts suggest that in each of these societies the state of drunkenness is a state of societally sanctioned freedom from the otherwise enforceable demands that persons comply with the conventional proprieties. For a while—but just for a while—the rules (or, more accurately, *some* of the rules) are set aside, and the drunkard finds himself, if not beyond good and evil, at least partially removed from the accountability nexus in which he normally operates. In a word, drunkenness in these societies takes on the flavor of *"time out"* from many of the otherwise imperative demands of everyday life.

Nor is it only the rare society that accords to its drunken members such a surcease from its normally operative demands. Thus, for instance, the anthropologist Ozzie Simmons (1959) reports that in the Peruvian mestizo community of Lunahuaná, "No one hides the fact that he has been drunk, nor has he any hesitation about excusing some defection by saying he was drunk. . . . it is considered much less reprehensible to have done so when drunk than when sober, and whatever act of aggression he commits seldom has serious or enduring consequences" (pp. 108–109).

So, too, with the already mentioned Indians of Chamula, Mexico, about whom Bunzel (1940) writes:

> A man has no hesitation in explaining an absence, or failure to complete any required task by saying he was drunk. . . . A person who is drunk is not responsible and his offenses are condoned. . . . Nor do drunken quarrels have further repercussions. Toward a drunken man everyone assumes a protective and conciliatory attitude. . . . No one, unless he too were drunk, would assume a belligerent or condemnatory attitude. . . . The man whose head is cracked knows that he himself is to blame. If he tried to air his grievance, he would get no support. 'He was drunk, why did you fight with him?' (p. 379).

Shifting continents now, we find the anthropologist Paul Bohannan (1960a) reporting that drunkenness also either excuses or mitigates both minor and major offenses among the BaLuyia of East Africa. Thus, he notes that in 27 cases of BaLuyia homicide in which alcohol was implicated, "Alcohol was, in all instances save one, considered a mitigating factor, and a plea for manslaughter was accepted" (p. 161). Bohannan's finding is paralleled by that of the anthropologist Gordon Wilson (1960), who investigated violence in another East African tribe, the Luo. Of twelve cases of Luo homicide that Wilson classified as "the result of excessive beer drinking . . . [all] were finally treated by the courts as manslaughter" (p. 180).

Turning now to a more general review of drunken transgressions, we find that Donald Horton (1943), in his often cited survey of the literature on drinking practices in 56 non-Western societies, states that in those societies in which drunken aggression occurs, it is frequently the case that such aggression is not "strongly" penalized: "Smaller fines, a shorter jail sentence, or some other moderation of punishment is often characteristic of the attitude toward drunken aggression. The drunken man is not to be held strictly accountable for his actions" (p. 255).[1] In a more recent survey of the literature on drinking in 16 non-Western societies, Chandler Washburne (1961) also concludes that "A person is not punished as severely for doing forbidden things while drunk" (p. 262). To this, Washburne adds the significant observation that "The feeling is nurtured that the best time to do such things is when drinking" (p. 262).[2]

Rather than continue with an endless panorama of synoptic depictions of the fact that the state of drunkenness is accorded the status of at least a partial *time out* in one culture or another, there is perhaps more to be gained at this point by examining a detailed treatment of the phenomenon. An unusually rich depiction of the

1. In Horton's rhetoric, all negative sanctions directed against the drunken transgressor are subsumed under the rubric "counteranxiety," which is the affect he presumes that such sanctions will evoke in the person against whom they are directed. Although he acknowledges that by failing to produce a constraining "amount" of counteranxiety, a laxity in the administration of negative sanctions constitutes "a form of permission," his theoretical preconceptions blind him to the full import of what he is saying; for he steadfastly holds that "we are dealing here with aggression released by intoxication" (p. 256).

2. However, Washburne, like Horton, seems unable to appreciate the full relevance of this state of affairs. Although Washburne regards the conventional disinhibition theory as but dubiously adequate, he variously recommends that this formulation be bolstered by stipulations as to the degree of repression of the "inhibited or repressed drives," the availability of opportunity for the expression of such "drives," and the severity of punishment that is meted out following their expression. He also proposes (1) a regression theory as an alternative to "the theory of release of inhibition" (sic) in which "drinking is viewed as bringing to the fore a less complicated individual who cannot deal with frustration on the same level as when he is sober" (p. 264), and therefore reacts to frustration with physical aggression; (2) a social role theory; and (3) an anxiety and/or tension-reduction theory. Having recommended such a hodgepodge of conceptual solutions, Washburne concludes on the following note: "As the present study was not intended to test any single hypothesis, it cannot come to any specific conclusion" (p. 273). And there he leaves the matter.

time out character of drunkenness is contained in the anthropologist John Kennedy's (1963) recent account of the role that the *tesguinada,* or drinking party, plays among the Tarahumara Indians of the pueblo of Aboreachi, Mexico. As we have already seen in Chapter 4, Bennett and Zingg (who studied the Tarahumara some thirty years before Kennedy) were singularly struck both by the extreme shyness of these Indians when they were sober, and by the metamorphic effect that alcohol had upon them. As Zingg (1942) put it, "It is only when the Tarahumara are drunk that they lose their wooden expressions. Then they are animated . . . and only then do individuals of the opposite sex lose their abysmal shyness for each other . . ." (p. 90). An even earlier reflection on this latter point is contained in the journals of Carl Lumholtz (1902), who traveled among the Tarahumara around the turn of the century. Lumholtz was so impressed by the Tarahumaras' inordinate shyness when they were sober that he was moved to suggest that *tesguino* played no small role in their very perpetuation as a tribe, it being his impression that the male had to become drunk before he could muster sufficient courage to enforce his marital rights (Vol. 1, p. 342). While doubtless overdrawn, such summary observations as these are vivid indications of the great importance that all observers have attributed to the state of drunkenness in the Tarahumara scheme of things.

It remained, however, for Kennedy to address himself specifically to this phenomenon. The *tesguinada,* Kennedy writes, is the basic social activity of the people. "Conversations frequently concerned *tesguinadas,* and they formed one of the dominant subjects of dreams. . . . this meaning and importance of *tesguino* interpenetrate all major sectors of the culture and social organization" (1963, p. 622). And again, "the *tesguinada* serves all the functions of social life outside those served by the household groups. It is the religious group, the economic group, the entertainment group, the group at which disputes are settled, marriages arranged, and deals completed" (p. 629). Indeed, it was Kennedy's conclusion that "the set of people defined by reciprocal *tesguino* invitation forms the meaningful 'community' for any particular individual" (p. 625).

And at every *tesguinada,* Kennedy goes on to assert, the participants get drunk:

The etiquette of *tesguino* drinking requires that all people present, both women and men, drink as much as possible. . . . Rarely is one allowed to beg off this drinking obligation, though rarely does one want to. . . . the Tarahumaras not only attach no shame to being drunk, but make drunkenness a matter of pride. A person is expected to get intoxicated and is proud to brag later of his degree of intoxication. The ideal of enjoyment is the state of complete inebriation (p. 629).

Since the Tarahumaras' settlement pattern is one of wide dispersal and since their daily activities—both the household duties of the women and the herding and agricultural pursuits of the men—are performed largely in isolation, the *tesguinada* is, first and foremost, a time of greatly telescoped interaction with one's fellows. And they go all out to make the most of it. Once drunk, the Tarahumara discard "their wooden expressions"; they relax, joke, sing, dance, etc. But there is a negative side to the coin as well. Although the participants were always enjoined at the beginning of the festivities neither "to fight or to engage in sexual intercourse with the unmarried or the mates of others" (Kennedy, 1963, p. 627), it was understood that such good advice would most probably be ignored, for they were also enjoined to keep their children away from the drinking area lest they "learn things beyond their stage of development." And their fears were not without basis, for Kennedy observed of the *tesguinadas* that "Fighting is frequent and adultery only a little less so" (p. 627), an observation that he elaborated as follows: "By frequent, I mean that at most large *tesguinadas* some kind of altercation ending in serious physical struggle occurs and one or more adulterous contacts" (p. 627). Indeed, he reports that at least 90 per cent of all social infractions take place in the context of *tesguinadas*. Fighting, for instance, "is correlated exclusively with drinking" (p. 632). And as for extramarital intercourse, "it is only in the context of the *tesguinada* that the permissive norm may be expressed" (p. 627).

What of the role of *time out* in all of this? As for fighting, Kennedy reports that:

Theoretically, formal sanctions may be invoked against people who fight. In practice, most fights are forgotten the day after the *tesguinadas,* unless they result in serious injury. If asked about his fighting the next day, the person almost always shrugs it off as due to *tesguino* (1963, p. 627).

And of the consequences of extramarital affairs, Kennedy states:

> The *tesguinada,* despite the sermons, is known by all to be an opportunity for intercourse with other than one's spouse. . . . No sanctions are brought to bear for adulterous behavior unless it results in actual breakup of marriage. *The unanimous opinion of informants was that tesguino was to blame for these infractions, as for fighting* (p. 627, emphasis ours).

Thus, while at least 90 per cent of all Tarahumara transgressions are *drunken* transgressions committed during drinking parties, they do not blame themselves for such occurrences. Instead, they blame the *tesguino;* more accurately, they blame the state of intoxication to which the ingestion of *tesguino* gives rise. And because of this, virtually all of these transgressions end up being *excused.* Clearly, then, for the Tarahumara, as for so many peoples, the drinking party is the sanctioned time and place for doing many things that would be categorically inexcusable under normal circumstances. While it would be idle to speculate as to what Tarahumara life would be like without the institution of the *tesguinada,* there can be no doubt that it would be radically different.[3]

But this "saving up" for the proper occasion may be a matter of pure discretion rather than the combination of discretion and necessity that it is with the Tarahumara. The Cubeo of the northwest Amazon, who are not so isolated from each other as are the Tarahumara, exemplify this possibility. Thus, the anthropologist Irving Goldman (1963) has recently written of them that:

> Fighting at a drinking party, although actually disliked by the Cubeo, is not a punishable offense, since the angry parties have had full opportunity to retaliate. When the fight is over the issue is usually closed, unless new threats and insults are uttered. Those will be remembered *at the next drinking party* and serve to start a new fight (p. 158, emphasis ours).

Nor is the comportment that ensues during periods of drunken

---

3. Only remember (from Chapter 4) that even for the Tarahumara, the state of drunkenness is accorded the status of *time out* only *within limits.*

time out necessarily limited to a bursting forth of what is normally quiescent. This point is nicely documented by the anthropologist Robert C. Suggs (1962, 1966) in his accounts of the sexual practices of the inhabitants of the Marquesas Islands of French Polynesia. Suggs, who lived among the inhabitants of the island of Nuku Hiva in the late 1950's, reports that for the Marquesans, sex "is something of a national sport—a culturally sanctioned pastime in a culture offering few recreational opportunities" (1966, p. 170). Not only is it considered normal for adolescents of both sexes to have frequent sexual relations (1962, p. 120), a similarly promiscuous pattern continues even after marriage, "the wife taking lovers from among the young boys and her husband's friends and relatives, while the husband may call upon his sisters-in-law, the young girls, or the valley's loose women" (1962, p. 123).

When the Marquesans get drunk it is all very much the same—only more so! Writing of their weekly lost weekends, Suggs (1962) notes that:

> During [these] periodic drinking bouts, the usual standards of sexual conduct dropped to even more casual levels. Often . . . bold proposals would be made [to me] by some of the women present without evoking any wrath from their husbands. . . . A woman whose husband had passed out could be assured of getting a large number of propositions from the young bucks, and any woman stepping into the brush to relieve herself or take a quick bath in the stream was throwing down a gauntlet that would without exception be taken up. Much of the really heavy drinking done by the adults was done in the spirit of a contest to see who could manage to drink under the table the husbands of the most accessible females and still remain conscious enough to possess the victor's prize. Many such contests soon became sexual orgies, with discretion and custom thrown completely to the winds; wives took lovers right beside their dead-drunk husbands; young boys lured women of their mothers' generation into the bush . . . (p. 116).

We shall have more to say of the Marquesans in a moment, but first we want to consider an example of *time out* in which, from the standpoints both of character and of custom, the change is truly antipodal. Our source is the Abbé J. A. Dubois' account of Hindu life and customs as he observed them in India between the years 1792–1823. At the time Dubois wrote, considerations of caste dominated Hindu thought and conduct to a degree that is difficult for the Westerner to appreciate. The comportment of all members of all castes was regulated by an astonishing number of rules and ritualized avoidances covering virtually every facet of life. These caste dictates were deeply implanted during the course of socialization. Furthermore, since their violation was presumed to pollute not only the transgressor, but all members of his caste as well, external and internal pressures combined to insure compliance.

As these strictures impinged upon the Brahmans (the highest caste), it was believed, for instance, that merely to be in physical proximity to the lowly pariahs was sufficient for pollution to occur. Regarding food, the Brahmans were required to observe the following strictures with scrupulous care: to refrain from eating meat, to refrain from all intoxicating liquors, and to refrain from even touching food that had been prepared by persons of a lower caste.

With this as background, Dubois' (1897) account of the Hindu rite of *sakti-puja,* as performed especially by the *Namadharis,* or followers of Vishnu, becomes particularly remarkable:

> People of all castes, from the Brahmin to the Pariah, are invited to attend. When the company are assembled, all kinds of meat, including beef, are placed before the idol of Vishnu. Ample provision is also made of arrack (brandy), toddy, and opium, and any other intoxicating drug they can lay their hands on. The whole is then offered to Vishnu. Afterwards the *pujari,* or sacrificer, who is generally a Brahmin, first of all tastes the various kinds of meats and liquors himself, then gives the others permission to devour the rest. Men and women thereupon begin to eat greedily, the same piece of meat passing from mouth to mouth, each person taking a bite, until it is finished. Then they start afresh on another joint, which they gnaw in the same manner, tearing the meat out of each other's mouths. When all the meat has been consumed, intoxicating liquors are passed round, every one drinking without repugnance out of the same cup. Opium and other drugs disappear in a similar fashion. They persuade themselves that under these circumstances they do not contract impurity by eating and drinking in so revolting a manner. When they are all completely intoxicated, men and women no longer keep apart, but pass the rest of the night together, giving themselves up without restraint to the grossest immorality without any risk of disagreeable consequences. A husband who sees his wife in another man's arms cannot recall her, nor has he the right to complain; for at those times every woman becomes common property. Perfect equality exists among all castes, and the Brahmin is not

of higher caste than the Pariah. The celebration of these mysterious rites may differ sometimes in outward forms, but in spirit they are always equally abominable (pp. 286–87).

Lest one think that such a concerted and, by all accounts, successful effort to stand the whole array of caste strictures on its head was but the disinhibited product of the participants' alcoholically impaired central nervous systems, note that the breaching of the proscriptions regarding physical proximity, the eating of meat, etc., occurred *before* they began to drink, and that the drinking (which must necessarily have commenced with all drinkers entirely sober) was itself among the caste proscriptions. In the rite of *sakti-puja,* then, we come upon an instance of ceremonially arranged *time out* in which the state of drunkenness, far from serving to excuse one's transgressions, was itself an excused transgression—and all in the name of religion.

But there is really nothing surprising in this, for throughout recorded history there are instances in which religious observance and ceremonially arranged license go hand in hand. Venus, Mitra, Osiris, Baal, and Moloch—all were the objects of "equally impure worship." [4] And while drinking was a frequent accompaniment of these observances, the resulting drunkenness was essentially incidental, for the license was an intrinsic part of the ceremonies themselves!

With this in mind, we want now to look again at the seemingly alcohol-induced sexual revels of the contemporary Marquesans. Although there is no doubt that the participants at these revels do get very drunk and that their comportment is orgiastic by anyone's standards, there *is* good reason to question whether the former is in any way causative of the latter. In fact, there is an abundance of evidence to indicate that although such get-togethers are now entirely secular, they were traditionally religious in nature:

> Ritual orgies played an important part in Marquesan society before the coming of the Europeans, but at that time they were generally a part of important religious ceremonies. . . . Licentiousness did not then disrupt the society; the role it played in organized religious activities further cemented social solidarity. Now native social and

4. The very word *orgy* derives from the Greek word *orgia,* meaning "secret rites, secret worship."

political organization is gone, and with it the elaborate and colorful
pagan religion (Suggs, 1962, p. 125).[5]

What is more, about these traditional observances—these periods
of *time out* by ceremonial arrangement—we can be certain that
alcohol played no part whatsoever, for prior to the coming of the
Europeans it was unknown to the Marquesans. What we are sug-
gesting, then, is that the sexual license that occurs during contemporary Marquesan drinking parties is to be understood not as an
alcoholically produced disjunctive state of affairs, but as the vesti-
gial and secularized expression of traditional non-drunken religious
practices.

That societies may call *time out* without benefit of alcohol is
evidenced by the fact that ceremonially arranged periods of license
generally similar to the above, but without intoxicants of any kind,
have been reported from various parts of the world. For example,
the anthropologist Evans-Pritchard (1929), in reviewing such
phenomena in sub-Saharan Africa, notes that many African tribal
societies provide their members with periods of what we are calling
time out in which drunkenness plays no part whatsoever, and
that during these occasions entirely sober African tribesmen engage in acts of "indescribable lewdness." And, as the anthropologist
Edward Norbeck (1963) has recently documented, such intoxica-
tion-free periods of suspension or relaxation of the normally operative rules of proper conduct are not at all limited to the sexual
sphere. Throughout much of Africa there are socially sanctioned
occasions associated variously with death, mourning, harvesting,
planting, initiation, housebuilding, drought, famine, political
change, etc., during which, in addition to the performance of sundry
kinds of illicit sexual behavior, obscenities, insults, physical assaults, theft, property destruction, and the like are also variously
allowed.

Actually, as long ago as 1909, Arnold van Gennep's epochal
book, *The Rites of Passage,* conclusively demonstrated the fact
that throughout the world, initiation rites were often set apart as
occasions during which many rules of proper conduct might be

5. For early explorers' accounts of Marquesan life, see P. F. de Quiros
(published 1904); A. J. von Krusenstern (1813), and D. Porter (1822). On
the colonial period, see Father M. Gracia (1843) and Father S. Delmas
(published 1927). For more recent anthropological accounts, see E. S. C.
Handy (1923) and the already cited R. C. Suggs (1962, 1966).

broken with impunity. At about the same time, Sir James Frazer's (1907–1915) monumental *Golden Bough* provided abundant documentation of the fact that the practice of ceremonial *time out* of one sort or another was confined neither to such status-transition rites nor to the "primitive" world, but had long been a part of both the religious and the secular life of the world's major civilizations as well. And for most of those examples cited by van Gennep and Frazer in which there was clear-cut evidence of *time out,* the drunkenness of the participants was neither a necessary nor a sufficient condition.

How does this fact—the fact that *time out* can occur independently of alcohol usage—relate to our proposal that whether or not drunkenness is accompanied by marked changes in comportment is a function of whether or not the state of drunkenness is defined as a state of being-in-the-world during which, in effect, a new array of options is available? Its relevance may be stated as follows: If societies have it in their power to define certain occasions in which alcohol plays no part whatsoever as occasions during which various of the normally operative prescriptions and proscriptions can be set aside, then certainly they can do the same for occasions in which alcohol *does* play a part.

Taken by itself, this line of argument is not, of course, sufficient to *prove* that changes in one's drunken comportment either do or do not occur as a consequence of the definition one's society accords to the state of drunkenness. It does, however, go a long way toward establishing the plausibility of our formulation. And when we recognize that only some such formulation as this is capable of making sense of the sundry "exceptions" which we have presented, things begin to look even better.

In the next two chapters we shall attempt to add further to the compellingness of our formulation by demonstrating that it and it alone is capable of providing an adequate framework for understanding the historical experience with alcohol of a people whose drunken changes-for-the-worse are commonly acknowledged to have been as spectacularly horrendous as any the world has ever seen—the Indians of North America.

6 "Indians Can't Hold Their Liquor"

A. The Conventional Wisdom and the Puzzles

EXCEPT FOR A FEW SOUTHWESTERN tribes, the North American Indians had no alcoholic beverages prior to the coming of the white man. With his arrival, however, alcohol was soon introduced; and once it took hold, it did so with a vengeance. Perhaps nowhere has alcohol had more profoundly adverse effects on both personal and social organization. Certainly, the history of these effects has nowhere been so amply and so variously documented. And from it all has come the guiding and abiding notion that "Indians can't hold their liquor."

It will be our purpose to show that within this massive body of materials on the North American Indians' historical experience with alcohol there are numerous observations that do not at all comport with the stereotype of the "drunken Indian." Indeed, it will be our contention that at one point or another in this historical panorama, the disinhibition theory of alcohol's workings is confronted with all of the puzzles that we have previously encountered.

THE CONVENTIONAL WISDOM

The application of the conventional wisdom to the case of the Indians of North America is founded upon two seemingly indisputable facts: (1) that these Indians craved the white man's liquor; and (2) that when they got drunk, their comportment was characterized by horrendous changes-for-the-worse.

Let us begin by presenting some examples of the sorts of documentation upon which this formulation relies. There is, for instance, Father Chrestien Le Clercq's late seventeenth-century account (published 1910) of alcohol usage among the Micmac Indians of Gaspé Harbor, located on the Gulf of St. Lawrence. According to Father Le Clercq, the Micmac "[find no] pleasure in this drink except so far as it makes them entirely lose their understanding and reason" (p. 257). And of their comportment once this occurs, Father Le Clercq provides the following characterization:

Lewdness, adulteries, incests, and several other crimes which decency keeps me from naming, are the usual disorders which are committed through the trade in brandy, of which some traders make use in order to abuse the Indian women, who yield themselves readily during their drunkenness to all kinds of indecency. . . . Injuries, quarrels, homicides, murders, parricides are to this day the sad consequences of the trade in brandy; and one sees with grief Indians dying in their drunkenness . . . (p. 255).

Nor is this mere hysterical exaggeration, for similar accounts of Indian drunkenness during the prereservation period are available in such profusion as to convince even the most skeptical that drunken disorders of like severity were once quite common. Thus, for example, this anonymous memorandum (*Collection de manuscrits,* 1883) on the Indians of Nova Scotia was written in 1693:

The brandy that they drink without moderation, carries them to obscenities and extremities of fury and cruelty which are unimaginable. They slaughter one another, they murder one another like ferocious beasts; being drunk they disfigure their faces. They burn and cripple in their scuffles, they sell all that belongs to them. . . . Many die in the flower of youth . . . parricides, incest, rape, prostitution and a thousand other infamies and detestable brutalities . . . are the ordinary results of drinking this beverage (Vol. 1, p. 541).

And in the same year, another anonymous observer (quoted in Eastman, 1915) wrote this account of the drunken comportment of the Indians of another part of eastern Canada:

> Savage men and women, drunken and naked, dragged each other into the streets, where in the sight and to the great scandal of everybody, they did publicly, like brute beasts, things shameful and infamous . . . that decency does not permit the author to relate (pp. 274–75).

In still another anonymous account (quoted in Blair, 1911) from the same area, written in 1705, considerations of decency were partially set aside, thereby permitting a somewhat more explicit reference to at least some of these "shameful and infamous" deeds:

> Every one knows the passion of the savages for this liquor, and the fatal effects that it produces on them. . . . The village or the cabin in which the savages drink brandy is an image of hell: fire [*i.e.*, burning brands or coals flung by the drunkards] flies in all directions; blows with hatchets and knives make the blood flow on all sides; and all the place resounds with frightful yells and cries. . . . They commit a thousand abominations—the mother with her sons, the father with his daughters, and brothers with their sisters. They roll about on the cinders and coals, and in blood (Vol. 1, p. 208).

Similar reports issued from scattered locations throughout the vast area to the south and to the west as well. This despairing letter written toward the end of the seventeenth century by Father Carheil (quoted in Parkman, 1901) of Marquette's old mission of Michilimackinac, located in the Upper Great Lakes region, is altogether characteristic:

> Our missions . . . are reduced to such extremity that we can no longer maintain them against the infinity of disorder, brutality, violence, injustice, impiety, impurity, insolence, scorn, and insult, which the deplorable and infamous traffic in brandy has spread universally among the Indians of these parts . . . nothing remains for us but to abandon them to the brandy-sellers as a domain of drunkenness and debauchery (Vol. 2, p. 119).

Some years later (in 1750), and still farther to the west, we find another French priest (*Jesuit Relations,* Vol. 69, 1896) writing that:

> The savages—especially the Illinois, who are the gentlest and most tractable of men—become when intoxicated, madmen and wild beasts. Then they fall upon one another, stab with their knives, and tear one another (pp. 201–203).

Nor was it only the missionaries who likened drunken Indians to "madmen" and "wild beasts." The fur traders—men who, as a group, were scarcely devoted either to religion or to temperance— regularly attested to the mayhem and debauchery they had observed to accompany Indian drunkenness. John Long, for instance, who spent most of the period between 1768 and 1782 trading with the far-flung Chippewa, recorded numerous episodes of Indian drunkenness of which the following (published 1904) are typical:

> We stayed here ten days, encamped by the side of the Lake; during which time a skirmish happened among the Indians, in which three men were killed, and two wounded, after a dreadful scene of riot and confusion, occasioned by the baneful effects of rum (pp. 86–87).

> The rum being taken from my house, was carried to their wigwaum, and they began to drink. The frolic lasted four days and nights; and notwithstanding all our precaution (securing their guns, knives, and tomahawks) two boys were killed, and six men wounded by three Indian women; one of the chiefs was also murdered . . . (p. 93).

> I traded for their skins and furs, and gave them some rum, with which they had a frolic, which lasted for three days and nights; on this occasion five men were killed, and one woman dreadfully burnt (p. 142).

Daniel Harmon, another fur trader, recorded this note in his journal for the year 1800 (published 1903):

> The last night, a squaw, in a state of intoxication, stabbed her husband, who soon after expired. This afternoon, I went to their tent, where I saw a number of Indians, of both sexes, drinking and crying over the corpse, to which they would frequently offer rum, and try to pour it down his throat, supposing him to be as fond of rum when

dead, as he was when alive. The Natives of this place are Chippeways (p. 17).

And in the same year, Harmon also recorded this description of a Cree drinking bout:

To see a house full of drunken Indians, consisting of men, women and children, is a most unpleasant sight; for, in that condition, they often wrangle, pull each other by the hair, and fight. At some times, ten or twelve, of both sexes, may be seen, fighting each other promiscuously, until at last, they all fall on the floor, one upon another, some spilling rum out of a small kettle or dish, which they hold in their hands, while others are throwing up what they have just drunk. To add to this uproar, a number of children some on their mothers' shoulders, and others running about and taking hold of their clothes, are constantly bawling, the older ones, through fear that their parents may be stabbed, or that some other misfortune may befall them, in the fray. These shrieks of the children, form a very unpleasant chorus to the brutal noise kept up by their drunken parents, who are engaged in the squabble (1903, pp. 35–36).

Peter Jones (1861), himself a Chippewa, had this to say, in his memoirs, of the drunken disorders that afflicted his tribe:

I have seen such scenes of degradation as would sicken the soul of a good man, such as husbands beating wives, and dragging them about by the hair of the head; children screaming with fright, the older ones running off with guns, tomahawks, spears, knives, and other deadly weapons, which they concealed in the woods to prevent the commission of murder by their enraged parents; yet, notwithstanding this precaution, death was not unfrequently the result (p. 167).

The early ethnographer Henry Schoolcraft (1847), who had traveled extensively among the Indians east of the Mississippi, summarized both his own observations and those of others as follows:

The effects of ardent spirits in the lodge are equal to the appearance of a grizzly bear amongst them. The men get drunk, and perfectly crazy; all at once, the Indian will grasp his gun and knife, and out he goes, in search of some one that has injured him. He drives through the women and children—they scream with fright and fly to the woods; the maniac, if he cannot find the object he wishes, will take after the women and children and many a night have they had to sleep out in the coldest winter nights, on account of these drunkards (pp. 241–42).

Still farther west, along the Missouri, a traveler (quoted in Blair, 1911) wrote of his observations of Indian drunkenness that:

One must be a witness to the orgies of these people in order to understand to what excess their brutal passion can carry them. Once the bounds of temperance are passed, their blood is inflamed, and a sort of rage consumes them. . . . Very often blood is mingled with their libations, and murder seasons the feast (Vol. 1, p. 209).

Continuing westward, we have the report of Rudolph Kurz (published 1936) who traveled among the Indians of the northern Plains in the years 1846–1862, a time when the warlike Plains tribes were at the height of their military prowess. Kurz noted, as did his predecessors and contemporaries in their depictions of the Eastern tribes, that "here as elsewhere, brawls, and murders not infrequently occur as a result of drinking" (p. 177).

By the early years of the nineteenth century, even the far West Coast had its share of what the Russian governor of Alaska (quoted in Rich, 1958) referred to as "horrible scenes of bloodshed arising from drunkenness" (Vol. 2, p. 479). Fort Simpson, in British Columbia, was reported to have been "in a constant drunken riot and . . . the scene of several murders" (Rich, 1958, Vol. 2, p. 857). So common did such reports from the Pacific Northwest of Canada and the United States become that the contemporary historian F. W. Howay (1942) could write without fear of contradiction that eventually the Indian of this area, too, "became inordinately fond of liquor, indulging in it to excess and becoming under its influence a perfect demon" (p. 159).

Thus in tribe after tribe and from one coast to the other, the baneful effects of alcohol on the Indians came to be recognized. As this recognition sank in, attempts began to be made to deny them access to liquor. Churches, townships, the military, etc.—all joined in an insistence on this prohibition. But the Indians' desire for alcohol was great, the satisfaction of this desire was highly profitable, and the outcome of these efforts was never in doubt. In Canada, the contest between the fur trade and the Church reached such proportions that it came to be known as the Brandy War. And to the south, the historical documents of all of the colonies and, later, of almost every state in the Union are replete with records of countless legislative attempts to accomplish what moral suasion could not. But although these efforts to deny alcohol to the Indians were often scarcely less vigorous than the efforts to deny them Winchesters, these same records contain ample evidence of the failure of this exercise in moral uplift. Entirely representative of what was to become a continent-wide lament are the following remarks of the historian John DeForest (1851) regarding liquor legislation in the earliest days of Connecticut:

> Nothing operated with more injurious effect upon the native than intoxicating liquors. . . . One law after another was passed, forbidding any person to furnish an Indian with such liquors under considerable penalties. In 1654, this penalty amounted to five pounds for every pint thus sold, and forty shillings for the least quantity (p. 203).

> As drunken natives used to prowl about the settlements, making attempts to get more liquor . . . all Indians were forbidden walking about towns after nightfall, under a penalty of a fine of twenty shillings, and a flogging of at least six stripes (p. 271).

However, as DeForest laconically observed, "Notwithstanding these laws the evil still went on increasing . . ." (p. 203).

Despite the repeated failures of such local legislative efforts, a federal law was enacted in 1832 under which it became illegal to provide alcohol to Indians throughout the United States and its territories. But this federal effort was no more successful than the earlier state and local ventures, and although some local laws against Indian drinking remain on the books, the year 1953 marked the final abandonment of the quest for a solution at the federal level.

As Henry Schoolcraft (1847) noted over a century ago:

> There is one vice which the Indians have fallen into since their acquaintance with the Christians, of which they could not be guilty before that time, that is, drunkenness. It is strange how all the Indian nations, and almost every person among them, male and female, are infatuated with the love of strong drink. They know no bounds to their desire, while they can swallow it down, and then indeed the greatest man among them scarcely deserves the name of a brute (p. 192).

Still, the passage of the years has produced a remedy of sorts, for as generation after generation of Indians has become, as it were, "domesticated" on the reservation, the awesome mayhem that characterized their earlier drunkenness has greatly diminished. Yet, while the drunken misconduct of modern reservation Indians is pallid in comparison with the sorts of transgressions that occurred during the prereservation era, even now their comportment often undergoes dramatic change when they get drunk. Thus, in a 1938 report by the Commissioner of Indian Affairs (quoted in Lindquist, 1944) we read that "Most of the serious crimes committed by Indians have intoxicating liquor as a contributing cause" (p. 85). And even more recently, federal crime statistics for the year 1960 document that the proportion of Indians arrested for all alcohol-related crimes is higher than that of any other ethnic category in the United States—the rate being more than twelve times greater than the national average.[1]

That drunken transgressions are almost everywhere a common feature of reservation life in both the United States and Canada is evidenced in numerous recent studies. From the Yankton Sioux of South Dakota (Hurt and Brown, 1965), from the Menomini of Wisconsin (Slotkin, 1953), from the Mescalero Apaches of New Mexico (Curley, 1967), from several Northwest Coast tribes (Lemert, 1954), from the Navaho of the Southwest (Heath, 1964; Kluckhohn, 1944), from the Standing Rock Sioux of the Dakotas (Whittaker, 1963), from the Chipewyans (Oswalt, 1966) and the Slaves (Helm, 1961) of the Canadian Northwest, from the Potawatomi (Hamer, 1965) of Michigan's Upper Peninsula, from the Chippewa of Wisconsin and Canada (Barnouw, 1950), and on and on—all speak to the points that Indians continue to drink heavily, and that when they become drunk, their comportment continues to undergo marked, although now relatively muted, changes-for-the-worse.

Clearly, the problem has not only long been with us, it shows no immediate signs of going away. While earlier students have interpreted the peculiarly disruptive effects of alcohol upon the Indian as resulting from some form of racial weakness, and while this con-

1. A compilation of such statistics as they relate to Indian drunkenness is contained in Stewart (1964). For a more general statement of the problem of drunken changes-for-the-worse among contemporary reservation Indians, see Dozier (1966).

ception still finds occasional voice, there is no evidence that such a constitutional vulnerability exists. This does not alarm most contemporary discussants, however, for they feel that when properly stated, the disinhibition theory is capable of providing an entirely adequate explanation.

For a consummate, and certainly a most influential, statement of this—the conventional—explanation, we turn to the now classic paper of the anthropologist A. I. Hallowell (1955), a leading authority on the Indians of the Eastern Woodlands.[2] Hallowell begins by noting that although the Indians were actually very hostile, under normal circumstances they placed great emphasis on restraint in the expression of all emotion, most particularly on the expression of aggression. Thus, the pattern of deference and politeness that characterized their everyday activities within the tribal unit was only rarely broken by visible anger and almost never by overt aggression. When hostility did come to the surface, it took such covert forms as malicious joking and gossip, slander, and witchcraft. According to Hallowell, then, although the Indians often gave vent to the most notorious extremes of cruelty in their warfare with other tribes, they were among the most "inhibited" of people in their relations with their fellow tribesmen. Given this, we can easily anticipate Hallowell's analysis of the effects of alcohol upon the "repressed" Indians:

> Alcohol, as we know, often releases inhibitions so that impulses are revealed which usually are kept in check when the individual is sober. Since there also appears to be a connection between personality organization, culture pattern and behavior under the influence of alcohol, the conduct of the Indian when drunk was, in a sense, a natural experiment, a cue to his character. If his basic emotional structure was one that led to the suppression of a great deal of affect, in particular aggressive impulses, then we would expect that these might be released in a notably violent form under the influence of alcohol. This seems to have been what happened. . . . The homicidal aspect of drunken behavior becomes still more significant when we recall that however implacable and cruel the Indian may have proved as a foe, in-group behavior was not only amicable, but, by

2. Although we have quoted from a relatively recent statement of Hallowell's thesis, his views on this subject became influential as early as 1943 when Donald Horton (1943), in his widely read, already mentioned, cross-cultural study of drinking practices, referred at some length to an unpublished version of Hallowell's formulation. Since that time various references to Hallowell's thesis have appeared in the anthropological literature.

and large, it was characterized by a remarkable absence of murder. . . . Thus, while individuals, projecting their own aggressive fantasies, often believed that they were the victims of witchcraft, in actual fact (when sober) physical violence among in-group members was a rarity. Drunkenness, however, leading as it did to release from the pattern of emotional restraint, permitted the discharge of suppressed hostility in the form of overt physical aggression which in the sober state was inhibited and overlaid by an effective facade of amiability (pp. 141–42).

Here, then, in what is perhaps its most influential statement, we find the conventional formulation of alcohol's workings invoked as *the* explanation of how and why these drunken changes-for-the-worse came to pass.

Yet, when we examine the record of Indian drunkenness more closely, we find that there are abundant grounds for challenging this explanation. Let us begin at the beginning by turning the record back to the earliest years of the Indians' experience with the white man's alcohol.

IT WASN'T ALWAYS THUS

Before European contact, the New World was not entirely without alcohol; alcoholic drinks were widespread in South America, throughout the Circum-Caribbean region, and in Meso-America. In Mexico, for example, the Indians had developed at least forty distinct alcoholic beverages (Driver, 1961). Alcoholic drinks were also known in scattered portions of what is now the southwestern United States. Such familiar tribes as the Apache and the Zuñi drank indigenously produced alcoholic beverages on secular occasions, and the Pima and the Papago (whom we have already encountered) drank ceremonially. Yet, as we have seen, the ceremonial drinking of the Papago was confined to a single peaceable annual ceremony, and the secular drinking of the other Southwestern Indians was also infrequent and apparently similarly peaceable in character (Lindquist, 1923, pp. 65–66; Curley, 1967). It is remotely possible that some tribes of the American Southeast (Virginia and the Carolinas) produced a persimmon wine, but it is more likely that it was of European origin (Driver, 1961, pp. 93–97). Certainly, if it was indigenous it did not spread among the neighboring tribes, for the rest of the Indians of the Eastern seaboard and the South were definitely without knowledge of alcohol.

So, too, were the rest of the Indians of North America, for outside the Southwest, the Indians of what is now the United States
and Canada had no alcoholic beverages before the coming of the
white man. Why alcohol did not spread farther north from Mexico
is a puzzling but unanswerable question. It was cherished in
Mexico and it later became sought all over North America. Yet the
fact remains that the vast majority of these North American Indians, although they possessed many wild and cultivated plants
suitable for fermentation, had not produced alcoholic beverages
prior to the period of European contact. Thus, when the first Europeans set foot upon the northeastern coast of this continent, upon
the "New Found Land," they introduced their "ardent spirits" to
an unknowing population.

The exact date at which this initial introduction took place is as
unknowable to history as that which marked the discovery of North
America itself. The discoverers of this continent were probably
Norsemen, sailing west from Greenland. They and subsequent
voyagers most likely landed near the mouth of either the Gulf of St.
Lawrence or Hudson Bay, and the land they saw they called "Vin-
land," after the wild grapes that they saw growing in such abundance. But the native "Skraelings" (Eskimos and Indians) whom
they encountered were neither friendly nor cowardly. Indeed, they
fought so well that if these Norsemen established colonies they
were probably very short-lived; and given the armed hostility of the
native inhabitants, it is highly unlikely that they traveled very far
inland.[3]

Those first Norsemen who sailed the coasts of North America
may have been in search of better lands, or they may have been
motivated merely by the spirit of exploration, but however this may
be, we know that later voyagers came to these shores in search of
fish. Throughout the Middle Ages, European fishermen from as far
south as Portugal and Spain fished vast portions of the North At-
lantic, often sailing to distant Iceland for their catches. Many his-
torians believe that these Basque, Breton, and Norman fishermen
had been drawn to the incredibly rich codfish banks off Newfoundland for centuries before John Cabot recorded their existence in
1497. If such fishermen set foot in North America before the time

3. The so-called Kensington Stone, long alleged to be a Norse rune left
behind in Minnesota by a band of beleaguered Norsemen in 1362, is almost
certainly a hoax (See Wahlgren, 1958).

of Cabot, however, it is unlikely that their landings went beyond hurried watering or hunting trips. And if they traded with the Indians in those early days (as we know some of them had prior to the visit of Verrazano in 1524) there is no indication either in record or in legend that liquor was involved.

John Cabot was the first European to record his visit (in 1497) to North America, but he makes no mention of alcohol. Neither do any of the several Portuguese explorers who followed hard on his heels. Not until Giovanni da Verrazano, captaining the French ship *La Dauphine,* sailed up the coast from the Carolinas to Newfoundland in 1524, do we have reason to believe that alcohol may have reached the Indians; for his vessel was well provisioned with liquor, and he spent several days with both the peaceable Mohicans of New York and the Indians of Narragansett Bay. Farther to the north, Verrazano met Indians who quite obviously had traded with Europeans before, and noted that they became truculent when their demands for trade goods were not adequately met. They did not demand alcohol, however, and he makes no mention that he offered them any.

Although other Europeans sailed the east coast of North America in the decade after Verrazano, and although fishermen continued their trips (even bringing captured Indians and Eskimos back with them to European ports), the first recorded instance in which alcohol was given to the Indians is contained in Jacques Cartier's journal for the year 1534. The Indians in question were those of Gaspé Harbor—the same Indians, be it noted, whose drunken disorders a hundred years later had so horrified Father Le Clercq. Cartier, however, had never heard that Indians could not hold their liquor, for on more than one occasion he gave it to them in "good cheer," and their reaction after trying it was anything but violent; once, for instance, the chief hugged and kissed Cartier as an expression of his pleasure! This so impressed Cartier that when he set sail, he gave these Indians additional quantities of liquor as a going-away present. What is more, on subsequent voyages Cartier continued to give liquor to the Indians without untoward incident (Biggar, 1924, p. 66; pp. 122–23).

While sporadic exploration along the east coast continued in the wake of Cartier's initial penetration, there is little or no mention of alcohol in the documents covering the remainder of the sixteenth century. There is no evidence, for instance, that the Spanish, who

were actively exploring in Florida, along the Gulf Coast, and
throughout the Southwest during this period, either gave the Indians alcohol or traded it to them. However, in the exploration of
Henry Hudson in 1609, we again find mention of alcohol. Landing
in New York, Hudson had reason to wonder about the good intentions of some of the Delawares and Mohicans whom he encountered and decided to test their intent by getting them drunk. Robert
Juet, who sailed with Hudson, recorded the event this way (published 1959):

> And our Master and his Mate determined to trie some of the chiefe
> men of the Countrey, whether they had any treacherie in them. So
> they tooke them downe into the Cabbin, and gave them so much
> Wine and Aqua vitae, that they were all merrie: and one of them had
> his wife with him, which sate so modestly, as any of our Countrey
> women would doe in a strange place. In the end one of them was
> drunke (p. 32).

Juet noted that the other Indians were alarmed by the stupor of this
"drunke" and departed the ship, leaving the "victim" behind where
"he slept all night quietly" (p. 32). This experience so impressed
the Indians that they told of it for many years, much to the amusement of subsequent travelers who recorded their stories. As these
Indians recalled the event according to one chronicler (Asher,
1860), when their companion staggered and then fell asleep, they
left the ship in fear, for they were certain that he had been poisoned
and that they would never see him alive again. To their amazement
however, the next morning "He awakes again, jumps up, and de-
clares that he never felt himself before so happy as after he had
drank the cup. Wishes for more. His wish is granted; and the whole
assembly soon join him, and become intoxicated" (p. 177). Juet
himself recorded this celebration, and although he noted that the
Indians became generally intoxicated, it is significant that he made
no mention whatsoever of any resultant misconduct, remarking
only that when the festivities had ended, Hudson's men went ashore
and began to trade. In none of this is there any indication that Hudson believed that alcohol would have a peculiarly adverse effect on
the Indians. And nowhere is there any indication that it had such
an effect.

Similar reports concerning the peaceable introduction of liquor
are available from the tribes of New England (Schoolcraft, 1848)

and from others far inland. The Ojibwa around Lake Superior (Warren, 1885) and the Menomini of Wisconsin (Skinner and Satterlee, 1915), for instance, give almost identical accounts of their first experience with alcohol. In both instances, white traders offered them brandy, but since the Indians feared that it might be a poison, they selected an elderly (ergo, an expendable) person to taste the strange new beverage. This hapless soul (a woman among the Ojibwa; a man among the Menomini) drank mightily, became stuporous, then passed out; and the watching Indians, assuming that their suspicion was correct and that the poison had taken effect, became both fearful and angry. After some time, however, the Indian recovered consciousness and extolled the virtues of drunkenness in such glowing terms that they all decided to give it a try. This they proceeded to do, but in neither the Ojibwa nor the Menomini accounts of what followed is there the least mention that these first drinkers manifested anything akin to changes-for-the-worse.

Clearly, the *initial* reaction of many Indians to liquor was anything but an epic of drunken mayhem, debauchery, and the like. Instead, we find account after account of these earliest days in which the Indians showed remarkable restraint while in their cups. Even the French Jesuits, who later spoke at such length about the disastrous consequences of the brandy trade, had little to say about the effects of alcohol upon the Indians' comportment when they first arrived in the New World. Thus, for example, when Father Pierre Biard (*Jesuit Relations,* Vol. 3, pp. 75–77) wrote of his experiences among the Eastern Algonquians between 1611–1616, he complained about their drinking not because of any misconduct that accompanied it, but because the low-quality French brandy that the traders supplied was causing stomach ailments! And in 1662–1663 another Jesuit priest (*Jesuit Relations,* Vol. 48) noted that while drunkenness had by that time become a "passion" for the Indians, during the earlier period "all [had] a loathing for our wines" (p. 63).[4]

Crossing the continent, we find very much the same pattern of

4. While the Indians' first experience with alcohol did not always produce "loathing," neither did it always result in "disinhibition." The journals of several traders and explorers contain many cryptic comments such as the following by Alexander Henry (published 1897): "We gave them half a keg of liquor, and they began the first drinking-match the natives have enjoyed here; but they were very quiet" (Vol. 2, p. 627).

events repeated on the Northwest Coast, where the introduction of liquor took place independently and much later in time. Thus, for example, from Vitus Bering (quoted in Howay, 1942) in 1741— as the Indian "tasted it he spat it out and returned the glass" (p. 157); from Captain James Cook in 1778—"when offered spiritous liquors, they rejected them as something unnatural and disgusting to the palate" (1784, Vol. 2, p. 323); and from the French explorer, Etienne Marchand in 1791—"the brandy of which they were prevailed on to make a trial, appeared not to be to their liking" (1798, Vol. 1, p. 221). From Vancouver in 1794—"At dinner they did not make the least scruple of partaking of our repast, with such wine and liquors as were offered to them; though of these they drank very sparingly, seeming to be well aware of their powerful effect" (1801, Vol. 5, p. 162); from Langsdorff in 1805—they rejected brandy "as a scandalous liquor, depriving them of their senses" (1817, p. 396); and from Ross Cox but a few years later— "All the Indians on the Columbia [river] entertain a strong aversion to ardent spirits, which they regard as poison. They allege . . . that drunkenness is degrading to free men" (1831, Vol. 1, pp. 291–92).

Nor is there any evidence that these Indians' earliest responses to liquor resulted in changes-for-the-worse, as witness, for example, Swan's (1857) account of a Chinook woman's description of the first drinking experience of several Indians of her tribe in 1793: "They drank some rum out of a wine glass—how much she did not recollect; but she *did* recollect that they got drunk, and were so scared at the strange feeling that they ran into the woods and hid till they were sober" (p. 155).

Thus, from one coast to the other the evidence points to the fact that *when the North American Indians' initial experience with alcohol was untutored by expectations to the contrary, the result was neither the development of an all-consuming craving nor an epic of drunken mayhem and debauchery.* But if alcohol did not instantaneously become a desired elixir, we must look elsewhere than to the substance itself for an understanding of how it eventually came to be so regarded. The villain, if we choose to see this transformation along the lines of a morality play, was the fur trade.

From early on, the traders recognized that alcohol was potentially the most potent trade-ware in their inventory, for unlike iron skillets, hatchets, etc. (the demand for which was clearly limited), they saw that if a desire for alcohol could be created it would be insatiable. They recognized, too, that if such a desire could be made strong enough, then they, who alone could satisfy it, would be able to assume near-dictatorial control over the Indians' activities. We can well understand, then, why the early trader John Macdonnell remarked that it was customary for the traders "to wet the whistle of every Indian they met on the way" (published 1965, p. 101). In fact, the literature on the fur trade abounds with instances in which every conceivable form of deceit and coercion was employed in forcing liquor upon the Indians (see, for example, Berry, 1961; Chittenden, 1954; and Lavender, 1964). And yet, as the historian Paul Phillips (1961) reports in his comprehensive survey of the fur trade in North America, despite the traders' most concerted efforts, "The use of alcohol in the Indian trade developed slowly. The Indians were . . . unwilling to use it at first, but the white traders persisted in offering it to them" (Vol. 1, p. 109).[5] Gradually this persistence paid off, for despite their initial reticence, the Indians eventually came to place themselves more and more at the traders' often less than charitable mercy—with what consequences, we have already seen.

Our point, however, is not that this finally came to pass, but that *it wasn't always thus*. The Indians' initial usage of liquor did *not* typically result in an insatiable craving for more. Where no preconceptions were operating, neither was its ingestion initially accompanied by marked changes-for-the-worse. All of this came later; for in the history of alcohol usage among the North American Indians, the early days were the *good* old days.

AN "ONLY SOMETIME" PROBLEM

Having now seen that the Indians were quite capable of "handling" their liquor at least in the early days of their contact with Europeans, we want next to show that even in later years—years during which their drunken disorders were at their most extreme—neither

5. Thus, from Sillery mission near Quebec, Father Jacques Bigot (*Jesuit Relations*, Vol. 63) wrote in 1685 that an Abnakis chief who had just brought his band to the mission asked protection against the liquor traders, saying "watch the french well, so that they may not intoxicate any of our people. We are going away from the English solely because they tormented us too much, and would give us nothing but liquor for all our peltries; and we see here many frenchmen who wish to do the same" (p. 117). Even in the beginning, however, the use of alcohol in the fur trade had certain built-in disadvantages; and this fact, about which we shall have more to say below, came to be ever more obvious as the years passed.

excessive drinking nor the disorders that so often accompanied it were universal features of the Indians' experience with alcohol.

Concerning the notion that the Indians of North America came universally to crave alcohol, we would first note that many Jesuit priests, even at the peak of their passionate outcry against the ravages created by the brandy trade, also recorded the existence of individual Indians who firmly abstained from liquor. These Jesuits also noted, sometimes in a tone of wonderment, that many Indians had either overcome "the vice" entirely or now drank only in moderation. Characteristic of such comments, which are scattered throughout their reports, is the following from the early 1680's (*Jesuit Relations,* Vol. 62): It seems that an Iroquois, after resisting the blandishments of his tribesmen to join in their drinking bout "found himself assailed on all sides with offers of flasks of wines. He received it all in his kettle, and afterwards poured it into the River, without touching it" (p. 249). And Father Jacques Bigot (*Jesuit Relations,* Vol. 62), who elsewhere noted that most of the Iroquois deserved their reputations as incorrigible drunkards, also noted that "Some drink merely out of human respect, without having any great craving for liquor" (p. 127). And again, Father Francois de Crepieul (*Jesuit Relations,* Vol. 63) wrote in 1686 of the by then widely accepted notion that all Indians had an uncontrollable craving for alcohol that, in his experience with the Algonkians, "This is not the general rule, as I have seen; and I think it untrue in the case of many" (p. 255).[6] Or consider this note on the Iroquois which was written in 1735 by another Jesuit priest (*Jesuit Relations,* Vol. 68): "Drunkenness is the great vice of the savage; but Thank God, we have many who never Touch intoxicating Liquor of any kind. [and] Those who do drink do not do so often . . ." (p. 269). Continuing on, we find this note written in 1730 by still another Jesuit priest (*Jesuit Relations,* Vol. 68) concerning the Montagnais, about whom, 100 years earlier, it had been reported (*Jesuit Relations,* Vol. 6, pp. 251–53) that drunkenness had reached "frightful" proportions:

6. By way of specification, Father Crepieul added that "I have known tall charles to keep it better than the French do, and even to Trade it to Others. I have seen Medartchis, an Etechemin, refuse it,—as did also some Savage women, although they had already drunk some; and there are many who would not take more than a drink or two. . . . I have seen Louÿs Kestabistichit, my host, keep a pint for more than ten days—and this on more than four or five occasions,—and not touch what I had put in a bottle to test him, although he knew Where it was" (p. 255).

Very different from the others, these savages do not, as a rule, like brandy; and if the Frenchman,—more eager for their goods than their salvation,—in spite of repeated prohibitions of our kings, overcomes their natural repugnance for that intoxicating liquor, they drink it only with ridiculous grimaces, and never return to the charge of their own accord. Their reason is,—to use their own language,—that the mind is shamefully lost when once it has been killed by firewater (pp. 45–47).

Traders, travelers, and explorers recorded many similar observations. Thus, Lewis and Clark (1904), writing in 1804 of their experiences with the Indians of the Great Plains, noted that although these Indians knew of liquor and had been in contact with traders, of all the tribes from the Mandan west to the Yellowstone, only the Assiniboine drank, and they did so with notable moderation (Vol. 1, p. 306). They report that other tribes, such as the Arikara, actively resisted alcohol: "The *recarees* (Arikara) are not fond of Spiritous liquers, nor do they appear to be fond of Receiving any or Thankfull for it. (*they say we are no friends or we would not give them what makes them fools*)" (Emphasis in original, Vol. 1, p. 199). Henry Schoolcraft reported in 1820 that he had encountered Chippewa who drank moderately, and others who drank but a taste (1953 edition, p. 448). Edwin Denig, who, in the first half of the nineteenth century, spent 21 years as a government scout and trader among the tribes of the upper Missouri, wrote as follows of the Assiniboine (a tribe into which he had married) and their neighbors: "They all drink whenever they can get it—men, women, and children—except the Crow Indians, who will not taste it" (published 1928, p. 529). And Thomas Farnham (1843) reported of the Shoshone Indians' response to liquor that:

They abjured it from the commencement of its introduction among them. And they give the best of reasons for this custom:—"It unmans us for the hunt, and for defending ourselves against our enemies; it causes unnatural dissensions among ourselves; it makes the Chief less than his Indian; and by its use, imbecility and ruin would come upon the Shoshone tribe" (Vol. 1, p. 263).[7]

7. Despite the quotation marks, this is clearly not a literal rendering. Other travelers of that period, however, have confirmed that the Shoshones typically abstained from alcohol for reasons of this general sort. See, for instance, the account of the trader Josiah Gregg (published 1904, pp. 342–343).

On the basis of observations such as these and innumerable others like them, we conclude that when Jeremy Belknap and Jedidiah Morse, in a government-sponsored fact-finding report dated 1796, wrote that it was "the character of all the savages of North America" to be "generally, and we fear incurably, addicted to intemperance, whenever they have the means in their power" (published 1955, p. 17), they were, shall we say, overzealous in their generalization. So much, then, for the fact that even when alcohol "caught hold," not all Indians fell hopeless victim to its fatal attraction.

We want now to show that even then the Indians did drink— and drink mightily—their comportment did not always undergo disastrous changes-for-the-worse. We turn first to the Menomini Indians of Wisconsin, who, by general agreement, were the equal of any Indians when it came to drunken disorder. Thus, we find an Indian agent (quoted in Keesing, 1939) writing in 1820 that "No quarrels, disturbances, or murders, have been known among the Menominees during the four years of my residence among them except such as have their origin in whiskey" (pp. 123–24). And in 1844, Colonel McKenney (McKenney and Hall, published 1934), who spent many years among the Menomini, reported of them that:

> Few of our tribes have fallen from their high esteem more lamentably than these Indians. They are, for the most part, a race of fine looking men, and have sustained a high character among the tribes around them. But the curse of ardent spirits has passed over them and withered them. They have yielded to the destructive pleasures of this withering charm, with an eagerness and recklessness even beyond the ordinary career of savages. There is, perhaps, no tribe upon all our borders so utterly abandoned to the vice of intoxication as the Menominies; nor any so degraded in their habits, and so improvident in all their concerns (Vol. 3, pp. 53–54).

But liquor also played a prominent religious role among the Menomini, and it is to this facet of their experience that we now turn. From the beginning, alcohol in certain contexts served as an aid in obtaining their much desired dreams and visions; and in these contexts, drunkenness typically was not accompanied by changes-for-the-worse.[8] Thus, Skinner (1915) reported performances of their

8. According to Skinner (Skinner and Satterlee, 1915), the first Menomini to become drunk described the experience in terms that are roughly comparable to those we often find used today in describing a "good" LSD

most important religious ceremony, the Medicine Ceremony, in which, despite continued drinking, there was no drunken misconduct. Skinner and Satterlee (1915) write, for instance, of one such observance, which occurred at Lake Poygan around 1850, that while the participants "kept drinking for days at a time," they confined themselves entirely to ceremonial singing in a search for visions and supernatural revelations (p. 497).

Elsewhere, we read that even where drinking was initiated as a part of a highly serious religious observance, the solemnity of the mood was subject to change on very short notice. Thus, Peter Pond, an early trader who in the 1760's and 1770's traveled widely in the East and the Midwest, reported (published 1965) that he once came upon a band of Fox Indians seated around the grave of one of their recently deceased members. When Pond chanced upon them, they had already made substantial inroads upon a keg of rum, and although they displayed evident sensorimotor signs of advanced intoxication, their demeanor was entirely somber and restrained—they cried, sang, and mourned their departed comrade in a maudlin recitation of their grief. They continued in this vein for some time until at last, upon what Pond called a "Moshan" (motion), their prevailing solemnity gave way almost instantaneously to gaiety, and the funeral was transformed into a party. Yet, while "thay ware More then Half Drunk," and while each woman selected a man of her choice and took him into the bushes, they showed not the least sign of aggression. Rather, as Pond put it, it was "as marey as a Party Could Bea" (pp. 35–36).

Indeed, it is virtually impossible to read the journals of men who traded with and lived among the Indians without discovering, interspersed among accounts of orgies and the most violent of drunken brawls, other accounts of drinking bouts at which *nothing* troublesome happened.[9] Archibald McLeod, for instance, whose journal (published 1965) reports his trading experiences over a vast area of north central Canada in the early 1800's, cited many such peaceable drinking parties conducted by many different bands of Indians. So, too, did Thomas Connor, who traded with the Ojibwa of the Upper Great Lakes region in 1804–1805. Among

trip: "It is very nice and good. There are funny feelings and a merry go of the brain and you can know more than you ever knew" (pp. 496–97).

9. For additional instances of this phenomenon, see Cameron (1960), Cox (1831), Du Ru (1934), Harmon (1903), Henry (1921), Lewis and Clark (1904), Lederer (1902), Long (1904), and Masson (1960).

many similar entries in Connor's journal (published 1965), we find these remarks: "They drank all night very peaceably" (p. 257); and of a different band, "They drank peaceably and gave me no manner of trouble" (p. 258). Yet, since in Connor's experience with Indian drinking it was more likely for "the Indians (to follow) their usual Custom of Stabbing" (p. 277), he expressed puzzlement concerning one such bout in which two stabbings occurred, for only two days earlier, these very same Indians "drank very peaceably" (p. 266).

One of the best sources for documenting the "now-you-see-it-now-you-don't" character of drunken changes-for-the-worse among the Indians of North America is the journal of the trader Alexander Henry (published 1897). Henry's journal spans the years between 1799 and 1814, when he was trading liquor for furs from Lake Superior to the Pacific Coast. If the decision to forgo self-aggrandizement is any index of veridicality, Henry's observations ought be taken particularly seriously, for he emerges by his own account as rather less than a hero: He admits, for instance, to "knowing" (in the biblical sense) his share of Indian maidens, and to watering his liquor with the best (or worst) of them.

What, then, does Henry say of Indian drunkenness? First, it is painfully clear that their drinking bouts were often accompanied by violence, for scattered throughout the pages of his journal are such entries as these: "What a different set of people they would be were there not a drop of liquor in the country! If a murder is committed among the Saulteurs, it is always in a drinking match" (Vol. 1, p. 209); "Wayquatchewine, in a drinking match, stabbed another Indian on the shoulder blade, but the knife was arrested by the bone, and the wound was not mortal" (Vol. 1, p. 205); "Grande Gueule (Big Mouth) stabbed Perdrix Blanche [White Partridge] with a knife in six places; the latter, in fighting with his wife, fell in the fire and was almost roasted, but had strength enough left, notwithstanding his wounds, to bite her nose off" (Vol. 1, pp. 238–39).

In short, where drunken disorder occurred, Henry saw it and reported it. But he also saw and reported a great many Indian drinking bouts during which bands of these same Indians drank heavily without displaying anything of the kind. The following entries from Henry's journal are not at all unusual: "The Indians were drinking all night but were not troublesome" (Vol. 1, p. 21); "The Indians did not once trouble me during the night" (Vol. 1, p. 57); "A band of Gens de Pied Assiniboines arrived. I gave them liquor, and they drank all night peaceably" (Vol. 2, p. 553); "This evening I gave the Piegans rum; they were not very troublesome, but drank quietly and soon went to sleep" (Vol. 2, p. 643).

For another example, we turn to the journal for the year 1800 (published 1903) of the trader Daniel Harmon, whose accounts of drunken mayhem we have already cited, for Harmon also reported drinking bouts at which there was not "the least affront or the smallest injury" (pp. 45–46). For example, he recorded one occasion at which a substantial number of Crees and Assiniboines of both sexes drank steadily for five days, yet their resulting comportment consisted in nothing more than talking, singing, and crying (p. 34). And he reported another occasion during which a band of Crees remained drunk for over 48 hours, but did not become aggressive *until their liquor supply was exhausted and they began to sober up* (p. 55).

Harmon's remark serves to introduce the last point we would make in refutation of the conventionally presumed inevitability of Indian aggression when drunk; viz., that alcohol sometimes had an effect more closely resembling that produced by a tranquilizer (rather than an exciter) of the passions. That increasing drunkenness sometimes gave rise not to increasing aggression, but to its opposite is indicated in Fortescue Cuming's account (published 1904) of his confrontation with a band of drunken and hostile Delawares in 1807. When Cuming and his party arrived on the scene, these Indians were already "quite drunk," and they "did not seem to like our intrusion" (p. 283). Yet when Cuming offered them more liquor, they accepted; and the heightened intoxication which this additional drinking produced, did not result in the slaughter of Cuming and his party, but in an entirely pleasant and uneventful encounter. What is more, Cuming related that he had a similar experience with a band of Shawnees (p. 284).[10]

10. Alexander Henry (published 1897), too, reported several experiences that reflect an essentially similar pattern. He made recurrent reference, for instance, to bands of Indians who were insolent and demanding while they were sober, but who, once he gave them the liquor they demanded, became tranquil. Thus, for instance, we read this concerning his "taming" of a band of Bloods and Sarcees: "I presented them liquor, which they drank during the night; all were quiet" (Vol. 2, p. 653). And this concerning a band of Blackfeet: "I gave them liquor, and they drank noisily all night, but were not troublesome" (Vol. 2, p. 656).

Indians, too, sometimes employed liquor to transform warlike relations into peaceable ones. For example, James Schultz (1962), who lived most of his life among the Blackfoot of the Northern Plains, recorded that in 1881 several hostile subtribes that were on the verge of war with each other came together in one large encampment in an effort to prevent the outbreak of hostilities. During these peace talks everyone drank copiously of whiskey (shades of the Urubu), but this time the result was anything but violent: "Strange it was, a thousand Indians, men and women, drinking, chatting, singing, dancing around their evening fires, and quarreling not at all" (pp. 56–57).

And, too, there is the not altogether uncommon frontier saga of sober Indians who set out to torture a white captive, are plied with alcohol, become drunk, and lose all aggressive inclination. The trader John Long reported such an instance in which an Englishman named Ramsey had been captured by a band of Potawatomies in the 1770's. Since at that time the Potawatomies were siding with the French against the English, the unfortunate Mr. Ramsey found himself tied to a pole in preparation for a premature cremation. However, the resourceful Ramsey deflected the Indians from their agenda by informing them that he had some rum hidden in his canoes. Hearing this, the Indians dropped what they were doing and went in search. Since the rum was indeed where Ramsey said it would be, the Indians soon came up with it. And with liquor in hand, all thoughts of Ramsey left them as they devoted themselves with singleminded attention to the pursuit of alcoholic stupor. This goal they soon achieved; and Ramsey, with his captors thus out of commission, freed himself and proceeded forthwith to cut their throats (Long, published 1904, pp. 182–84).

So, in account after account we are informed of the whimsical effects that alcohol had upon the Indians of North America. Sometimes the changes in comportment that accompanied drunkenness were highly dramatic, and sometimes they were virtually nonexistent; moreover, when changes did occur, while the typical transformation was from sober tranquility to drunken hostility and violence, exactly the opposite order was not infrequently observed.

Nevertheless, present-day discussants appear to be oblivious to all of this, for they continue to write, as does the historian Otto F. Frederickson (1932), that:

When alcoholic drink came into the red man's possession . . . he flung aside all restraint and became a fool, a madman, or a murderer as chance and his now unbridled nature might direct. . . . While they were under the influence of liquor, their passions controlled them absolutely. . . . Yet the same Indians who in their drunken paroxysms were reckless, savage and murderous in the most extreme sense, and void of every consideration except that which conduced to the indulgence of the moment were, when sober, tractable, peaceable, civil and capable of improvement (pp. 5–6).

In this section we have attempted to demonstrate that the facts of the matter require that such talk be taken with a rather large grain of salt, for it is indisputably the case that not all North American Indians were irresistibly drawn to alcohol, nor did they, even if they drank it, always become uncontrollable as a consequence. While drunken changes-for-the-worse did characterize the comportment of some of the Indians some of the time, alcohol most certainly did *not* give rise to such a result in all of the Indians all of the time. In a word, "disinhibition" was an "only sometime" accompaniment of Indian drunkenness.

AGAIN, THE WITHIN-LIMITS CLAUSE

In this concluding section we shall take still further and final issue with the conventional view that the changes-for-the-worse that so often characterized the comportment of drunken Indians were simply the uncontrolled eruptions of their toxically released sexual and aggressive impulses. Specifically, we shall attempt to show that the comportment they exhibited when drunk was quite other than a species of mindless impulsivity that, once set off, they were powerless to direct.

Early accounts of the drunken doings of the Indians of North America were, of course, written by white men rather than by the Indians themselves. And because of this, these early accounts tended to become detailed and specific only when the authors or their fellow white men were immediately involved. Thus, information concerning the operation and sway of the *within-limits clause* as it pertained to intra-Indian comportment is virtually nonexistent for the whole of the prereservation period. However, once the Indians became the objects of detailed treatment in their own right, all of this changed, and there now exists a large body of reports documenting the existence of such intra-Indian *within-limits* provisions among present-day Indians.[11] But for the prereservation period, there are only scattered comments such as the following by Edwin Denig, the already cited chronicler of Indian life on the Upper Plains in the first half of the nineteenth century (published 1928): "They are not quarrelsome in their families when inebriated, generally sing or cry for their dead relations; but among those who are not of kin quarrels often occur which occasionally result in the death of one of them" (p. 530).

However, this lack of detailed examples of the *within-limits* character of intra-Indian drunken changes-for-the-worse is more than made up for by the wealth of available material addressed to the relations between the white man and the drunken Indian. Such accounts are sufficiently numerous, detailed, dramatic, and of a piece to document the controlled character of Indians' drunken comportment many times over.

Let us look first at the experiences of the early Jesuit priests who braved all to bring salvation to the indigenous heathen of New France. Often alone and always unarmed, these churchmen were, in the truest sense, emissaries of civilization in a savage wilderness. Ejected from Acadia (Nova Scotia) by the British, they moved into Huronia—the land of the Hurons, south of Georgia Bay—in 1625. Here Champlain had already established a French presence and formed an alliance with the Hurons and the Algonquians against these Indians' mortal enemy, the Iroquois. But alcohol had preceded the Jesuits, and throughout the period of their ill-fated work with the Hurons, it remained a constant focus of their opprobrium. Thus, Father Paul LeJeune (*Jesuit Relations,* Vol. 5) observed in 1632 that "since I have been here, I have seen only drunken

11. The anthropologist J. S. Slotkin (1953), for example, wrote of the Menomini that "When spouses are drunk they usually quarrel or fight with each other . . . (but) this does not occur between parents and children" (p. 14). And Dwight Heath (1964), in summarizing his observations of 405 Navaho drinking occasions, notes that while fighting was the "normally expected outcome of prolonged drinking" (p. 131) and while "shooting, knifing and ostentatiously spiteful destruction of property was not uncommon" (p. 126) at such times, nevertheless, "although they often drank together, cross-cousins and biological brothers never fought" (p. 126). For additional examples of the *within-limits* character of intra-Indian drunken changes-for-the-worse in the contemporary reservation period, see Hamer (1965, p. 294), Helm (1961, pp. 104–106), Honigmann and Honigmann (1945, p. 180 ff.), Hurt and Brown (1965, pp. 223–28), and Lemert (1954, p. 347 ff.).

savages . . ." (p. 49), and in the following year he again noted of the Hurons that "drunkards are continually seen among them, shouting, fighting, and quarreling" (p. 231). And to this, an anonymous correspondent (quoted in *Jesuit Relations,* Vol. 6), also writing in 1633, added that:

> Our savages—not only men, but women and girls—are such lovers of brandy that they get swinishly intoxicated . . . which causes numberless quarrels among them. When they get tipsy, they fight, and batter each other with their fists; they break into cabins, and tear them to pieces; and in this state they may do some foul deed and murder us . . . (p. 328).

Yet the Jesuits survived it all. And in 1639 Father Jerome Lalemant (quoted in Parkman, 1885), after referring to the received maxim that the blood of martyrs is the seed of the church and after extolling the glory of such martyrdom, wrote that "it would be a kind of curse if this part of the world should not participate in the happiness of having contributed to the brilliancy of this glory" (p. 126). But if it was "a kind of a curse" that preserved the Jesuits of New France from slaughter, it appeared to Father Lalemant (*Jesuit Relations,* Vol. 17) that this curse would soon be lifted, for in the following year he wrote that:

> We have had five Missions in these regions of the Hurons,—preaching the Gospel to more than 10,000 barbarians. . . . Nevertheless, they have become nowise better,—nay, they are even more incensed at us than usual, and have turned upon us as if we were the authors of all their troubles. I know not with what calumnies they have not loaded us; they have come to threats, to hostility, to private and public councils respecting our slaughter, and finally to blows, —but light ones, and not yet stained with much blood. We suspect and look for something further. . . . Certainly, we cannot sufficiently wonder that we are even now alive; for . . . we are even without any soldier or local defense . . . (p. 227).

It was another nine years, however, before the Hurons provided this "something further"—this "glory"—which Father Lalemant desired. Commencing approximately with the arrival of the Jesuits among them, the Hurons began to suffer a series of unprecedented disasters. Decimated by wave after wave of pestilence, and sometimes too besodden to defend themselves, they fell easy victim to the Iroquois who, in a series of savage attacks, exterminated all but scattered remnants of this once proud tribe. Thus scattered, the Hurons continued to be picked off by Iroquois raiding parties, and many of those who escaped these mopping-up operations lived only long enough to die of starvation. It was in 1649, at this time of consummate defeat that the first and only Jesuit, Father Noel Chabanel, died at the hands of a Huron. The killer, however, was entirely sober at the time, being an apostate who came to hate the Faith because he believed it responsible for the ruin of his tribe (Parkman, 1885, pp. 408–10; Du Cruex, 1951, Vol. 2, pp. 551–55).

But if the Huron were reticent to provide Father Lalemant his martyrs, the Iroquois were more willing to oblige. Beginning with Father Issac Jogues in 1646, seven additional martyrs were added to the toll in the succeeding decade, including Father Jerome Lalemant's nephew, Father Gabriel Lalemant. In each case, however, there is no indication that the Iroquois who were responsible for these killing were other than entirely sober at the time.

With the French position in the New World perilously close to extermination, hostilities with the Iroquois continued in an on-again, off-again fashion until in 1666 the Marquis de Tracy, but recently arrived in New France at the head of a regiment of experienced soldiers, marched into the Mohawk Valley and destroyed village after village, thus bringing a short-lived peace to French-Iroquois relations and allowing the Jesuits, for a time at least, to establish missions among them. And this leads to the next segment of our saga. How fared these Jesuits who set up missions in the midst of the very Iroquois who but two decades earlier had savagely murdered seven members of their order? In a word, the Iroquois added the names of no additional Jesuits to the list of Christian martyrs. That they had ample opportunity, both drunk and sober, to do so if they had been of such a mind is clearly evident in the accounts of those priests who manned these "advance bases." For example, Father LeMercier (*Jesuit Relations,* Vol. 51), writing in 1668 from his lonely mission at Agnié, had this to say to the depredations to which the drunken Iroquois regularly forced him to submit:

> It seems sometimes as if all the people of the village had become insane, so great is the license they allow themselves when they are

under the influence of liquor. Fire brands have been thrown at our heads, and our papers set on fire; our Chapel has been broken into; we have been often threatened with death; and during the three or four days while these disorders last,—and they take place very often,—we have to suffer a thousand acts of insolence without complaint, without eating, and without repose. Meanwhile, these furious creatures overthrow everything they come to, and even massacre one another, without sparing either relatives or friends, compatriots or strangers (pp. 217–19).

Clearly it was not a newly developed awe of the Frenchmen's God or of His representatives that saved Father LeMercier from coming to harm at the hands of these drunken Iroquois. Nor does it appear that a concern for things reverential is of any relevance in explaining an identical Iroquois reticence to do in Father Jacques Bruyas of the mission St. Francis Xavier. In a letter also dated 1668, Father Bruyas (*Jesuit Relations,* Vol. 51) described his experiences as follows:

They have such a mania (for brandy) that they do not complain of going 200 leagues, to bring three or four pots of it into their own country; and the worst of it is that when they have drunk it, they are demons. Last summer, a Drunken man presented himself at the door, and asked where the black gown was. "I will kill him," said he, "he is a demon, who forbids us to have several wives," but when he saw the door closed, he went home, shouting like a madman. This is not the only time that they have sought to kill me; but God always preserved me . . . (p. 125).

Barring recourse to such a notion of divine intervention, one must conclude that these "attempts" were even less than half-hearted, for similar accounts continue over the next several years. In 1682, for instance, Father Jean de Lamberville (*Jesuit Relations,* Vol. 62, pp. 65–101) wrote page after page detailing the unconsummated reign of terror to which drunken Iroquois subjected him while he served at Onnontagué mission. And in the same period, Father Thierry Beschefer (*Jesuit Relations,* Vol. 62) wrote that:

These nations (the Iroquois) are opposed more strongly than any other to Christianity . . . they are at the same time very maliciously disposed toward the French, which causes us to feel great apprehensions. . . . Drunkenness prevails [among them] to such an extent,

and so continuously, that it often makes their villages veritable
images of hell. Then one sees only madmen, who destroy the Cabins
and everything in them; who strike all whom they meet; and who
Fall upon one another, Biting and tearing each other with Their
teeth—attacking chiefly their faces, whereon many bear marks of
These quarrels. Many even have been killed in Combats of this kind,
which are always bloody. At such times no Captain [Chief] or
Elder Can repress these lawless acts; they themselves are compelled
to flee from the violence of these madmen, to avoid being ill treated
by them. On such occasions a poor missionary must open his
house to all who take a fancy to enter it, unless he choose to run the
risk of having it torn down or Burned; and he has no rest by day or
by night, while he listens to all their insolent words, and endures all
their insults, to which often The death-Blow alone is wanting (pp.
223–25).

And yet, once again, the death-blow did not come; although "Many
even have been killed in Combats of this kind," Father Beschefer
reports that he and his fellow Jesuits suffered only "insolent words"
and "insults."

And so it continued to be. Indeed, so unquestioning did this pattern of selective immunity become that approximately 75 years
later, when another priest (*Jesuit Relations,* Vol. 70) wrote (in
1757) of his experiences among his frequently drunken Indian
parishioners, he did not once indicate the slightest concern for his
own safety. This anonymous priest began what, for adherents to
the conventional wisdom, must be a truly remarkable tale by recounting that on the occasion in question his parishioners together
with some visiting Indians from other tribes began to drink and
that:

> . . . . very soon their brains were deranged. Savage drunkenness is
> rarely quiet, nearly always boisterous. This time it burst forth in-
> stantly into songs, dances, and noise; and, in short, it ended with
> blows. At daybreak it was at the height of its wildness; this was the
> first news brought to me on awaking. I promptly ran to the place
> hence the tumult proceeded. There everything was in alarm and
> agitation. This was the work of drunken men. Everything was soon
> restored to order . . . I took them without ceremony by the hand,
> one after another, and led them unresisting to their tents, where I
> ordered them to rest (pp. 133–35).

Nor is this the end of this intrepid priest's story, for he then went on to report that:

> The tumult seemed to be quieted when a Moraigan [Mohican], naturalized and adopted by the Abnakis tribe, renewed the uproar in a more serious manner; after having had bad words with an Iroquois, his companion in the debauch, they came to blows. The former, who was much more vigorous, having thrown his adversary to the ground, dealt him a storm of blows, and, what is more, tore with his teeth his enemy's shoulders. The contest was at its hottest point when I reached them; I could not obtain help other than that of my own arms to separate the contestants, the Savages fearing each other too much ever to intrude, at any cost, in disputes among themselves. But my strength did not correspond to the greatness of the undertaking, and the victor was too excited to release his prey immediately. I was tempted to let these furious creatures be punished by their own hands for their intemperance; but I feared that the scene might be stained with blood by the death of one of the champions. I redoubled my efforts, and by dint of shaking the Abnakis he at last perceived that he was being shaken; then he turned his head, but it was only with much difficulty that he recognized me. Nevertheless, he did not recover his senses; he needed a few moments to come to himself, after which he gave the Iroquois full liberty to escape, of which the latter readily availed himself (p. 135).

Here, then, is an instance in which two drunken savages were to all appearances so hell-bent upon killing each other that their fellow Indians did not dare to intervene. Yet, a lone and unarmed priest was able successfully to do so with total impunity. Thus, although drunken Indians sometimes subjected the "Black Robes" to sundry forms of abuse, not only did they refrain from killing them, they often granted them a remarkable immunity.

Still, one might propose that following "the decade of slaughter" (1646–1656) that the Jesuits suffered at the hands of the (sober) Iroquois, these men of God came to occupy in some unspecifiable way a uniquely inviolable position in the eyes of the Indians. But what, then, of the fur traders? Although these traders, unlike the priests, were armed and generally able-bodied, they were loaded down with trade wares that the Indians much desired; and, armed or no, they were but a paltry handful among literally hundreds of armed savages. Furthermore, their excursions usually carried them scores and sometimes hundreds of miles from their nearest source of armed support. We want now to show that in spite of all this, the fur traders, too, were typically immune from drunken attack.

We begin our documentation of this point by quoting from the journal of the already cited trader John Long (published 1904). Writing in the late 1770's, Long made the following remarkable observation regarding the Indians' character and the effects of alcohol upon it:

> It seems to be the constant attention both of the male and female part of the Indians to instil ideas of heroism into the minds of the rising generation, and these impressions they carry far beyond the line of reason or of justice. Is it then surprising that every action of their lives should tend to satisfy their thirst for revenging offences committed against them, and that these sentiments should operate so powerfully in directing their future conduct? There is, nevertheless one exception to these observations—their conduct to traders, who are obliged on some occasions, when intoxication runs high, to beat them very soundly;—to their credit, in these instances, I must confess I never knew them to resent this severity when sober. . . . With regard to [such] severity when they are perfectly sober, I am convinced it would be highly dangerous, and should be cautiously avoided (pp. 114–15).

Remarkable, indeed! Drunken Indians could be beaten with impunity, but to beat a sober Indian was "highly dangerous" and to be "cautiously avoided." The fact that the trader was able to wade with complete safety into a group of drunkenly raging savages and, using only as much force as was necessary, restore order among them, was too frequently and too matter-of-factly recorded to doubt its authenticity. Thus, from the trader Thomas Connor's journal for the years 1804–1805 (published 1965) we find such jottings as these: ". . . they were very Quarrelsome amongst themselves. I was obliged to interfere to prevent Murder being Committed" (p. 261); "Indians Drunk and peaceable except [one] who behaved himself so ill that I was forced to drub him" (p. 257); "Cold Weather. Indians Drunk & troublesome. threaten to leave me if I refuse them [more] Rum. put them to a defiance. they flew to Arms. we prepared to receive them and they thought proper to be peaceable" (p. 260).

And so, in the journal of one fur trader after another, there is only rare mention that drunken Indians ever assaulted either the traders themselves or members of the traders' parties. For instance, the journals of the traders McLeod (published 1965, p. 172), Harmon (published 1903, p. 89) and Connor (published 1965, p. 261) each report only one instance in which a drunken Indian attempted to stab a white man; and significantly, in each case the Indian somehow "missed" his mark.

But rather than skip haphazardly from the journal of one trader to another, it might be better to look at one such chronicle in some detail. For this purpose we select the journal of Alexander Henry (published 1897), whose experiences in the liquor trade, as we have already mentioned, spanned fifteen years and a continent, and brought him into contact with tribes from the Canadian Saulteaux in the East to the salmon fishermen of the Pacific Northwest. In addition to the length and variety of Henry's experiences in the fur trade, there is another reason for selecting his journal for special attention. Although charges that he hated the Indians (Saum, 1965, p. 212) are doubtless overdrawn, no one could reasonably say of him that he was an "Indian-lover." It is thus impossible to attribute Henry's longevity to the charismatic force of an angelic character. Yet, from the detailed record he kept of his many years in the trade, one fact stands out above all others: while Henry recorded numerous instances of intra-Indian violence during the drinking bouts of the many Indians with whom he traded, and while his journal has often been recommended as a particularly rich source of such accounts (Wissler, 1940, p. 266; Saum, 1965, p. 211), both he and his French Canadian assistants were immune to injury from such ones.

This is not to suggest, however, that all was blissful in his dealings with them. Indians of this or that tribe frequently annoyed Henry by the infernal racket they made during their nocturnal drinking bouts, and when they exhausted their supply of liquor they often threatened him with death if he did not accede to their demands for more. But when they did so, Henry merely told them, in so many words, to shut up, or else . . . ! And, on occasion after occasion, Henry reported that they did just that. On other occasions the Indians proved less willing to listen to "reason," and Henry found himself forced to give this or that drunken Indian a "good beating"—and this, too, met no serious resistance. For example, when confronted with one especially bellicose and particularly obnoxious Indian who was well into his cups, Henry (published 1897, Vol. 1, pp. 250–51) reported that he seized him by the hair and dragged him out of the fort, at which point the Indian threatened him with a knife, but, predictably enough, did not use it. And reports of instances such as the following dot the pages of his journal:

> They traded for liquor, and all began to drink, men and women. . . . The Indians grew much more than usually troublesome. I quarreled with Maymiutch, and took his gun away. About midnight I heard one of them chopping the gate with an ax, and bawling out to let him in, as he wanted liquor. Desmarais (one of Henry's men) took the ax from him, and told him if he cut the gate again he might depend upon receiving a sound beating (Vol. 1, pp. 105–106).

While taking guns, axes, etc., away from drunken Indians may have been in the daily run of things for Henry and his men, it should not be presumed from the ease with which they did so that the Indians involved were "devoid of aggressive impulses." In the example which we have just quoted, Henry went on to report that only a few hours after Maymiutch passively allowed his gun to be taken from him, he attacked and seriously wounded two of his fellow Indians.

Indeed, so complete was their immunity to drunken assault that in the whole of his journal Henry reported only two occasions during which a drunken Indian either attacked or killed a member of his entourage. In the first case, after learning that an Ojibwa had stabbed an Assiniboine to death during a drinking bout being held just outside the camp, Henry and several of his colleagues rushed to the scene, only to have the supposedly drunken Indian attempt to stab one of them. When they tried to club the Indian into submission, however, he proved so nimble as to twice evade their blows and then sprint for the woods "like a deer." Although they tried to overtake him, they could not, for "he was too fleet for us" (published 1897, Vol. 1, pp. 257–58). About the first of Henry's two cases, then, we would only suggest (as did Henry himself by implication) that it is difficult to imagine anyone so agile and fleet of foot to have been very intoxicated.

In the second case that Henry reported, a drunken Indian did in fact do in one of Henry's French colleagues. But when we examine Henry's account of the matter, an entirely different picture emerges than this bare fact would suggest. Henry reported that several Ojibwas and Assiniboines with whom he had earlier established trade relations paid him a visit and, together with some Frenchmen who were in his employ, they sat down with a good deal of rum for a bout of drinking. They drank and conversed quietly for some time, but toward midnight the Indians began to discuss their past exploits against the Sioux. Henry's narrative (published 1897, Vol. 1) picks up the story at this point:

> During this discourse they sang their war songs, recounted their exploits, and performed the manoeuvres usual in battle. These repeated exertions so agitated their minds, and the fumes of liquor had taken such effect, that they were transported to a degree of frenzy. They could not remain seated . . . but attempted to rise up . . . to fight their battles over again in pantomime (p. 270).

As this was going on, the fire burned down, and with the darkness the Indians became increasingly agitated. Suddenly, as one of them was reviling the Sioux, a gun went off and a Frenchman fell gravely wounded. Henry rushed to the scene, prepared to execute a speedy justice, but what he found was not the raging Indian he expected. Instead, he reported that:

> The Indian, although very drunk, on seeing the mischief he had done fell a-crying and lamenting, assuring the bystanders that he did not do it intentionally, and that, if they were of a different opinion, they were welcome to kill him. . . . The Indian remained seated upon the earth entirely naked, with his head between his legs, every moment expecting to have his brains knocked out . . . (pp. 271–72).

After interrogating those who were present and being assured that it was an accident, and after examining the gun (which he found to have a hair-trigger), Henry concluded his report of this second and final case of "drunken violence" by stating that "I could not punish the fellow with death, as it appeared to me that it was plainly an accident" (p. 272). Thus, although over a period of fifteen years there were scores of occasions when the Indians with whom Henry traded became drunk while camped around his trading post, and although the Indians often maimed and sometimes killed each other at such times, in the single instance in which one of his own party died at their hands, the death was clearly accidental. As for Henry himself, not once over all these years was he ever harmed, and when he finally did meet his death, it was in a small boat that capsized during a gale in the Columbia River. Neither liquor nor Indians had anything to do with his demise.

To be sure, the fur trade was not without its perils, and some traders were killed by Indians in the course of plying their wares during the many decades in which the trade flourished. However, when deaths did occur, they came about for a wide variety of reasons which, with but the rarest exception, were eminently practical in character. Political intrigue, economic competition, intertribal warfare, etc., were matters of life and death importance to the traders, while the threat posed by merely drunken Indians was a matter of much lesser moment. Thus, when the traders raised their voices against the excessive use of liquor in the trade, as some of them came to do in later years, it was *not* because they felt that their lives were endangered by drunkenly disinhibited savages. Rather it was either because of the havoc they believed alcohol to have created among the Indians or because the Indians had become too slothful and generally besodden to obtain sufficient furs to sustain the trade.

But we are not the first to have noticed the general inviolability of the trader to drunken assault. Phillips (1961), in what is perhaps the best available overview of the fur trade throughout the continent, refers on more than one occasion to the fact that the traders seemed to have lived "charmed lives;" Bailey (1937), after surveying the first two centuries of the fur trade amongst the Eastern Algonquians, concludes that the French traveled among the Indians "without fear, arms or danger" (p. 11); and Barnouw (1950) summarizes the experiences of the fur traders with the Ojibwa (or Chippewa) by noting of their drunken violence that "the victims were always Indians. The drunken Chippewa turned upon their own relatives, wives, and children, but not upon the white men" (pp. 60–61). Thus, the general inviolability of the white man—Jesuit and fur trader alike—to the assault of drunken Indians is not our own original discovery. By the same token, neither is it our own invention.

In the present chapter we have attempted to show that within the history of alcohol usage among the Indians of North America we find all the puzzles that we have previously encountered in other parts of the world. And once again we would note that in the face of a myriad of instances that stand in essential contradiction to the most basic tenet of the conventional wisdom, its adherents have elected, in effect, to look the other way.

It is our contention, however, that the puzzles we have here presented are far too general and pervasive to be put down as but so many minor oddments of frontier existence. In the next chapter we shall attempt to apply to their solution the formulation we advanced in Chapter 5.

7 *"Indians Can't Hold Their Liquor"*

B. Our Formulation Applied

IN CHAPTER 5 WE proposed, as an alternative to the disinhibition theory of alcohol's workings, that in the course of socialization persons learn about drunkenness whatever their society presumes to be the case; and that, comporting themselves in consonance with what is thus imparted to them, they become the living confirmation of their society's presumptions. But how can this formulation apply to the American Indian societies which, at the time of their initial contact with the Europeans, had no experience with drunkenness and thus could not possibly have had anything to impart to their members on the subject? It will be our contention that the Indians of this continent took as their exemplars of alcohol's effects on comportment the drunken doings of the very white men who introduced alcohol to them. But while the role of the seed is crucial, so, too, is that of the soil in which it is sown. Thus, before we examine the nature of the model of "what happens to you when you are drunk" that these early traders and frontiersmen provided, we shall want to say something concerning the receptivity of the existing Indian society to these "teachings."

THE NOBLE SAVAGE—BEFORE HIS "FALL"

We began the last chapter with a series of accounts of the mayhem and debauchery that so frequently accompanied Indian drunkenness. Implicit, and sometimes explicit, in those accounts is the notion that but for the Indians' fatal attraction to alcohol and the horrendous effects its ingestion produced upon them, their lot would have been both very different and infinitely better than it turned out to be. That is, it was presumed that before the coming of the white man, the American Indian was a person of essentially noble character and that when he behaved ignominiously, it was because of alcohol's shattering effect upon this pristine continence. For many reasons—guilt undoubtedly not the least among them—this portrait of the American Indian *qua* Noble Savage has been promulgated and progressively enlarged upon over the years as the unquestioned version of what the Indian was initially like. In fact, however, as contemporary scholars are well aware, even a most cursory examination of the early literature leads to a very different conclusion.

What, then, was the Indian of this continent like in his pristine state? Just as we would expect in any society, Indians had their fair share of intratribal quarrels, murders, treachery, avarice, jealousy, hate, sexual "irregularities," etc.—all without benefit of alcoholically produced "disinhibition." So jaundiced, for instance, was Father LeJeune's (*Jesuit Relations,* Vol. 16) impression of his Huron parishioners—actual and potential—that in 1634 he was moved to write of them that "I would not dare to assert that I have seen one act of real moral virtue in a Savage. They have nothing but their own pleasure and satisfaction in view" (p. 239). This judgment found frequent echo not only among his fellow Jesuits, but among many secular writers as well. Furthermore, many tribes had established traditions of ceremonially arranged *time out* long before the coming of the white men. The nature of these occasions is indicated in the following description of the Huron's version of the Dream Feast (*Jesuit Relations,* Vol. 17) written in 1639: "They . . . have during the time of the feast, in all the evenings and

nights of the three days that it lasts, liberty to do anything, and no
one dares say a word to them . . ." (p. 179).[1]

As for the Indians' intertribal relations, we would note that examples of base treachery and deceit everywhere abounded. And in
their relations with the white men, it is abundantly evident that ne-
gotiating in bad faith was in no way the exclusive prerogative of
the latter; in fact, there was little to choose between them on this
score. In sum, if we count it an index of honor that a man's word
is his bond, the phrase "Ignoble Savage" would on this score seem
to be closer to the mark. And in the degree to which they molded
their actions to the prevailing balance of forces, the Indians proved
themselves masters of *realpolitik*.

When we examine the Indians' treatment of their prisoners, there
is precious little indication that the quality of charity had reached
even "primitive" development. Although scalping is typically supposed to have been the Indians' preferred manner of dealing with
their enemies, many tribes went to great lengths to take prisoners
so that they might savor the process of accomplishing their demise.
This process—"caressing" the prisoners, the Iroquois jocularly
termed it—was developed to a point of elaborate refinement in
many tribes, entailing the participation, each in his own way, of
men, women and children alike. The horrors the Indians thus visited upon each other practically defy belief.[2] And the treatment to
which the Iroquois subjected Fathers Jean de Brébeuf and Gabriel

---

1. Parkman (1885) has summarized several first hand accounts of this
feast that the Hurons called *Ononhara* ("turning of the mind") as follows:
"The time and manner of holding it were determined at a solemn council.
This scene of madness began at night. Men, women, and children, *all
pretending to have lost their senses,* rushed shrieking and howling from
house to house, upsetting everything in their way, throwing firebrands, beating those they met or drenching them with water, and availing themselves
of this time of license to take a safe revenge on any who had ever offended
them. This scene of frenzy continued till daybreak. No corner of the village
was secure from the maniac crew. . . . It usually took place in February,
occupying about three days, and was often attended with great indecencies"
(emphasis ours, pp. 67–68). Almost identical versions of this feast were
practiced by the tribes of the Iroquois confederation and by the Algon-
quian-speaking tribes; and similar ceremonially arranged (and alcohol-free)
periods of *time out* were early reported throughout much of the North
American continent.

2. If the reader entertains any doubt on this score, and if he is of strong
stomach, Thwaites' index to the *Jesuit Relations* (Vol. 72, pp. 399–401)
contains two full pages of citations on the subject of the Indians' treatment
of their prisoners which, if consulted, will resolve all uncertainty.

Lalemant, who suffered the fatal misfortune of becoming their captives, has seldom been equalled and probably never surpassed in the annals of man's inhumanity to man (See, for instance, Talbot, 1949; Du Creux, 1951, Vol. 2, pp. 518–525). Although the likelihood that a prisoner would finally be cannibalized by his captors varied from one tribe to another, the few Hurons who survived this instance of Iroquois blood-letting reported that Father Brébeuf was far more pleasing to the palate of his captors than Father Lalemant.

We do not want to belabor the point, but along with the most barbaric torture and sometimes the cannibalization of their captives, many tribes also had institutionalized the practices of slavery, human sacrifice, ritual orgy, prostitution, and, in sum, all that is usually counted as least ennobling of our species. Thus, when James Isham (published 1949), an employee of the Hudson's Bay Company, lamented that,

> I think as others has, itts a pitty they was allow'd to taste that Bewitching spirit called. Brandy, or any other Spiritious Liquor's —which has been the Ruing of a Great many Indians, and the Chief Cause of their Ludness and bad way's they are now given to . . . (p. 103),

we would only note that their "Ludness and bad way's" long predated the introduction of alcohol amongst them. We would suggest that Isham's error in presuming alcohol to have been the "Chief Cause" of their "Ruing" derived from the fact that, by the time he wrote, the Indians had long since learned to reserve their "Ludness and bad way's" only, or at least primarily, for those occasions when they were drunk. Unaware that such or similar comportment was not uncommon prior to their introduction to alcohol, and seeing that such comportment occurred for the most part only when they were drunk, it was only natural that Isham, like so many others, should have presumed that alcohol was the responsible agent. By contrast, it is our contention that if there is any truth at all to the proposition that alcohol brought about the fall of the Noble Savage, then certainly, the pedestal from which he fell did not tower far above ground level.

MODELS FOR MAYHEM

This, however, is only half the story; for if the Indian was not a paragon of virtue before the coming of the white man, neither was the white man himself. Although by the year 1600 the fur trade had extended inland at least as far as the Eastern Great Lakes region, the records of this early period are very scanty, and next to nothing is known about these first traders or their experiences. It is when the priests, with their penchant for detailed records, began their work in New France—in Huronia in 1625 and in Acadia even earlier—that we begin to learn something of the character of these first emissaries of Western commerce. And there can be no doubt that in these churchmen's eyes, the traders with whom they came into contact were, by and large, a most unsavory lot.

Recruited largely from the impoverished of Europe, these "wood runners" or *coureurs de bois,* as they were called, were only too happy to depart the squalid existence of their homeland for the unshackled freedom the wilderness offered them. For as the contemporary historian J. Bartlett Brebner (1960) put it, in the New World "They could hunt, as only aristocrats could at home; they could gorge themselves frequently and idle for considerable periods; a different set of sexual morals invited their endless indulgence . . ." (p. 32).

Nicolas Perrot (quoted in Blair, 1911), one of the few early *voyageurs* to leave a record of his experiences, wrote of the life of the *coureurs de bois* that it "is a perpetual idleness, which leads them to all kinds of debauchery. They sleep, they smoke, they drink brandy at whatever cost; and often they seduce the wives and daughters of the savages . . ." (Vol. 1, p. 229). And Parkman (1901) likened their comportment on returning from months in the wilds to that of "the crew of a man-of-war paid off after a long voyage. As long as their beaver-skins lasted, they set no bounds to their riot . . . gambling and drinking filled the day and the night" (Vol. 2, p. 112).

Thus it is not surprising that from the time of the Jesuit's first arrival in New France, they were fated to remain in perpetual conflict with these men of the wilderness. "Would to God," said one priest (quoted in Brebner, 1960) in speaking of Champlain, "that all the French who first came to this country had been like him; [for then] we should not so often have to blush for them before our savages" (p. 36). But though their efforts to convert the Indians were everywhere made more difficult by the unsaintly examples of their fellow countrymen, the Jesuits were largely without power to control their excesses. For as Perrot put it (Blair, 1911), "They live in entire independence; they do not have to render account to any one for their actions; they recognize neither superior nor judge, neither laws nor police, nor any subordination" (Vol. 1, p. 229). And Parkman (1901), too, noted that the priests could not "venture to bear too hard on their unruly penitents, lest they should break wholly with the Church and dispense thenceforth with her sacraments" (Vol. 2, p. 112).

But the Jesuits were less prone to moderation in the admonitions they addressed to their native parishioners, and this de facto double standard did not escape the Indians' notice. Thus, in 1636, Father LeJeune dutifully related (*Jesuit Relations,* Vol. 9, p. 145) the Hurons' not unreasonable demand that the Jesuits cease complaining about the drunken transgressions of the Indians until they put an end to the drunken excesses of their own countrymen. Similarly, nine years later, Father Lalemant wrote (*Jesuit Relations,* Vol. 27) that the Algonquians "complain much and stoutly that the French get drunk and are bad, and that not a word is said about it" (p. 101).

There was no help for it, however, for as the years passed, economic and geopolitical considerations continued to take precedence over things spiritual, and although New France never really prospered while under French control, this once beleagured colony did grow. With its growth, an additional model of drunken mayhem came before the Indians' view—the French soldiers who had been sent to protect France's fledgling North American Empire. Thus, Sister Morin (quoted in Parkman, 1901), who wrote in what appears to have been a sublime ignorance of all that had transpired in New France previous to her arrival, had this to say concerning the drunken comportment of the soldiers who had saved the colony from almost certain extinction at the hands of the Iroquois: "Our good King has sent troops to defend us from the Iroquois, and the soldiers and officers have ruined the Lord's vineyard, and planted wickedness and sin and crime in our soil of Canada" (Vol. 2, p. 171). And in truth, while in the provinces of "wickedness, sin, and crime" matters had never been in very good shape, the arrival of a relatively large number of soldiers certainly did nothing to improve the situation. In at least one respect, matters seem to have gone from bad to worse in the ensuing years, for by 1699 the situation had gotten so bad that the King felt compelled personally to order his officers and men to cease their "debauchery and public

are the most disagreeable; for excessive drinking generally causes them to quarrel and fight, among themselves. Indeed, I had rather have fifty drunken Indians in the fort, than five drunken Canadians (p. 73).

Along the Texas frontier, H. B. Cushman (1899), who had wide experience with the Choctaw, Chickasaw, and Natchez Indians, had this to say of the relative "fiendishness" of the two groups:

Much has been said to prove the drunken Indian to be a fiend incarnate; and though I have seen drunken Indians yet my experience has taught me that a drunken white man is far worse than a drunken Indian, and more to be feared ten to one, than the Indian (p. 105).

That the white man everywhere throughout his westward march provided the Indians with such a model of drunken changes-for-the-worse is beyond dispute. No account of the fur trade, for instance, is without extended comment on the drunken disorders of the traders themselves, and this regardless of their nationality or the area in which they plied their wares.[3] To mention only one example of what Phillips (1961) referred to as this "long and sordid story" (Vol. 1, p. 402), we turn to the journal of the trader John Long (published 1904), wherein he recorded that once while drunk aboard a riverboat he became angered by a French priest and seized him, beat him into a state of semiconsciousness, and threw him overboard (p. 195). While most traders were not so candid as Long in relating their own drunken excesses, we have just seen in the above comparisons of the drunken comportment of Indians and whites that many were less reticent to record the drunken excesses of other white men in their retinues.

Some idea of what happened when many traders got together is provided by Alexander Ross who was an active member of John Jacob Astor's Pacific Fur Company. Writing in the early 1800's (published 1923) of the same Michilimackinac where the drunken comportment of the French soldiery had so incensed

3. Testimony to the misconduct of the traders is everywhere available. For some representative accounts, see the following general historical reviews of the fur trade: Berry (1961, p. 299 ff.); Chittenden (1954, Vol. 1, p. 22 ff.); Lavender (1964, p. 314 ff.); Phillips (1961, Vol. 2, p. 377 ff.); Rich (1958, Vol. 2, p. 476 ff.); Saum (1965, p. 3 ff.); and Sunder (1965, p. 56 ff.).

Father Carheil a century earlier, Ross makes it clear that the ensuing years had brought little in the way of improvement. This once remote trading post and settlement had by Ross's time become a major staging area for trade and exploration and was a prominent "rest and recreation" haven for traders from much of the midcontinent and beyond. What Ross saw was what Carheil had seen, only on a much larger scale:

> To see drunkenness and debauchery with all their concomitant vices, carried on systematically, it is necessary to see Mackinac. . . . for in the morning they were found drinking, at noon drunk, in the evening dead drunk, and in the night seldom sober. Hogarth's drunkards in Gin Lane and Beer Alley were nothing compared to the drunkards of Mackinac at this time. Every nook and corner in the whole island swarmed, at all hours of the day and night, with motley groups of uproarious tipplers and whiskey hunters. Mackinac at this time resembled a great bedlam, the frantic inmates running to and fro in wild forgetfulness . . . (p. 186).

The traders, however, were not the only white men to provide the Indians with such a model of drunken changes-for-the-worse. The whole frontier, as it advanced westward, abounded with such exemplars, as is evident, for instance, in the account of one F. A. Michaux (published 1904). Michaux was a member of the French Society of Natural History who was commissioned by his government to conduct a tour of inspection of the America that lay west of the Alleghenies. This he did in 1802, and everywhere he went he was appalled by the drunkenness he saw. One illustration is contained in his depiction of some of the white inhabitants of western Pennsylvania with whom he happened one night to lodge:

> The lower class of people . . . made the most dreadful riot, and committed such horrible excesses, that [they are] almost impossible to form the least idea of. The rooms, stairs, and yard were strewn with drunken men; and those who had still the power of speech uttered nothing but the accents of rage and fury (p. 144).

At about the same time (1807–09), the Englishman Fortescue Cuming, who traveled farther inland through the frontier areas of Ohio and Kentucky, indicated that the white inhabitants of these areas were at least equally hard-drinking, that they were similarly

prone to drunken violence, and that, in short, they provided the Indians "an example of selfishness and knavery which they [the Indians] *attempt to follow"* (emphasis ours, 1904, p. 285).

To move still further westward, the remarks of John K. Townsend (published 1904) on his observations of the drunken comportment of the white frontiersmen and trappers were equally unequivocal in their import. A physician and naturalist from Philadelphia, Townsend traversed the plains to the Rocky Mountains in 1833–1834 and gave this account of what he saw at Fort Hall, Idaho, on one occasion when everybody got liquored up:

> The consequence was a scene of rioting, noise, and fighting, during the whole day; some became so drunk that their senses fled them entirely, and they were therefore harmless; but by far the greater number were just sufficiently under the influence of the vile trash, to render them in their conduct disgusting and tiger-like. We had "gouging," biting, fisticuffing and "stamping" in the most "scientific" perfection; some even fired guns and pistols at each other, but these weapons were mostly harmless in the unsteady hand which employed them. Such scenes I hope never to witness again . . . (p. 324).

But witness them again he did, for in the following year he wrote of the drunken doings of a different group:

> These people, with their obstreperous mirth, their whooping and howling and quarreling . . . their crashing into and through our camp, yelling like fiends, the barking and baying of savage wolf-dogs, and the insistent crackling of rifles and carbines, render our camp a perfect bedlam (pp. 363–64).

Thirty years later, in 1864, Special Indian Agent H. T. Ketcham (quoted in Berthrong, 1963), after observing the comportment of the soldiers and citizenry of Forts Larned and Lyon in Colorado Territory, concluded a letter of report to the then Governor Evans on the following pessimistic note:

> While citizens and soldiers are permitted to enter their villages with whiskey in day time and at night; to make the men drunk and cohabit with the squaws, disseminating venerial diseases among them; while the Commanding Officer at the Post [Fort Larned] continues

to get drunk every day and insult and abuse the leading men of the Tribes, and make prostitutes of their women; you cannot expect to have any permanent peace with these Indians . . . (p. 174).

And at the same time, an unnamed traveler (quoted in Lumholtz, 1912) described the fort at Tucson as "the headquarters of vice, dissipation, and crime" (p. 3). And to this he added, "There was neither government, law, nor military protection. The garrison at Tucson confined itself to its legitimate business of getting drunk or doing nothing" (p. 3).

Thus, from the beginning of the white man's presence on this continent and throughout his westward march, he drank; and when he got drunk his comportment often changed in such a manner and to such a degree that it could not possibly have escaped the attentive gaze of the ever-present Indian. That the Indians' first observations of the dramatic changes-for-the-worse that so often occurred when white men got drunk were "lessons" not soon forgotten is vividly documented in an account by Daniel Harmon in which he described what happened when a band of Carrier (Sicannie) Indians first witnessed this phenomenon in 1811:

> This being the first day of another year, our people have passed it, according to the custom of the Canadians, in drinking and fighting. Some of the principal Indians of this place, desired us to allow them to remain at the fort, that they might see our people drink. As soon as they [the whites] began to be a little intoxicated, and to quarrel among themselves, the Natives began to be apprehensive, that something unpleasant might befall them, also. They therefore hid themselves under beds, and elsewhere, saying, that they thought the white people had run mad, for they appeared not to know what they were about. . . . [the Indians] appeared not a little surprised at the change; for it was the first time that they had ever seen a person intoxicated (1903, pp. 162–63).

But what happened next? A remarkably concise recapitulation of the natural history of a process that we propose must have occurred innumerable times throughout this continent in the wake of the Indians' observations of these drunken changes-for-the-worse is contained in the journal of George Simpson (published 1931). Simpson, who was in charge of all the operations of the Hudson's Bay Company throughout the Pacific Northwest, made the following observations of the Indians of the Columbia Valley early in the nineteenth century:

> Until these last two or three years the use of Spiritous Liquors was unknown among the Natives and nothing gave them such a contemptible opinion of the Whites as seeing them (the common men) deprive themselves of reason thereby on particular occasions; but I am concerned to say that *as they got familiarized to those scenes they became fond of indulging themselves in like manner* and are now getting as much addicted to Drunkenness as the tribes on the East side of the Mountain; this baneful habit arose from the Custom of giving a Dram every time they brought Furs *which at first there was some difficulty in prevailing on them to accept; it however very soon became agreeable,* they were then allowed a present of a Bottle of Rum for every 10 Skins they brought and latterly they have traded Provisions and even Furs for this article which has been so injurious throughout the Indian Country (p. 109, emphasis ours).

We must confess that we could not have said it better. For in the confines of these few sentences there is reference to the model of drunken "mindlessness" that the white man presented, the contempt that this transformation initially engendered in the Indians, and their progressive enchantment with the idea of "indulging themselves in like manner." And paralleling this transformation in the Indians' view of the desirability of drunkenness, we are informed that at first rum practically had to be forced upon them, that then it became a "bonus" for work well done, and that, finally, it became their preferred unit of payment.

Thus, across a continent, the Indian observed the dramatic transformation that alcohol seemed to produce in the white man; and, reaching into his repertoire of available explanations, he concluded, as the historian A. G. Bailey (1937) put it, that "Brandy was the embodiment, or was the medium through which an evil supernatural agent worked" (p. 73). Thus it was that the Indian came to see that changes-for-the-worse were to be expected during drunkenness, for at such times the drinker was temporarily inhabited by an evil supernatural agent. And from this, the Indian reached the entirely reasonable conclusion that since he was thus "possessed," his actions when drunk were not his own and he was not responsible for them. After all, the Indians' precontact cultures already contained an ample array of *time out* ceremonies and supernatural agents (*e.g.,* witchcraft, dreams, spirit possession, etc.) under whose "influence" a man became less than strictly responsible for his actions. What is more, the notion that the state of drunkenness was excusing of those transgressions committed while "under the influence" was entirely consonant with the model the white man provided, for in regard to his own drunken transgressions and those of his fellows, the white man, too, ignored much and forgave still more on the grounds that when drunk, one is "under the influence." In sum, so vivid were the examples of drunken mayhem and so well did such changes-for-the-worse mesh with precontact notions that it is difficult to imagine how a consciously conceived program of instruction about alcohol's "influence" on conduct could possibly have improved on the "lesson plan" that the Indians' white tutors provided.

DRUNKENNESS AS AN EXCUSE

That the Indians early came to honor the state of drunkenness as excusing was recognized from the first by the Jesuits. As early as 1632, for instance, Father LeJeune noted that when he accused a Huron of killing some Indian prisoners—a practice, be it remembered, that was entirely conventional *prior* to the coming of the white man—the Indian replied that "it is thou and thine who killed him; for, if thou hadst not given us brandy or wine, we would not have done it" (*Jesuit Relations,* Vol. 5, p. 49). To this, Father LeJeune added the following observation regarding the manner in which reconciliation was accomplished following an intratribal bout of drunken fighting:

> When they have returned to their senses, they say to you, "It is not we who did that, but thou who gavest us this drink." When they have slept off their drunkenness, they are as good friends with each other as ever, saying to each other: "Thou art my brother. I love thee; it is not I who wounded thee, but the drink which used my arm" (p. 49).

Again in the following year he returned to this theme when, on questioning some Indians about the recent murder of one of their tribesmen, he reported that the Indians reproached him, saying:

> It was brandy and not the Savage who had committed this murder, meaning to say that [their tribesman] was drunk when he struck the

blow. "Put thy wine and thy brandy in prison," they say: "It is thy drinks that do all the evil, and not we." They believe themselves to be entirely excused from crimes they commit, when they say that they were drunk (*Jesuit Relations,* Vol. 5, p. 231).

In 1659, Father Lalemant also noted of the Indians throughout New France that "everything is permitted them, for they give as satisfactory excuse that they were bereft of reason at the time" (*Jesuit Relations,* Vol. 46, p. 101). And in 1663, Father Francis Ragueneau observed of the Iroquois that "drunkenness . . . introduces the liberty of killing or beating, with impunity, those against whom they have any spite" (*Jesuit Relations,* Vol. 48, p. 67). Still another priest wrote of the Iroquois in the latter 1660's that:

When our Savages have received an injury from any one, they get half drunk and do with impunity all that passion suggests to them. All the satisfaction one receives from them is embraced in two words: "He was drunk; He had lost his reason" (*Jesuit Relations,* Vol. 53, p. 257).

And another commentator noted of the Indians throughout New France that while "the brandy they drink without moderation, carries them to obscenities and extremities of fury and cruelty which are unimaginable," all of this they "satisfy without punishment [by claiming] that drunkenness excuses all" (*Collection de Manuscrits,* 1883, Vol. 1, pp. 541–42). Finally, in the journal of Louis de Bougainville—the same Bougainville who later explored the Pacific —we find this entry regarding the Iroquois:

They pardon murder committed by drunkards. A drunken man is a sacred person. According to them it is a state so delicious that one is not responsible for his acts. But ordinarily, they themselves calmly punish cold-blooded murderers with a speedy death neither preceded nor followed by any formalities (1964, pp. 224–25).

That the Iroquois—who had clearly carried the excuse to its outer limits—had long given formal recognition to this principle of drunken irresponsibility is forcefully evidenced in Father Louis Hennepin's account of the remarkable rationale for their late seventeenth-century practice of getting their executioner drunk before he performed his task:

> When they would put any body to death for an enormous Crime, which they are persuaded he is guilty of, they hire a Man, whom they make drunk with Brandy, (for these People are very greedy of it) that the Kinsfolks of the Criminal may not seek to revenge his Death. After this drunken man has kill'd him whom they judge culpable, they give this account of it, that he that slew him was mad and drunk when he struck the blow (1903, Vol. 2, pp. 513–14).

Acceptance of the excusing character of drunkenness was in no way limited to the Indians of New France. Thus, in the early 1760's Lt. Henry Timberlake (published 1927) reported of the Cherokees (who inhabited large portions of the American Southeast) that "the follies, nay the mischief, they commit when inebriated, are entirely laid to liquor; and no one will revenge any injury (murder excepted) received from one who is no more himself . . ." (pp. 78–79). And Alexander Mackensie, who in the 1790's became the first known white man to traverse the continent, observed of the Indians he had encountered that "a state of intoxication sanctions all irregularities" (1962 ed., p. 76). Thus, by the first quarter of the nineteenth century, both drunkenness and the acceptance of the excuse conferred by drunkenness had spread over most of the continent. And in the following half century, a multitude of explorers, traders, trappers, missionaries, and soldiers would record—sometimes in passing, and sometimes in detail—that with few exceptions the Indians in every part of the continent had come to revel in drunkenness and to excuse the changes-for-the-worse that occurred at such times.

It is on the basis of this whole mass of firsthand accounts that Reuben Gold Thwaites (1903), a major historian of early white-Indian contact, concluded, as the Jesuits had so many years before:

> Drunkenness was regarded by the Indians as a sufficient excuse for a crime committed under its influence; they held that the liquor, and not the man who drank it, was responsible for the deed (Vol. 2, p. 514).

And to this conclusion we would only add that, as the Indians were

defeated and settled upon their many reservations, the state
of drunkenness continued, as it does to this day, to be both claimed
and honored as an excuse.[4]

TAKING ADVANTAGE OF THE EXCUSE

It is widely recognized that in order to cheat them in trade, to de-
bauch their women, etc., the whites often found it to their advantage to get the Indians drunk while only pretending to be drunk
themselves. Quickly mastering the intricacies of such deception, the
Indians early came to emulate their white teachers in this regard,
too. For a remarkably lucid example of this phenomenon from the
earliest period of which records are available, we turn to the account (published 1908) of Nicholas Denys, the owner-proprietor
of a trading station which he set up in Acadia in 1633. After reporting how the French seamen would use brandy to bring the Indian women "into so favourable a condition that they can do with
them everything they will" (p. 449), Denys added:

> In addition to all the wickedness of which I have spoken, the
> [French] fishermen have taught them [how] to take vengeance upon
> one another. He who may desire ill to his companion, will make him
> drink in company so much that it makes him drunk, during which
> time he holds himself in restraint. He acts as if he were as drunk as
> the others, and makes a quarrel. The fight being commenced, he has
> an axe or other weapon, which he had hidden before the drinking;
> this he draws and with it kills his man. He continues to make
> drunken orgie, and he is the last to awaken. The next day he is told
> that it is he who has killed the other man, at which he expresses
> regrets, and says that he was drunk (p. 450).

Thus, from the earliest years of which we have record, we find not
only that the Indians had come to feign drunkenness in order to
avail themselves of the excuse that this state conferred, but that
they learned this practice from the whites. Indeed, in the matter of
feigning drunkenness, it would appear that the pupil soon outdid his
teacher, for Denys reported that some of the Indians with whom he
had contact were so well able to hold their liquor when trading that

---

4. For evidence that reservation Indians continue to excuse drunken misconduct, see, for example: Curley (1967, pp. 121–22), Hamer (1965, pp.
293–98), Helm (1961, p. 105), Hurt and Brown (1965, p. 229), Lemert
(1954, pp. 336–57; 1958, p. 101), and Whittaker (1963, p. 89).

they often turned the tables and made "dupes" of the French (p. 448).

Nor were the Jesuits so otherworldly as to have missed the Indians' talent for pretense. Father LeJeune, after noting that the Indians entirely excused themselves from crimes that they committed by saying that they were drunk, added "I do not readily believe in this, because they feign this madness very well when they wish to hide their malice" (*Jesuit Relations*, Vol. 5, p. 231). The comments of another French priest show that by 1659 the Indians had developed this strategy in full. After noting as a general proposition that anything they did while they were drunk was excused, he wrote that "those that have any quarrels pretend to be intoxicated, in order to wreak vengeance with impunity" (*Jesuit Relations*, Vol. 46, p. 105). Nor were Dollier and Galinée (quoted in Kellogg, 1917) deceived. During their travels between the years 1660–1670, these two French noblemen-turned-missionaries had this to say of drunken murder among the Algonquians in Ontario:

It is a somewhat common custom amongst them when they have enemies, to get drunk and afterwards go and break their heads or stab them to death, so as to be able to say afterward that they committed the wicked act when they were not in their senses (p. 183).

And again, the pattern once established proved enduring. Thus, the trader Duncan Cameron wrote in 1804 of the Chippewa that "when mischievously inclined, they feign to be drunk, expecting that no one will lay their crimes to their account when in that state" (1960 reprint, pp. 248–49). And John Tanner, in an account commencing in 1789 of his many years as a captive first of the Ottawa and then of the Chippewa, reported the following experience when the group of Chippewa he was with encountered a large band of Crees with whom "in times long past" the Chippewa had quarreled:

They were part of a considerable band, strangers to us, and in themselves were far too powerful for us. We heard of their intention to kill Wa-me-gon-a-biew [Tanner's "brother"], and as we could not avoid being thrown more or less into their power, we thought best to conciliate their good will, or at least purchase their forbearance by a present. We had two kegs of whiskey, which we gave to the band, presenting one particularly to the head of the family who had threatened us. When they began to drink, I noticed one man, who, with great show of cordiality, invited Wa-me-gon-a-biew to drink, and pretended to drink with him. The more effectually to throw my brother off his guard; this man, in due time, began to act like a drunken man, though I could perceive he was perfectly sober, and knew that he had drank very little, if anything, since we had been together. I had no difficulty to comprehend his intentions, and determined, if possible, to protect Wa-me-gon-a-biew from the mischief intended him (Tanner, 1940 ed., pp. 88–89).

Additional accounts of the Indians' ability to feign drunkenness are contained in the journal of the trader John Long (published 1922). Long never really recognized that Indians often feigned their drunkenness, and he was thus genuinely puzzled at what he took to be their unique capacity to "sober up" in an instant when it was in their interest to do so. He reports one occasion, for instance, in which he and a lone companion were threatened by a band of drunken Ojibwas. He forestalled this threat by acceding to the Indians' demand for rum, but the crisis was only temporarily averted, for:

In about an hour they returned very much intoxicated, singing their war-songs, and every warrior naked, painted black from head to foot. . . . As our situation was truly critical, we acted with as much coolness as men devoted to destruction would. A fortunate thought came into my head, which I instantly put in practice. I went into the store, and rolling a barrel of gunpowder into the outer room knocked out the head. I had scarcely finished it before the savages arrived, and advancing to the door, armed with spears and toma-hawks, said to each other, "You go first." We stood ready to receive them, and gave them to understand we were not afraid of them. One of the band entered the house and I said to him sternly, "Who now among you old women is a brave soldier?" and immediately pointing my pistol cocked to the barrel of gunpowder, cried out with great emphasis, "We will all die this day." On hearing these words they ran from the door, crying, "The Master of Life has given the Beaver great strength and courage." The women fled with the ut-most precipitation, pushed their canoes into the water, and got off as fast as they could. *The men, who before were intoxicated, be-came sober,* and making as much haste as possible paddled to an island opposite the house (emphasis ours, pp. 90–92).

Rather than present additional accounts of such feigning, we shall let Francis Parkman (1901) provide a summary view of the extent to which the Indians of North America engaged in this practice:

> A drunken Indian, with weapons within reach, was very dangerous, and all prudent persons kept out of his way. This greatly pleased him; for, seeing everybody run before him, he fancied himself a great chief, and howled and swung his tomahawk with redoubled fury. If, as often happened, he maimed or murdered some wretch not nimble enough to escape, his countrymen absolved him from all guilt, and blamed only the brandy. Hence, if an Indian wished to take a safe revenge on some personal enemy, *he would pretend to be drunk; and not only murders but other crimes were often committed by false claimants to the bacchanalian privilege* (emphasis ours, Vol. 2, pp. 123–24).[5]

But although the Indians' proclivity to feign drunkenness in order to take advantage of the excuse this state provided was very real, and doubtless often invoked, there is something deeply puzzling here. When we dig into the early materials we find that this puzzle, too, was long ago recognized. Indeed, we can introduce what we have in mind in no better way than by quoting from Father Bruyas' reflection, voiced in 1668, concerning the Iroquois:

> Although they often become intoxicated with the intention of killing those to whom they bear ill-will, yet all is forgiven, and you have no other satisfaction than this: "What woudst thou have me do? I had no sense; I was drunk." Thus they atone for a man's death. There is among them neither prison nor gibbet; each one lives according to his fancy; and *I am surprised that, in so great impunity, they are not daily cutting each others throats* (emphasis ours, *Jesuit Relations*, Vol. 51, p. 125).

In fact, if *something* had not been operating to restrain them,

5. That the process of "feigning-drunkenness-in-order-to . . ." was not unique to the Indians of this continent is indicated, for example, in Paul Bohannan's (1960b) discussion of African homicide: "Killings that occur at drinking parties are seldom random. Seldom, when the information is complete, is a victim a stranger to his killer. The relationship of killer to victim is too often not given in the records of such cases—we think because the stereotype of killing wantonly in a drunken brawl is so commonly held by European officials that it is deemed sufficient explanation. At least some tribes know this and may take advantage of it." (p. 257).

there would never have been a need for either the United States
Cavalry or the Bureau of Indian Affairs, for "The Indian Problem"
would have achieved its final solution at the hands of the Indians
themselves. In the next section we want to look at this "something"
that "saved" the Indians from this self-inflicted genocide.

THE LIMITS OF THE EXCUSE

If alcohol did in fact transform the Indians into mindless perpetra-
tors of wanton slaughter as the conventional wisdom contends, then
there is no escaping the conclusion that the original inhabitants of
this continent were among the most incompetent killers the world
has ever seen. For while Alexander Henry, for instance, could say
of some Indians with whom he traded that "[drunken] murders
among these people are so frequent that we pay little attention to
them" (published 1897, Vol. 1, p. 429), with most tribes, even
during drinking bouts extending over several days and characterized
by wholesale drunken violence, it was only rarely that any of the
participants were actually killed. Thus, while Nicholas Denys said
of the Micmac Indians, "They do not call it drinking unless they
become drunk, and do not think they have been drinking unless
they fight and are hurt" (1908 edition, p. 444), he reported that
the number of Indians who were killed per year in such drunken
brawls along the entire Nova Scotian coast was only "some six,
seven, or eight" (p. 445). How are we to make sense of this fact—
that in a full year of opportunity, several hundred of these drunkenly violent Indians failed to produce a more "impressive" record
than this?

Denys himself, although unknowingly, provided us with one element of the solution to this puzzle when he noted of the Micmacs:

> If it is found that any one among them is hurt, he who will have
> done it asks his pardon, saying that he was drunk; and he is pardoned
> for that. But if some one has been killed, it is necessary that the
> murderer, aside from the confession of his drunkenness and the par-
> don he asks, should make to the widow some present to which all
> the others condemn him. And to make peace complete he must pay
> for another drinking bout" (1908 edition, pp. 444–45).

That is, for an injury, the excuse of drunkenness was exonerating,
but for a death, atonement did not come cheap. The killer had not
only to plead drunkenness in extenuation and to apologize for his

crime, he had also to make a present to the surviving kin (the nature and value of which was determined by others) and personally
to bear all expenses entailed in giving another drinking bout. In a
word, among the Micmacs, the drunkard could "get away with
murder" only figuratively, not literally, for the excuse of drunkenness had its limits.

This practice of purchasing the aggrieved's forgiveness was common to many tribes. Thus, for instance, Daniel Harmon mentioned
a case (published 1903) in which an Assiniboine atoned for stabbing a Cree in a drunken altercation by giving the victim a horse,
and reported that "now, they appear to be as great friends, as they
were before the quarrel took place" (p. 104). And to this he added:

> Even murder is sometimes, in this way atoned for; but not com-
> monly. In ordinary cases, nothing but the death of the murderer, or
> of some of his near relations, will satisfy the desire of revenge in an
> Indian, whose relative has been murdered (p. 104).

In this remark we find the second element that operated to limit
the severity of drunken violence—the presence of concerned relatives who could be counted upon to retaliate if a kinsman were
harmed. Both the potency and the generality of this factor are suggested by Harmon in his comments concerning the perilous circumstances in which an Indian without such relatives near-by often
found himself:

> Yesterday, six families of Crees came to the fort; and they have
> been drinking, ever since. An Indian had a few wrangling words
> with a squaw, belonging to another man, to whom he gave a slight
> beating. At that time, the chief, who was a friend of the Indian, was
> passing by; and he was so enraged at the abusive language given by
> the woman to his friend, that he commenced beating her on the
> head with a club, and soon terminated her life. This morning, the
> Indian women buried her corpse; and no more notice is taken of her
> death, than if a dog had been killed; for her relations are at a con-
> siderable distance, in another part of the country. An Indian is not
> much regarded or feared by his fellows, unless he has a number of
> relations to take part with him in his contests while in life, or to
> avenge his death, in case he should be murdered. This is true among
> all the Indian tribes, with whom I have been acquainted (1903, p.
> 69).

For another example of the "sobering" role that relatives often played, we turn to the Iroquois. It will be recalled from a previous section that, other things being equal, the Iroquois tended to excuse even murder if it had been committed by a drunkard. But even among the Iroquois, things were not always equal, as is evidenced in the following narrative written in 1679 by Father Claude Dablon (*Jesuit Relations,* Vol. 61). In this account we find reference not only to the excusing character of drunkenness and to the probable feigning of this state, but to the fact that here, too, kinsmen at least sometimes took it upon themselves to avenge wrongs that drunkards might have done a relative:

> After marrying another woman, he made himself drunk—or pretended to be so, as those do who desire to injure others with greater impunity. Bursting into his first wife's cabin, he upset and broke in pieces all the furniture; carried off all her clothes; and also beat her, declaring that he would kill her. She was wrested from his hands, and enabled to escape. She came immediately to the Chapel to pray, and to tell me what I have related above. These outrages went on for several Days, and did not cease until the relatives of this Christian woman, not able any longer to stay their resentment, also made themselves drunk, and avenged the cruel treatment inflicted on their relative (p. 173).

Alexander Henry provides still another example in which the excuse of drunkenness failed to carry the day. It seems that an elderly Indian who suspected his young wife of infidelity got "blind drunk" and attacked her, inflicting "three terrible stabs." Her relatives became extremely angry at this, for the girl had been seriously wounded, but they quieted their rage and waited. After several months the girl recovered from her wounds and, with the connivance of her relatives,

> [she] . . . held a drinking match, during which the lady gave her old husband a cruel beating with a stick, and then, throwing him on his back, applied a fire brand to his privates, and rubbed it in, until somebody interfered and took her away. She left him in a shocking condition with the parts nearly roasted. I believe she would have killed him, had she not been prevented; if he recovers it will be extraordinary (published 1897, Vol. 1, pp. 105–106).

Henry reported other instances as well in which Indians refused to honor the excuse that drunkenness typically conferred. One such case involved Henry, one might say, intimately, for it concerned the fate of an Ojibwa woman who had gotten drunk and spent the night with him. The next morning her husband, who was by then quite sober, learned of his wife's nocturnal escapade and, although she pleaded drunkenness in defense, he was so outraged that he picked up a firebrand and burned her face terribly (Vol. 1, pp. 71–72). Evidently in this case, too, the aggrieved decided that as far as he was concerned, the limits of the excuse had been exceeded.[6]

But while the Indians set up limits among themselves beyond which the excuse of drunkenness did not hold, in cases where their drunken transgressions impinged on the health and welfare of the white man, the matter was taken entirely out of their hands. For, typically, if the white men had sufficient force available with which to retaliate—and sometimes even when they didn't—they saw to it that the score was evened in full measure. And it mattered not a whit whether the Indian had been drunk or sober at the time he committed the deed that incurred their wrath.

Consider, for instance, the way the Dutch handled one such situation. The episode began in late 1642 when some Dutch traders used brandy to stupefy a Hackingsack Indian and then proceeded to steal several of his beaver skins. When the victim came to, he was enraged at his loss and vowed to shoot the first white man he met. And he more than kept his word, killing first an Englishman who resided on Staten Island and, a few days later, a Dutchman. Hearing of this outburst, and already aware of its possibly serious repercussions, a deputation of local Indian chiefs collected a great quantity of wampum and hastened to New Amsterdam to make reparation before things got out of control. With propitiatory offering in hand they pleaded that "You ought not to sell brandy to the Indians to make them crazy for they are not accustomed to your liquors" (quoted in O'Callaghan, 1846, Vol. 1, p. 264). Their plea was to no avail, however, for the Dutch demanded that the Indians surrender the murderer. This the Indians refused to do, for he was the son of a chief. And there matters stood while the Dutch feuded among themselves over what policy to pursue.

6. And, of course, whether or not the excuse of drunkenness would be honored in any specific case was *always*, at least in principle, a matter for individual discretion. So long as the generally agreed limits were not exceeded, however, the excuse *was* typically honored—at least until the next drinking party.

Finally, after much debate, the militants prevailed and in February, 1643, Governor Kieft, having resolved to exact vengeance sent out two bands of Dutchmen to avenge these killings. They left under the cover of darkness, and before the night was over they had slaughtered eighty Indians—men, women and children—at Pavonia and thirty at Corlaer's Hook. The next morning, those who had somehow lived through the night's carnage presented the following picture:

> Some [had] their hands cut off; some lost both arms and legs; some were supporting their entrails with their hands, while others were mangled in other horrid ways, too horrid to be conceived (quoted in O'Callaghan, 1846, Vol. 1, p. 268).

The immediate consequence of this act of slaughter was to cause the surrounding Indian tribes to unite in indignation and to destroy most of the outlying Dutch settlements. The following year, however, brought peace; and the longer-range consequence of this savage reprisal was to impress on the Indians that killing a white man was a project not to be lightly undertaken.

The French, too, when they had sufficient force to do so, were quick in their application of the law of the talion. Thus, for instance, Father Nau matter-of-factly recounted the following episode which occurred in 1735:

> Not three months ago, an Algonquin, in a drinking bout, killed with three stabs of a knife, a poor [French] soldier who was quietly working in a house at Montreal. Arrested on the spot, the Algonquin thought he would escape punishment because he was drunk and did not know what he was doing. He was condemned notwithstanding to be hanged; but as the executioner was away he was killed by a blow on the head (*Jesuit Relations*, Vol. 68, pp. 267–69).

Thus the Indians of New France also came to appreciate the virtue of restraint. That they learned their lesson well is illustrated in a report written some years later by W. W. Warren (1885) of what followed after a drunken Chippewa murdered a fur trader at Lac Court Oreilles. The French warned the Indians that if they did not hand over the murderer, all trade in the area would cease forthwith. After considerable discussion, the murderer was given up; and once he was in French hands, he was summarily hanged before a large throng of his fellow tribesmen. Although Jean Cadotte, an experienced trader who was in charge of the post, was certain that the Indians would not attempt to take revenge, others at the post were less sanguine. Thus:

> . . . to satisfy his men, as well as to discover if the relatives of the executed Indian indulged revengeful feelings, he presented a quantity of "eau de vie" [brandy] to the Indians, knowing that in their intoxication they would reveal any hard feelings or vengeful purposes for the late act, should they actually indulge them (p. 297).

That the Indians had achieved a proper appreciation of their circumstances is indicated by Warren's laconic commentary on what happened next: "The Indian camp was that night drowned in a drunken revel, not a word of displeasure or hatred did they utter against the traders" (p. 297).

And it can be generally said of the fur trade that where the white men established regular trade relations with the Indians, were reasonably fair in their dealings, and operated with sufficient strength and organization to insure the likelihood that murder would be punished—as was the case, for instance, with the men of the Hudson's Bay Company (in its later years) over the length and breadth of their vast domain—the probability that a white man would fall victim to a drunken Indian was very small indeed. Contrariwise, where the trade was sporadic and was in the hands of largely unorganized and often ruthless individual freebooters—as it was throughout most of the American area of the Great Plains and of the eastern slopes of the Rockies—the lives of the frontiersmen and trappers were in infinitely greater jeopardy.

This distinction between London monopoly-paternalism and St. Louis freebootery as it arose in the nineteenth century deserves elaboration, for the lesson it provides is an important one. Briefly, then, following a bitter trade war between the Northwest Company and the Hudson's Bay Company—a war that saw each side incite Indians to violence against the other company's posts and traders, and that succeeded finally in bringing both companies to the verge of bankruptcy—considerations of self-interest (and of British national policy) finally prevailed and the two companies merged their operations into one giant monopoly. Upon their merger, Parliament (in 1821) gave this reorganized giant, the *new* Hudson's Bay Company, exclusive trading rights to almost the whole of Canada and to all of what is now the American Pacific Northwest. In consequence, whereas a century earlier the Company had been guided by a vision no more illustrious than maintaining a few trading stations and, hopefully, increasing the immediate profitability of the enterprise, now, with its monopoly position established, it came to recognize that it had a *permanent* stake both in the Indians and in the country's resources. In contrast to this, the independent American trappers saw their interest in the land and its people as only transitory. They saw it as an "opportunity" that, so long as it lasted, ought be made the most of. The result was relative safety for the former and grave danger and not infrequently death for the latter.

The consequences of these two disparate orientations remained profound—not only during the period in which the fur trade flourished, but for later years as well. Frederick Merk (1931) has summarized the longer range historical impact of these two approaches to "doing business" as follows:

> This striking contrast between British and American Indian relations was no mere temporary phenomenon disappearing with the passing of the fur trade. It persisted as long as the red man and the white faced each other in the coveted land of the Far West. Trapper and trader gave way on both sides of the international boundary to miner and cattleman and they in turn to the pioneer farmer. These harbingers of a new day on the American side entered a region of already established strife and perpetuated there traditions two centuries old of Indian massacre and border retaliation. On the Canadian side civilization entered a region reduced by the Hudson's Bay Company to a tradition of law and order and the history of this frontier was one of almost unbroken peace (p. xxxiv).

While Merk has overly sublimed the Canadian record in the interest of making his point, nevertheless the main lines of his comparison are essentially correct. We would add only that this contrast held no less for drunken Indians than it did for sober ones.

THE UPSHOT OF IT ALL

Having found the conventional wisdom regarding Indian drunkenness to be subject to all of the puzzles that we have previously encountered, we have here attempted to provide some indication of the relevance of our formulation to their solution. We have suggested that in a soil already hospitable to its cultivation, the seed—the model of drunken changes-for-the-worse—that white traders, trappers, and frontiersmen provided the Indians readily took root and flourished. Seeing the dramatic transformation that alcohol seemed to produce in the white man, the Indians took it—some literally and others only figuratively—that alcohol contained or was the embodiment of an evil spirit, and that when they drank it this evil spirit took possession of them. By thus equating drunkenness and spirit possession, the Indians understood themselves to be innocent of whatsoever this spirit "caused" them to do while they were under its influence. We have also seen how the Indians came to take advantage of this excuse by feigning intoxication in order to do with impunity things that under normal circumstances would result in punishment. We have seen, too, that while the excuse of drunkenness was honored over a wide range of transgressions, it was not without its limits. Finally, we have seen that where these limits were consistently enforced, they were seldom breached.

We do not suggest that this account of Indian drunkenness is in any sense definitive, nor even that it makes much sense (in this connection or in any other) to speak of the Indians of this continent as if they were all cast from the same mold, although for reasons of economy we have sometimes spoken as if this were the case. Rather, we have attempted to recommend the relevance of our formulation in a very general sense. Seen in this light, our disproportionate reliance on examples from French Canada was neither proper nor improper per se, for *all* the accounts of drunken comportment that we have presented are intended to be but so many *intimations* of what we believe was really going on. A truly *definitive* application of our formulation, in contrast, would necessarily have been studiously time- and tribe-specific and infinitely more attuned to the socially organized character of the participants' understandings of the circumstances in which they found themselves.

While ours is certainly not the last word on so enormous a subject, we do hope to have demonstrated that it is impossible to account for the puzzles that are subsumed under the phrase "Indians can't hold their liquor" with the single conceptual presumption that the conventional wisdom brings to the task. For here, as elsewhere, the disinhibition formulation succeeds only in raising questions, not in answering them.

Indeed, if anything is clear from this brief overview of the history of drunken conduct among the Indians of this continent, it is that truly significant advances in our understanding of why people do what they do when they are drunk will come only from a more fully informed grasp of societies' differing understandings of the nature of drunkenness.

8 *Some Concluding Remarks*

IN THE FOREGOING CHAPTERS we have attempted to document the inadequacy of the conventional understanding of the effects of alcohol on human conduct and to present a radically social-psychological formulation in its stead. Rather than viewing drunken comportment as a function of toxically disinhibited brains operating in impulse-driven bodies, we have recommended that what is fundamentally at issue are the learned relations that exist among men living together in a society. More specifically, we have contended that the way people comport themselves when they are drunk is determined not by alcohol's toxic assault upon the seat of moral judgment, conscience, or the like, but by what their society makes of and imparts to them concerning the state of drunkenness. This, then, is our thesis, and it will stand or fall on the basis of the materials we have already presented.

Certain questions, however, have doubtless occurred to the reader as he has followed the unfolding of our argument, and it is to at least the more obvious of these questions that we wish to address our concluding remarks. To begin with, then, what if the "worst" should happen? What, that is, if some day someone should convincingly demonstrate that alcohol does in fact possess some

sort of capacity to disinhibit? Animal studies are highly equivocal
on this point, but what if they were not? Would such a demonstration render our effort irrelevant? We hardly think so, for now that
the host of "exceptions" to the disinhibition theory that have filled
our earlier chapters have been assembled, they can not honestly be
ignored. And once these "exceptions" *are* recognized, they compel
the conclusion that insofar as man's comportment is concerned, the
manifestations of such an alcohol-induced disinhibiting effect are
demonstrably subject to social channeling and even to outright
veto, should one's socially acquired understandings of the nature of
drunkenness so dictate. Regarding human comportment, then, the
most that one could possibly claim on the basis of such a demonstration would be that in certain places, at certain times, and under
certain circumstances, the ingestion of alcohol produces certain
kinds of disinhibited conduct. And this, we submit, is a very weak
statement indeed. Having come this far with us, we trust that the
reader, too, sees that even if the "worst" should happen, it would
not really challenge the supremacy of social factors over physiological ones.

But if the learned practice we have termed drunken *time out* is
both real and very widespread, this brings us to a second question.
Why is it so widespread? Certainly such a practice did not arise in
a vacuum, and we want now to say a few words about the broader
social context in which it occurs. To this end, we begin with a
truism to the effect that in every society it is a governing presumption that the overwhelming majority possess both sufficient competence and inclination to conduct their affairs in accordance with
whatever is counted as correct and proper. At the same time, it is
everywhere recognized that in no society is the socialization process
so wholly efficacious as to produce persons who will do and will
want to do only those things their society would have them do.
Since this disjunction between the ideal and the reality is a universal
one, it follows that living in a society—living in *any* society—is
never without conflict. Nor can any society ever wholly escape the
possibility that this conflict might at any moment break out into the
open.

How do societies respond to this perennial challenge? Before
addressing this question directly, let us first say a word about what
they do *not* do. At one extreme, it may be said that no society—at
least no society now extant, and no society for which records re-

main—has ever simply abandoned its quest for order. Societies
have crumbled, and at such times power vacuums have sometimes
arisen; but new power centers have always emerged, and upon their
emergence they have immediately directed their energies to the
task of reinstituting some version of the social order. Never has a
state of anarchy been allowed to assume the status of a way of life.
At the other extreme, neither has any society ever achieved long
range stability by resorting to the systematic application of the
doctrine of strict liability. People do things accidentally, inadver-
tently, while under duress, and so on, and to deny persons
the right ever to plead one or another such defense would be much
the same as to deny an engine its necessary lubricants. In both
cases, the result would be disastrous. It is our contention, then, that
the social fabric is inherently far too fragile for any society either
to allow its members to give unbridled play to their inclinations
(as in anarchy) or to operate on the premise that a transgressor's
intent is of no relevance in judging his blameworthiness and thus
in determining how his "case" ought be "adjudicated" (as in the
doctrine of strict liability).

Between these two unworkable extremes, however, there are
many ways in which societies have come to terms with the problem.
We have said that living in a society requires that persons abide by
standards. Yet in every society, persons have available to them a
wide range of what in the broadest sense of the term might best be
called "excuses." While it would take us too far afield to develop
the point in proper depth, we submit that the alternative approaches to which we have just referred *are* the sundry ways in
which different societies have organized the interplay between their
respective versions of the accountability system and the excuses
they make available to their members.

There are several broad categories into which these alternative
approaches can be ordered, but we shall here limit ourselves to a
brief consideration of two of them—Ineligibility and Time Out.
Every society has come up with some version of Ineligibility in
order to account for and to deal with certain of those classes of
troublesome or potentially troublesome persons (the profoundly
mentally retarded, for instance) who are considered chronically or
permanently incapable of living up to their society's minimal standards of competence. Since it is presumed of these people either that
"they know not what they do" or that they are incapable of doing

otherwise than they do, the approach that we have termed Ineligibility consists in setting them off as a class apart and granting
them one or another form of *long-term* or *permanent immunity*
from the demands of their society's accountability system.

In the case of Time Out—which, in one form or another, is
similarly universal—the demands for accountability are also set
aside, but only briefly. In Chapter 5 we saw how Time Out could
be "called" by ceremonial arrangement. We would now note that it
can be instituted in many other ways as well. In some societies,
people are allowed to call Time Out by temporarily assuming one
or another alteration in their social positions. (In the New Guinea
highlands, for example, one can escape burdensome economic re-
sponsibilities by exhibiting "wild man" behavior [Newman, 1964],
and in Hindu India this escape can be accomplished by donning the
orange robes of the *sanyasi* [Dumont, 1960].) In other societies,
conduct can come under the heading of Time Out by virtue either of
the willful action of another (as in the case, for example, of witchcraft, sorcery, and the like) or by the action of a supernatural agent
who might briefly take "possession" of one's will for "alien" purposes. Though the ways in which Time Out can be instituted are
far more numerous than this brief list would indicate, we would
conclude by noting that in many societies persons have available
to them the option of calling Time Out by producing "an altered
state of consciousness" in themselves. Concerning this last mentioned procedure, we would make the following points: (1) while
such an "alteration in consciousness" can be brought about in many
ways, it is most frequently achieved by the ingestion of one or another presumably psychoactive agent, and (2) alcohol is far and
away the most frequently used substance for this purpose.

But in what sense can it be said that recourse to the option of
drunken Time Out constitutes a solution to the conflicts to which
living in a society inexorably gives rise? The essence of our answer
is beautifully exemplified by the words of an Australian Aborigine
(quoted in Warner, 1958) who, when asked to explain the practice
of mandatory wife swapping that culminates his tribe's annual
Gunabibi ceremony, stated matter-of-factly that "It is better that
everybody comes with their women and all meet together at a Gunabibi and play with each other, and then nobody will start having
sweethearts the rest of the time" (p. 308). In effect this Aborigine
was saying that if people reserve the expression of their conflict-

engendered transgressions for occasions that fall under the purview of one or another form of sanctioned Time Out, not only are the adverse repercussions that would normally ensue either eliminated or significantly reduced, so too is the likelihood that such disruptions will occur at other times. Applying this insight to the phenomenon of drunken Time Out, the argument would run that if people have been brought up to believe that one is "not really oneself" when drunk, then it becomes possible for them to construe their drunken changes-for-the-worse as purely episodic happenings rather than as intended acts issuing from their moral character. So construed, not only can the drinker explain away his drunken misbehavior to himself ("I never would have done it if I had been sober"), those around him too can decide, or can be made to see, that his drunken transgressions ought not—or at least, *need* not—be taken in full seriousness ("After all, he was drunk"). We are arguing, then, that the option of drunken Time Out affords people the opportunity to "get it out of their systems" with a minimum of adverse consequences.

We are not, however, attempting here to pass off some simplistic version of sociocultural functionalism, for societies do not always "have their wits about them" when they set the outer limits to such transgressions, and they are sometimes brought near to ruination on this account. As the Kaingáng, for instance, so vividly exemplify (see above, pp. 70–71), although the option of drunken Time Out may provide a solution to one problem, it may at the same time give rise to other even more severe problems.

Considerations of the broader efficacy of drunken Time Out aside, if we are correct in contending that drunken changes-for-the-worse occur not because of alcohol's toxic assault on the higher brain centers but because the state of drunkenness is accorded the status of Time Out, we are left with the question "Why alcohol?" Why, that is, should alcohol any more than any other substance have come into such widespread use as a Time-Out-producing agent if its ingestion does not result in disinhibition?

The answer, of course, hinges on the fact that alcohol is *not* simply an inert placebo. At the sensorimotor level, we all know that alcohol is an incompetence producer. We all know, too, that at least certain of the adverse sensorimotor effects to which its ingestion gives rise often impinge on the drinker's comportment in ways that are clearly untoward. Its effects on the drinker's equilibrium, for instance, may result in his stumbling, bumping into things, knocking them over, falling down, etc. In addition, things may be dropped or otherwise broken, judgments of time and distance may be thrown askew, tasks may be poorly executed, etc.; and when the comatose state is approached, the drinker may fail to meet even the most imperative of his obligations. What is more, we all know that when a person is drunk, these sorts of alcohol-produced failings are both unintentional and beyond the drinker's power to overcome by sheer volition. From the acceptance of so obvious a fact-of-life as this, it certainly requires no great inferential leap to suppose that all other sorts of drunken "incompetencies" are similarly alcohol-caused and are thus similarly unintentional and similarly beyond the drinker's voluntary control. Man, after all, is man, and gray matter is gray matter. Why, then, it might be argued, ought one suppose that some kind of physiological Iron Curtain is capable of isolating the effects of alcohol to only certain "areas of the brain" so that only certain "functions" are adversely affected?

Nor does the case for alcohol rest only on this plausibility argument. Many additional factors have doubtless operated in support of its widespread utilization as a Time-Out-producing agent. On the technological side, it need only be mentioned that suitable materials for its production are almost everywhere close at hand and that their fermentation typically requires little in the way of time, effort, or skill. What is more, because this technology is so simple, it is easily transmitted—both from one generation to another and from society to society. Returning to alcohol's adverse effects on the drinker's sensorimotor performances, we would now note that these impairments have the important "cueing" property of being easily recognizable by all concerned. The existence of the state of drunkenness is self-monitorable in the sense that the drinker can simply "look within" and determine whether or not—and if so, to what degree—he is "under the influence." By the same token, since many of alcohol's effects on the drinker are highly visible to those around him, his "condition" is publicly monitorable as well. Nor should we overlook the advantages connected with the onset and duration of these effects. Because alcohol is readily soluble in the body, the onset of its effects is relatively sudden. And because the drinker need not wait long in order for these effects to make themselves known, in deciding when and where he will drink he at the same time decides when and where he will be drunk. As for duration, because alcohol is quickly oxidized once inside the body, the drinker knows that when he elects to "alter his state of consciousness" by ingesting alcohol, this alteration will not be longlasting unless, by continuing to drink, he chooses to make it so. Finally, the very act of drinking itself has the quality of a "warning sign" about it, and this, too, is very much in its favor. Since in those societies in which drunken changes-for-the-worse occur everybody knows that drinking often leads to drunkenness and that drunkenness is frequently accompanied by untoward conduct, those who wish to avoid the possibility of "becoming involved" have ample opportunity to depart the scene. And since to be forewarned is to be forearmed, there is an important sense in which those who remain have only themselves to blame should any mishap befall them. Add to all of this the fact that no single drinking bout, nor even a series of drinking bouts, produces in the drinker any easily identifiable long-term impairment in his health, and one can begin to see how well alcohol satisfies the criteria that might reasonably be proposed for an *ideal* Time-Out-producing agent. For since alcohol is a predictable, relatively harmless, and easily monitorible sensorimotor incompetence producer, it remains for societies but to "declare" that its ingestion produces an involuntary and thus an uncontrollable *moral* incompetence as well. Such, in brief, is our answer to the question, "Why alcohol?"

It is our contention, then, that if we are ever to understand drunken comportment, we must focus on the shared understandings of the nature of drunkenness that obtain among men living together in societies. It is our further contention that in those societies in which drunken changes-for-the-worse occur, these changes must be viewed in terms of the increased (though variously defined and never unlimited) freedom that these societies accord to their members when they are drunk. But if Time Out is so important a factor in so many societies, this raises still another question. Ought we conclude that in such societies people drink only or primarily in order to avail themselves of the increased freedom that drunkenness provides them? Our answer to this question is an emphatic No! Although we have presented several instances in which persons do so, it does not follow from this that most drinkers are typically acting in bad faith either with themselves or with their fellows when they commit drunken transgressions. Indeed, we would argue that to suppose that drunkenness is nothing but an institutionalized con game is even more one-sided than to suppose (as we conventionally do) that a drinker's "grift sense" is never operative.[1]

One last question and we shall be through. While the social channeling of drunken comportment is abundantly clear in the relatively small and homogeneous societies such as those we have drawn our examples from, what of the application of our formulation to the large and polymorphous national societies of the modern age? What, specifically, of its application to our own ethnically, religiously, occupationally, and in so many other ways heterogeneous society? Although it would take a book of greater length than the present one even to begin to do justice to this question, we would be remiss if we did not at least indicate the general lines along which our answer would proceed. Briefly, then, our basic thesis has been that persons learn about drunkenness what their societies impart to them, and comporting themselves in consonance with these understandings they become living confirmations of their societies' teachings. We would propose that this formulation is similarly applicable to our own society, but with this difference: our society lacks a clear and consistent position regarding the scope of the excuse and is thus neither clear nor consistent in its teachings. Because our society's teachings are neither clear nor consistent, we lack unanimity of understanding; and where unanimity of understanding is lacking, we would argue that uniformity of practice is out of the question. Thus, although we all know that in our society the state of drunkenness carries with it an "increased freedom to be one's other self," the limits are vague and only sporadically enforced, and hence what (if anything) the plea of drunkenness will excuse in any specific case is similarly indeterminant. In such a situation, our formulation would lead us to expect that what people actually do when they are drunk will vary enormously; and this is precisely what we find when we look around us. Thus, paradoxical as it may sound, we would argue that in our society this very unpredictability is the clearest possible confirmation of the essential correctness of our thesis.

1. Thus, we are *not* proposing, for instance, that "alcoholism" is to be understood solely (or in most cases even primarily) on the basis of the chronic propensity of persons so diagnosed to take advantage of the excuse that drunkenness affords. On this general point see MacAndrew, 1969.

On this note, we conclude what we have to say on the subject of man *qua* drunkard. The moral of the piece—and there is a moral —is neatly exemplified in the following anecdote, which dates from the England of the early 1600's. The story goes that not long after James I acceded to the throne, a certain English nobleman gave a dinner party to which he invited a large number of luminaries. After the goblets had been filled and refilled several times and the liquor had taken hold, an English general named Somerset rose from his chair and proclaimed: "Gentlemen, when I am in my cups, and the generous wine begins to warm my blood, I have an absurd custom of railing against the Scottish people. Knowing my weakness, I hope no gentlemen in the company will take it amiss."

Having thus delivered himself, he sat down, and a Highland chief, one Sir Robert Blackie of Blair-Atholl, rose and with singular dispassion addressed his fellow celebrants as follows: "Gentlemen, when I am in *my* cups, and the generous wine begins to warm my blood, if I hear a man rail against the Scottish people, I have an absurd custom of kicking him at once out of the company, often breaking a few of his bones in the process. Knowing my weakness, I hope no gentlemen will take it amiss."

The story concludes, we need scarcely add, that General Somerset did not that night follow his usual custom of denigrating the Scottish people.

The moral, then, is this. Since societies, like individuals, get the sorts of drunken comportment that they allow, they deserve what they get.

References

Amich, J. 1914. "An account of the first voyage of the Aguila under Captain Don Domingo de Boenechea to Tahiti:1772–1773." In *Quest and occupation of Tahiti by emissaries of Spain in 1772–76.* Series 2, Vol. 2, 36. London: The Hakluyt Society.

Asher, G. M. 1860. *Henry Hudson the navigator. An original document in which his career is recorded.* London: The Hakluyt Society.

Ashton, H. 1952. *The Basuto.* London: Oxford University Press.

Bailey, A. G. 1937. *The conflict of European and Eastern Algonkian cultures, 1504–1700.* Publications of the New Brunswick Museum, No. 2. St. John, N.B., Canada.

Banks, Sir Joseph. 1963. *The Endeavor Journal of Joseph Banks, 1768–1771.* 2nd ed. Edited by J. C. Beagelhole. 2 vols. Wellington, New Zealand: The Trustees of the Public Library of New South Wales in association with Angus and Robertson.

Barnouw, V. 1950. *Acculturation and personality among the Wisconsin Chippewa.* Memoirs of the American Anthropological Association, No. 72. Menasha, Wis.: American Anthropological Association.

Barton, R. F. 1930. *The half-way sun: Life among the headhunters of the Philippines*. New York: Brewer & Warren.

Barton, R. F. 1946. *The religion of the Ifugaos*. Memoirs of the American Anthropological Association, No. 65. Menasha, Wis.: American Anthropological Association.

Barton, R. F. 1963. *Autobiographies of three pagans in the Philippines*. New Hyde Park, N.Y.: University Books.

Bates, M., and Abbott, D. P. 1958. *Coral island: Portrait of an atoll*. New York: Charles Scribner's Sons.

Beals, R. 1945. *Ethnology of the Western Mixe*. University of California Publications in American Archeology and Ethnology, Vol. 42 (Whole No. 1).

Belcher, Sir E. 1843. *Narrative of a voyage around the world*. 2 vols. London: H. Colburn.

Belknap, J., and Morse, J. 1955. *Report on the Oneida, Stockbridge and Brotherton Indians, 1796*. Museum of the American Indian, Indian Notes and Monographs, No. 54. New York: Heye Foundation.

Bennett, F. D. 1840. *Narrative of a whaling voyage round the globe, from the year 1833 to 1836*. 2 vols. London: Richard Bentley.

Bennett, W. C., and Zingg, R. M. 1935. *The Tarahumara: An Indian tribe of Northern Mexico*. Chicago: University of Chicago Press.

Berry, D. 1961. *A majority of scoundrels. An informal history of the Rocky Mountain Fur Company*. New York: Harper & Bros.

Berthrong, D. J. 1963. *The Southern Cheyennes*. Norman, Okla.: University of Oklahoma Press.

Biggar, H. P. 1924. *The voyages of Jacques Cartier*. Publications of the Public Archives of Canada, No. 11. Ottawa: F. A. Acland.

Blair, E. H. 1911. *The Indian tribes of the upper Mississippi Valley and region of the Great Lakes*. 2 vols. Cleveland: A. H. Clark.

Block, M. A. 1965. *Alcoholism: Its facets and phases*. New York: John Day.

Bohannan, P. 1960a. "Homicide and suicide in North Kavirondo." In P. Bohannan (Ed.), *African homicide and suicide*. Princeton, N. J.: Princeton University Press.

Bohannan, P. 1960b. "Patterns of murder and suicide." In P. Bohannan (Ed.), *African homicide and suicide*. Princeton, N.J.: Princeton University Press.

Bougainville, L. A. de. 1964. *Adventure in the wilderness. The American journals of Louis Antoine de Bougainville 1756–60*. Edited by E. Hamilton. Norman, Okla.: University of Oklahoma Press.

Brebner, J. B. 1960. *Canada: A modern history*. Ann Arbor: University of Michigan Press.

Bunzel, R. 1940. The role of alcohol in two Central American cultures. *Psychiatry*, 3:361–387.

Burrows, E. G. 1952. From value to ethos on Ifaluk atoll. *Southwestern Journal of Anthropology*, 8:13–35.

Burrows, E. G., and Spiro, M. E. 1953. *An atoll culture: Ethnography of Ifaluk in the Central Carolines*. New Haven: Human Relations Area Files.

Cameron, D. 1960. "The Nipigon Country, 1804—with extracts from his journal." In L. R. Masson (Ed.), *Les bourgeois de la Compagnie du Nord-Ouest, recits de voyages, lettres et rapports inédits relatifs au Nord-Ouest Canadien*. (Reprint.) New York: Antiquarian Press.

Chafetz, M. E., and Demone, H. W. 1962. *Alcoholism and society*. New York: Oxford University Press.

Chittenden, H. M. 1954. *The American fur trade of the far west*. 2 vols. Stanford, Calif.: Academic Reprints.

Christian, F. W. 1899. *The Caroline Islands. Travel in the sea of the little lands*. London: Methuen & Co.

Collection de manuscrits contenant lettres, mémoires, et autres documents historiques relatifs à la nouvelle-France. 1883. 4 vols. Québec: Imprimerie D'A. Coté, sous les auspices de la législature de Québec.

Connor, T. 1965. "The diary of Thomas Connor." In C. M. Gates (Ed.), *Five fur traders of the Northwest*. St. Paul, Minn.: Minnesota Historical Society.

Conrad, B. 1962. *Tahiti*. New York: Viking Press.

Cook, J. 1784. *Voyage to the Pacific Ocean, 1776–1780.* Folio ed., 3 vols. London: Richard Phillips.

Cox, R. 1831. *The Columbia River.* 3rd ed., 2 vols. London: Henry Colburn and Richard Bentley.

Cuming, F. 1904. "Sketches of a tour to the Western Country." In R. G. Thwaites (Ed.), *Early western travels, 1748–1846,* Vol. 4. Cleveland: A. H. Clark.

Curley, R. T. 1967. Drinking patterns of the Mescalero Apache. *Quarterly Journal of Studies on Alcohol,* 28:116–131.

Cushman, H. B. 1899. *History of the Choctaw, Chickasaw and Natchez Indians.* Greenville, Tex.: Headlight Publishing House.

Davis, C. N. 1962. Human equation in alcoholism. *Malvern News,* 1 (May):1.

Davis, E. H. 1920. "The Papago ceremony of Vikita." In F. W. Hodge (Ed.), *Indian notes and monographs,* Vol. 3, No. 4. New York: Museum of the American Indian—Heye Foundation.

DeForest, J. W. 1851. *History of the Indians of Connecticut from the earliest known period to 1850.* Hartford: W. J. Hamersley.

Delmas, S. 1927. *La religion ou le paganisme des Marquisiens d'apres les notes des anciens missionaires.* Braine-le-Comte: Maison-mère des pères des Sacrés-Coeurs de Picpus.

Denig, E. T. 1928. *Indian tribes of the upper Missouri.* Forty-sixth Annual Report of the Bureau of American Ethnology. Washington, D.C.: Smithsonian Institution.

Denys, N. 1908. *The description and natural history of the coasts of North America (Acadia).* Edited by W. Ganong. Toronto: The Champlain Society.

Dobrizhoffer, M. 1822. *An account of the Abipones, an equestrian people of Paraguay.* 3 vols. London: John Murray.

Dozier, E. P. 1966. Problem drinking among American Indians: The role of sociocultural deprivation. *Quarterly Journal of Studies on Alcohol,* 27:72–87.

Driver, H. E. 1961. *Indians of North America.* Chicago: University of Chicago Press.

Dubois, J. A. 1897. *Hindu manners, customs and ceremonies.* 3rd ed. Edited by H. K. Beauchamp. Oxford: Clarendon Press.

Du Creux, F. 1951. *The history of Canada or New France.* Edited by P. J. Robinson and J. B. Conacher. 2 vols. Toronto: The Champlain Society.

Dumont, L. 1960. World renunciations in Indian religions. *Contributions to Indian Sociology,* 4:33–61.

Du Ru, P. 1934. *Journal of Paul Du Ru.* Edited by R. P. Butler. Chicago: The Caxton Club.

Eastman, M. 1915. *Church and state in early Canada.* Edinburgh: University of Edinburgh Press.

Ellis, W. 1853. *Polynesian researches.* Rev. ed. 4 vols. London: Henry G. Bohn.

Evans-Pritchard, E. E. 1929. Some collective expressions of obscenity in Africa. *Journal of the Royal Anthropological Institute,* 59:311–331.

Farnham, T. J. 1843. *Travels in the great western prairies.* 2 vols. London: Richard Bentley.

Frederickson, O. F. 1932. The liquor question among the Indian tribes in Kansas, 1804–1881. *Bulletin of University of Kansas Humanistic Studies,* 4:1–17.

Garfinkel, H. 1967. *Studies in ethnomethodology.* Englewood Cliffs, N.J.: Prentice-Hall.

Godwin, G. 1930. *Vancouver—a life, 1757–1798.* London: Philip Allan.

Goldman, I. 1963. *The Cubeo: Indians of the Northwest Amazon.* Urbana: University of Illinois.

Gorer, G. 1938. *Himalayan village: An account of the Lepchas of Sikkim.* London: Michael Joseph Ltd.

Gracia, M. 1843. *Lettres sur les îles Marquises, ou memoirs pour servir à l'étude religieuse, morale, politique et statistique des îles Marquises et de l'Océanie Orientale.* Paris: Gaumefrères.

Greenberg, L. A. 1953. Alcohol in the body. *Scientific American,* 189(12): 86–90.

Gregg, J. 1904. "Commerce of the prairies, or, the journal of a Santa Fé trader," part II. In R. G. Thwaites (Ed.), *Early western travels, 1748–1846*, Vol. 20. Cleveland: A. H. Clark.

Group for the Advancement of Psychiatry, Committee on the College Student. 1966. *Sex and the college student.* New York: Atheneum.

Hakluyt Society. 1913. *Quest and occupation of Tahiti by emissaries of Spain in 1772–76.* Series 2, Vol. 2, No. 32. London: The Hakluyt Society.

Hallowell, A. I. 1955. *Culture and experience.* Philadelphia: University of Pennsylvania Press.

Hamer, J. H. 1965. Acculturation stress and the functions of alcohol among the Forest Potawatomi. *Quarterly Journal of Studies on Alcohol,* 26:285–302.

Handy, E. S. C. 1923. *The native culture in the Marquesas.* Bernice P. Bishop Museum, Bulletin 9. Honolulu: Bishop Museum.

Harger, R. N. 1959. The pharmacology and toxicology of alcohol. In American Medical Association, Committee on Medicolegal Problems (Ed.), *Chemical tests for intoxication: Manual.* American Medical Association.

Harmon, D. W. 1903. *A journal of voyages and travels.* New York: A. S. Barnes.

Heath, D. B. 1958. Drinking patterns of the Bolivian Camba. *Quarterly Journal of Studies on Alcohol,* 19:491–508.

Heath, D. B. 1964. Prohibition and post-repeal drinking patterns among the Navaho. *Quarterly Journal of Studies on Alcohol,* 25:119–135.

Hellmann, E. 1948. *Rooiyard. A sociological survey of an urban native slum yard.* Rhodes-Livingstone Papers, No. 13. Capetown, Union of South Africa: Oxford University Press.

Helm, J. 1961. *The Lynx Point people: the dynamics of a Northern Athapaskan band.* National Museum of Canada, Bulletin No. 176. Ottawa: Department of Northern Affairs and National Resources.

Hennepin, L. 1903. *A new discovery of a vast country in America.* Edited by R. G. Thwaites. 2 vols. Chicago: A. C. McClurg and Co.

Henry, A. 1897. *New light on the early history of the greater Northwest. The journals of Alexander Henry and David Thompson.* Edited by E. Coues. 3 vols. New York: F. P. Harper.

Henry, A. 1921. *Alexander Henry's travels and adventures in the years 1760–1776.* Edited by M. M. Quaife. Chicago: R. R. Donnelley & Sons.

Henry, J. 1941. *Jungle people: A Kaingáng tribe of the highlands of Brazil.* Richmond, Va.: J. J. Augustin.

Holmberg, A. 1950. *Nomads of the long bow: The Sirionó of Eastern Bolivia.* Smithsonian Institute of Social Anthropology, Publication No. 10. Washington, D.C.: United States Government Printing Office.

Honigmann, J. J., and Honigmann, I. 1945. Drinking in an Indian-white community. *Quarterly Journal of Studies of Alcohol, 5:575–619.*

Horton, D. 1943. The functions of alcohol in primitive societies: A cross-cultural study. *Quarterly Journal of Studies on Alcohol, 4:199–320.*

Howay, F. W. 1942. The introduction of intoxicating liquors amongst the Indians of the Northwest Coast. *British Columbia Historical Quarterly, 6:157–169.*

Hunter, M. 1961. *Reaction to conquest: Effects of contact with Europeans on the Pondo of South Africa.* London: Oxford University Press.

Hurt, W. R., and Brown, R. M. 1965. Social drinking patterns of the Yankton Sioux. *Human Organization, 24:222–230.*

Huxley, F. 1957. *Affable savages: An anthropologist among the Urubu Indians of Brazil.* New York: Viking Press.

Isham, J. 1949. *James Isham's observations on Hudson's Bay, 1743.* Edited by E. E. Rich. London: The Hudson's Bay Record Society.

Jesuit Relations and Allied Documents. 1896. Edited by R. G. Thwaites. 74 vols. Cleveland: Burrows Bros.

Jones, P. 1861. *History of the Ojebway Indians.* London: A. W. Bennett.

Joseph, A., Spicer, R. B., and Chesky, J. 1949. *The desert people: A study of the Papago Indians.* Chicago: University of Chicago Press.

Juet, R. 1959. *Juet's journal. The voyage of the Half Moon from 4 April to 7 November 1609.* Edited by R. Lunny. Newark: New Jersey Historical Society.

Junod, H. A. 1962. *The life of a South African tribe.* 2 vols. New Hyde Park, N.Y.: University Books.

Keesing, F. M. 1939. *The Menomini Indians of Wisconsin.* Memoirs of the American Philosophical Society, vol. 10. Philadelphia: American Philosophical Society.

Kellogg, L. P. (Ed.) 1917. *Early narratives of the Northwest, 1634–1699.* New York: Charles Scribner's Sons.

Kennedy, J. G. 1963. Tesguino-complex: The role of beer in Tarahumara culture. *American Anthropologist,* 65:620–640.

Kessel, N., and Walton, H. 1965. *Alcoholism.* Harmondsworth, Eng.: Penguin Books.

Kluckhohn, C. 1944. *Navaho witchcraft.* Vol. 22. Cambridge, Mass.: Peabody Museum of American Archeology and Ethnology.

Krige, E. J., and Krige, J. D. 1943. *The realm of a rain-queen: A study of the pattern of Lovedu society.* London: Oxford University Press.

Krusenstern, A. J. von. 1813. *Voyage round the world, in the years 1803, 1804, 1805 & 1806, by order of His Imperial Majesty Alexander the First, on board the ships Nadeshda and Neva, under the command of Captain A. J. von Krusenstern.* London: Printed by C. Powarth for J. Murray.

Kuhn, T. 1962. *The structure of scientific revolutions.* Chicago: University of Chicago Press.

Kurz, R. F. 1936. *Journal of Rudolph Friedrich Kurz.* Bureau of American Ethnology, Bulletin No. 115. Washington, D. C.: Smithsonian Institution.

Langdon, R. 1959. *Island of love.* London: Cassell.

Langsdorff, G. H. 1817. *Voyages and travels in various parts of the world during the years 1803, 1804, 1805, 1806, and 1807.* Carlisle, Pa.: George Phillips.

Lavender, D. 1964. *The fist in the wilderness.* New York: Doubleday & Co.

LeClercq, C. 1910. *New relation of Gaspesia: With the customs and religion of the Gaspesian Indians.* Edited by W. F. Ganong. Toronto: The Champlain Society.

Lederer, J. 1902. *The discoveries of John Lederer.* Edited by Sir W. Talbot. Rochester, N. Y.: George P. Humphrey.

Lemert, E. M. 1954. *Alcohol and the Northwest Coast Indians.* University of California Publications in Culture and Society, Vol. 2, No. 6. Berkeley: University of California Press.

Lemert, E. M. 1958. The use of alcohol in three Salish Indian tribes. *Quarterly Journal of Studies on Alcohol,* 19:90–107.

Lemert, E. M. 1964. Forms and pathology of drinking in three Polynesian societies. *American Anthropologist,* 66:361–374.

Lemert, E. M. 1967. Secular use of kava in Tonga. *Quarterly Journal of Studies on Alcohol,* 28:328–341.

LeVine, R., and LeVine, B. B. 1963. "Nyansongo: A Gusii community in Kenya." In B. B. Whiting (Ed.), *Six cultures: Studies of child rearing.* New York: Wiley.

Levy, R. I. 1966. Ma'ohi drinking patterns in the Society Islands. *Journal of the Polynesian Society,* 75:304–320.

Levy, R. I. (in press) "On getting angry in the Society Islands." In W. Caudill and T. Lin (Eds.), *Mental health research in Asia and the Pacific.*

Lewis, M., and Clark, W. 1904. *The original journals of the Lewis and Clark expedition 1804–1806.* Edited by R. G. Thwaites. 8 vols. New York: Dodd, Mead & Co.

Lindquist, G. E. E. 1923. *The Red Man in the United States.* New York: George Doran & Co.

Lindquist, G. E. E. 1944. *The Indian in American life.* New York: Friendship Press.

Long, J. 1904. "John Long's journal: 1768–1782." In R. G. Thwaites (Ed.), *Early western travels, 1748–1846,* Vol. 2. Cleveland: A. H. Clark.

Long, J. 1922. *John Long's voyages and travels in the years 1768–1788.* Edited by M. M. Quaife. Chicago: R. R. Donnelley & Sons.

Longmore, L. 1959. *The dispossessed.* London: Jonathan Cape.

Lumholtz, C. 1902. *Unknown Mexico.* 2 vols. New York: Charles Scribner's Sons.

Lumholtz, C. 1912. *New trails in Mexico.* New York: Charles Scribner's Sons.

MacAndrew, C. 1969. "On the notion that certain persons who are given to frequent drunkenness suffer from a disease called alcoholism." In S. Plog and R. Edgerton (Eds.), *Changing perspectives in mental illness.* New York: Holt, Rinehart & Winston.

Macdonnell, J. 1965. "The diary of John Macdonnell." In C. M. Gates (Ed.), *Five fur traders of the Northwest.* St. Paul, Minn.: Minnesota Historical Society.

McKenney, T. L., and Hall, J. 1934. *Indian tribes of North America.* 3 vols. Edinburgh: J. Grant.

Mackensie, A. 1962. *First man West: Alexander Mackensie's journal of his voyage to the Pacific Coast of Canada in 1793.* Edited by W. Sheppe. Berkeley: University of California Press.

McKinlay, A. P. 1945. The Roman attitude toward women's drinking. *Classical Bulletin,* 22:14–15.

McLeod, A. 1965. "The diary of Archibald McLeod." In C. M. Gates (Ed.), *Five fur traders of the Northwest.* St. Paul, Minn.: Minnesota Historical Society.

Madsen, W. 1967. "Acculturation and drinking patterns in a Mexican Indian village." (Unpublished manuscript)

Mangin, W. 1957. Drinking among Andean Indians. *Quarterly Journal of Studies on Alcohol,* 18:55–66.

Marchand, E. 1798. *Voyage autour du monde, pendant les années 1790, 1791, et 1792.* 6 vols. Paris: Imprimérie de la République.

Maretzki, T. W., and Maretzki, H. 1963. "Taira: An Okinawan village." In B. B. Whiting (Ed.), *Six cultures: Studies of child rearing.* New York: Wiley.

Masson, L. R. (Ed.) *Les bourgeois de la Compagnie du Nord-Ouest, recits de voyages, lettres et rapports inédits relatifs au Nord-Ouest Canadien.* (Reprint.) New York: Antiquarian Press.

Meinertzhagen, R. A. 1957. *Kenya diary, 1902–1906*. Edinburgh: Oliver & Boyd.

Merk, F. (Ed.). 1931. Introduction to *George Simpson's journal. Fur trade and empire*. Cambridge: Harvard University Press.

Michaux, F. A. 1904. "Travels to the west of the Alleghany Mountains." In R. G. Thwaites (Ed.), *Early western travels, 1748–1846*, Vol. 3. Cleveland: A. H. Clark.

Moerenhout, J. A. 1837. *Voyages aux îles du Grand Ocean*. 2 vols. Paris: Bertrand.

Morris, J. 1938. *Living with Lepchas: A book about the Sikkim Himalayas*. London: William Heinemann.

Morrison, J. 1935. *The journal of James Morrison*. London: Golden Cockerel Press.

Mortimer, T. 1838. *The night of toil: Or, a familiar account of the labours of the first missionaries in the South Sea Islands*. London: J. Hatchard and Son.

Nash, T. 1592. "Pierce Penilesse, his supplication to the Diuell." Reprinted in *Quarterly Journal of Studies on Alcohol*, 4:462–469 (1943–44).

Neil, W. H. 1962. Influence of drugs on driving. *Texas State Journal of Medicine*, 58:2–7.

Netting, R. McC. 1964. Beer as a locus of value among the West African Kofyar. *American Anthropologist*, 66:375–384.

Newman, P. L. 1964. "Wild man" behavior in a New Guinea highlands community. *American Anthropologist*, 66:1–19.

Nimuendajú, C. 1948. "Tribes of the lower and middle Xingú River." In J. H. Steward (Ed.), *Handbook of South American Indians*. Vol. 3. *The tropical forest tribes*. Washington, D.C.: U.S. Government Printing Office.

Norbeck, E. 1954. *Takashima: A Japanese fishing community*. Salt Lake City: University of Utah Press.

Norbeck, E. 1963. African rituals of conflict. *American Anthropologist*, 65:254–279.

O'Callaghan, E. B. 1846. *History of New Netherland: Or, New York under the Dutch.* 2 vols. New York: D. Appleton & Co.

Oswalt, W. 1966. *This land was theirs. A study of the North American Indian.* New York: Wiley.

Parkman, F. 1885. *The Jesuits in North America in the seventeenth century.* Boston: Little, Brown, and Co.

Parkman, F. 1901. *The old régime in Canada.* 2 vols. Boston: Little, Brown, and Co.

Phillips, P. C. 1961. *The fur trade.* 2 vols. Norman, Okla.: University of Oklahoma Press.

Poe, C. 1964. *Angel to the Papagos.* San Antonio, Tex.: Naylor Co.

Pond, P. 1965. "The narrative of Peter Pond." In C. M. Gates (Ed.), *Five fur traders of the Northwest.* St. Paul: Minnesota Historical Society.

Porter, D. 1882. *Journal of a cruise made to the Pacific Ocean, by Captain David Porter, in the United States Frigate Essex, in the years 1812, 1813, and 1814.* 2nd ed. New York: Wiley & Halsted.

Quiros, P. F. de. 1904. *The voyages of Pedro Fernandez de Quiros, 1595 to 1606.* Edited by Sir C. Markham. London: The Hakluyt Society.

Ramos, E., and Apilis, A.: 1940. Nabukyag, an Ifugao hero. *The Philippine Magazine,* 37:104–106.

Reichel-Dolmatoff, G., and Reichel-Dolmatoff, A. 1961. *The people of Aritama.* London: Routledge & Kegan Paul.

Rich, E. E. (Ed.) 1949. Introduction to *James Isham's observations on Hudson's Bay, 1743.* London: The Hudson's Bay Record Society.

Rich, E. E. 1958. *The history of the Hudson's Bay Company, 1670–1870.* 2 vols. London: The Hudson's Bay Record Company.

Ritchie, J. E. 1963. *The making of a Maori: A case study of a changing community.* Wellington, New Zealand: A. H. & A. W. Reed.

Romney, K., and Romney, R. 1963. "The Mixtecans of Juxtlahuaca, Mexico." In B. B. Whiting (Ed.), *Six cultures: Studies of child rearing.* New York: Wiley.

Ross, A. 1923. *Adventures of the first settlers on the Oregon or Columbia River.* Edited by M. M. Quaife. Chicago: R. R. Donnelley & Sons.

Rowe, N. A. 1955. *Voyage to the amorous islands.* London: Andre Deutsch.

Ruey, Y., Ho, T., Tao, S., Hsu, S., and Ch'iu, C. 1955. Ethnographical investigation of some aspects of the Atayal Chin-shui Ts'un Miaoli Hsien. *Bulletin of the Department of Archeology and Anthropology,* National Taiwan University, 5:118–127.

Rush, B. 1811. *An inquiry into the effects of ardent spirits upon the human body and mind.* 6th ed. New York: Printed for the subscribers.

Rutter, O. 1929. *The pagans of North Borneo.* London: Hutchinson & Co.

Saum, L. O. 1965. *The fur trader and the Indian.* Seattle: University of Washington Press.

Schoolcraft, H. R. 1847. *Inquiries respecting the history, present condition and future prospects of the Indian tribes of the United States.* Washington, D.C.: U.S. Government Printing Office.

Schoolcraft, H. R. 1848. *The Indian in his wigwam, or characteristics of the red race of America.* New York: Dewitt & Davenport.

Schoolcraft, H. R. 1953. *Narrative journal of travels through the northwestern regions of the United States, extending from Detroit through the great chain of American lakes to the sources of the Mississippi River, in the year 1820.* Edited by M. L. Williams. East Lansing: Michigan State College Press.

Schultz, J. 1962. *Blackfeet and buffalo. Memoirs of life among the Indians.* Norman, Okla.: University of Oklahoma Press.

Shapiro, H. L. 1964. *The heritage of the Bounty.* 2nd ed. New York: Doubleday, Anchor Books.

Simmons, O. G. 1959. Drinking patterns and interpersonal performance in a Peruvian mestizo community. *Quarterly Journal of Studies on Alcohol,* 20:103–111.

Simpson, G. 1931. *Fur trade and empire. George Simpson's journal.* Edited by F. Merk. Cambridge: Harvard University Press.

Sinclair, A. 1962. *Prohibition: the era of excess*. Boston: Little, Brown, and Co.

Skinner, A. B. 1915. *Associations and ceremonies of the Menomini Indians*. Anthropological Papers of the American Museum of Natural History, Vol. 13, part 2.

Skinner, A. B., and Satterlee, J. V. 1915. *Folklore of the Menomini Indians*. Anthropological Papers of the American Museum of National History, Vol. 13, part 3.

Slotkin, J. S. 1953. Social psychiatry of a Menomini community. *Journal of Abnormal and Social Psychology*, 48:10–16.

Society of Friends. 1935. *Alcohol: our personal responsibility*. London: Headley Brothers.

Stevenson, R. L. 1912. *The works of Robert Louis Stevenson*. Vol. 18. *In the South Seas*. London: Chatto and Windus.

Stewart, O. 1964. Questions regarding American Indian criminality. *Human Organization*, 23:61–66.

Stout, D. B. 1947. *San Blas Cuna acculturation: An introduction*. New York: Wenner-Gren Foundation for Anthropological Research, Inc. Viking Fund Publication in Anthropology No. 9.

Suggs, R. C. 1962. *The hidden worlds of Polynesia*. New York: Harcourt, Brace & World.

Suggs, R. C. 1966. *Marquesan sexual behavior*. New York: Harcourt, Brace & World.

Sunder, J. E. 1965. *The fur trade on the upper Missouri, 1840–1865*. Norman, Okla.: University of Oklahoma Press.

Swan, J. G. 1857. *The Northwest Coast; or, three years residence in Washington Territory*. New York: Harper and Bros.

Talbot, F. X. 1949. *Saint among the Hurons, the life of Jean de Brébeuf*. New York: Harper and Bros.

Tanner, J. 1940. *A narrative of the captivity and adventures of John Tanner, during thirty years residence among the Indians in the interior of North America*. Edited by E. James. San Francisco: California State Library, Sutro Branch.

Teuber, H. 1959. "Some alterations in behavior after cerebral lesions in man." In A. D. Bass (Ed.), *Evolution of nervous control from primitive organisms to man: A symposium.* Publication No. 52. Washington, D.C.: American Association for the Advancement of Science.

Thwaites, R. G. (Ed.) 1903. L. Hennepin, *A new discovery of a vast country in America.* 2 vols. Chicago: A. C. McClurg and Co.

Timberlake, H. 1927. *Memoirs, 1756–1765.* Johnson City, Tenn.: Watauga Press.

Toomin, P. R., and Toomin, P. M. 1963. *Black robe and grass skirt.* New York: Horizon Press.

Townsend, J. K. 1904. *Narrative of a journey across the Rocky Mountains.* In R. G. Thwaites (Ed.), *Early western travels, 1748–1846,* Vol. 21. Cleveland: A. H. Clark.

Turnbull, J. 1813. *A voyage round the world.* London: A. Maxwell.

Underhill, R. M. 1936. *The autobiography of a Papago woman.* Memoirs of the American Anthropological Association, No. 46. Menasha, Wis.: American Anthropological Association.

Underhill, R. M. 1938. *Singing for power: the song magic of the Papago Indians of Southern Arizona.* Berkeley: University of California Press.

Underhill, R. M. 1939. *Social organization of the Papago Indians.* New York: Columbia University Press.

Vancouver, G. 1801. *A voyage of discovery.* New ed. 8 vols. London: Stockdale.

Wafer, L. 1934. *A new voyage and description of the isthmus of America.* Series 2, No. 73. Oxford: The Hakluyt Society.

Wahlgren, E. 1958. *The Kensington Stone: A mystery solved.* Madison: University of Wisconsin Press.

Warner, W. L. 1958. *A black civilization. A social study of an Australian tribe.* Rev. ed. New York: Harper and Bros.

Warren, W. W. 1885. History of the Ojibways. *Collections of the Minnesota Historical Society,* 5:21–394.

Washburne, C. 1961. *Primitive drinking: A study of the uses and functions of alcohol in preliterate societies.* New York: College and University Press.

Whittaker, J. O. 1963. Alcohol and the Standing Rock Sioux Tribe. II. Psychodynamic and cultural factors in drinking. *Quarterly Journal of Studies on Alcohol,* 24:80–90.

Williams, J. 1837. *A narrative of missionary enterprises in the South Sea Islands.* London: J. Snow.

Wilson, G. 1960. "Homicide and suicide among the Joluo of Kenya." In P. Bohannan (Ed.), *African homicide and suicide.* Princeton, N. J.: Princeton University Press.

Winch, P. 1958. *The idea of a social science and its relation to philosophy.* London: Routledge & Kegan Paul.

Wissler, C. 1940. *Indians of the United States: four centuries of their history and culture.* Garden City, N.Y.: Doubleday.

Wittgenstein, L. 1953. *Philosophical investigations.* New York: Macmillan.

Zingg, R. M. 1942. The genuine and spurious values in Tarahumara culture. *American Anthropologist,* 44:78–92.

Index